Films of th
French Extremity

Films of the New French Extremity

Visceral Horror and National Identity

ALEXANDRA WEST

Foreword by Andrea Subissati

McFarland & Company, Inc., Publishers
Jefferson, North Carolina

Library of Congress Cataloguing-in-Publication Data

Names: West, Alexandra, 1985– author.
Title: Films of the new French extremity : visceral horror and national
identity / Alexandra West ; foreword by Andrea Subissati.
Description: Jefferson, North Carolina : McFarland & Company, Inc.,
Publishers, 2016. | Includes bibliographical references and index.
Identifiers: LCCN 2016018019 | ISBN 9781476663487
(softcover : acid free paper) ∞
Subjects: LCSH: Violence in motion pictures. | Motion
pictures—France—History—21st century.
Classification: LCC PN1995.9.V5 W47 2016 | DDC 791.43/6552—dc23
LC record available at https://lccn.loc.gov/2016018019

British Library cataloguing data are available

ISBN (print) 978-1-4766-6348-7
ISBN (ebook) 978-1-4766-2511-9

Front cover: Beatrice Dalle in the 2001 film
Trouble Every Day (Lot 47 Films/Photofest)

Manufactured in the United States of America

*McFarland & Company, Inc., Publishers
Box 611, Jefferson, North Carolina 28640
www.mcfarlandpub.com*

For my parents

Table of Contents

Acknowledgments

My first encounter with New French Extremity was renting Alexandre Aja's *High Tension* a few years after its initial release. I had heard breathless reviews of the spellbinding yet highly violent pseudo-slasher film and decided to see it as soon as possible. When I finally got my hands on a DVD of the film I rushed to my best friend Alice's house to watch it with her. It was as sunny a day as you could ask for and we settled in to watch the film after, oddly enough, watching a copy of François Truffaut's *Jules and Jim* (1962) which one of her older brothers had left lying around the house. My first viewing of *High Tension* was stupefying. I felt betrayed, angry, and incomplete after watching it. The bizarre twist in the film had rendered what I thought to be in the world of the film irrelevant. My friend had a similar reaction, yet we kept talking about it.

It was these conversations that led to this book. Initially they began with friends, family, and fellow writers about these films that I could not shake from my mind. The most important of these conversations was with Andrea Subissati and Paul Corupe, who not only encouraged my thought process but asked me to do a lecture on the very subject for their Black Museum series. Without Paul and Andrea's initial belief in this subject, this book would not exist. In researching the lecture, which was given in March 2014, I realized there were books that dealt thoughtfully and intelligently with contemporary French films but none that focused on the movement from art-house films to full-fledged horror films. In this book, I attempt to explore this transition. This transition happened because of the demands of the film industry and I was lucky enough to speak with TIFF Midnight Madness programmer and *Shudder* curator Colin Geddes. Colin generously introduced me to Peter

Block, former vice president of acquisitions at Lionsgate Films and current "film fixer." Both Colin and Peter's insights and generosity contributed to a deeper understanding of the movement within this book.

While writers tend to write in solitude, which was the case with this book, I am deeply grateful to my family, friends, and colleagues who willingly engaged in a dialogue about all things French and horrifying: Patrice Baillargeon, Alice Berg, Adam Driscoll, Paul Erlichman, Jennifer Frees, Chris Hayes, Liisa Ladouceur, Alison Lang, Darren McLennan, Stacie Ponder, Neil Rankin, Giles Sander, Peter Sander, Joanne Sarazen, Kim Snider, Diana West, Lindsay Wilson, Emma Yardley, Sam Zimmerman & Zuzu.

Foreword
by Andrea Subissati

Parlez-Vous Horror?

If I could trace the origin of my friendship with Alexandra West, I'd say it started with our mutual love for Pascal Laugier's *Martyrs*. I met Alex in the summer of 2011, when we were both invited to be interviewed as female journalists working in horror. I got to know a fair bit about Alex through that guest spot—I can't recall any of the answers I gave that day, but I remember all of hers, particularly with regard to the aforementioned film. *Martyrs*, which would come to be recognized as a pivotal title in the New French Extremity movement, is brilliant, but it's also a challenging watch; apart from the dual-narrative that significantly changes gears midway through, there are unflinchingly graphic scenes where a young woman, captive and bound, is mercilessly beaten by a large man. Oddly enough, *Martyrs'* unabashed display of physical brutality against women is neither exploitative nor misogynistic. The scenes are necessary point plots of a deeply inventive and philosophical story: a narrative device that made sure the movie hit you right in the gut, and hard. These images were terribly shocking to Western audiences, and even the most hardened of horror fanatics had to confront the fact that the film was something different, and indeed, something special. When Alex revealed that she read it the same way, she earned an automatic seal of approval from me: a test she didn't realize she aced.

We were tadpoles in the industry back then, and our careers emerged through different but parallel paths. By 2014, I was running a horror lecture series with Paul "Canuxploitation" Corupe out of Toronto called The Black Museum, a monthly event where we'd host a talk with a local pro on a given horror-related topic. Alex had lectured the year prior on her master's thesis research on found footage films, so when she approached us to do another talk, we already knew she had the skills necessary to hold an audience of over 60 with just a mic and a slideshow. This time, she wanted to talk about a movement in French horror that took place between the early '90s and the late 2000s dubbed the New French Extremity. I had seen (and greatly enjoyed) such films as *Calvaire*, *Inside*, and *High Tension*, but I hadn't considered them as part of a cohesive movement. Naturally, I was all ears at her lecture titled "Quelle Horreur! The Films of New French Extremity." In the presentation, she outlined the social context of 20th century France and explained how a country, world-renowned for high culture and romance, drew from a history of political discord and strife to churn out the darkest, ugliest nightmares to be committed to film. The lecture was a hit, of course, and I like to flatter myself by thinking that in hosting that talk, I helped Alex start on what would eventually culminate in this book.

What makes Alex's perspectives on film so unique is that her arguments are not only articulate and insightful, they're deeply personal. Horror speaks to her directly and she has the gumption as well as the literary chops to look beyond the technical and superficial to the cultural implications of these films and the cinematic movement they comprised. It's a talent she brings to the table every month when we get together to record our academic horror podcast, *The Faculty of Horror*, and I think it's largely the reason our listeners continue to tune in to each episode. Visually, Alex and I couldn't be more different—I look like a Kat Von D impersonator and she could have stepped right off of an H&M billboard—but we've become close colleagues (as well as dear friends) because we share an inclination to approach horror from these larger cultural and social perspectives.

Our work together on *The Faculty of Horror* has made us so close that I revel in her accomplishments as if they were my own, and I'm terribly pleased to provide the foreword to this comprehensive volume on a cinematic movement that grew out of turmoil and resistance; a movement so gritty and unprecedented that it requires the brainy zeal that Alex consistently brings to our show. Horror movies have always been about breaking taboos, and in the case of the New French Extremity movement, it's about breaking taboos that even *horror movies* wouldn't touch. Alexandra West breaks taboos, too; James Quandt may have coined the term "New French Extremity," but Alex is among the first to have given it proper appreciation such as this book. If you take anything away from my little *amuse-bouche*, let it be that a ride through the New French Extremity with Alexandra West is one well worth taking, and you won't find a more qualified guide.

Andrea Subissati is a Toronto-based sociologist and journalist whose writing has appeared in *The Undead and Theology* (2012) and *The Canadian Horror Film: Terror of the Soul* (2015). In addition to co-hosting and producing *The Faculty of Horror Podcast*, she is also co-founder of The Black Museum horror lecture series and is a regular contributor to *Rue Morgue Magazine*.

Introduction

I propose a theater whose violent physical images pulverize, mesmerize the audience's sensibilities, caught in the drama as if in a vortex of higher forces.—Antonin Artaud

France began mad and wild. From revolutions, both cultural and bloody, to the innovations and aspirational lifestyle that made it a world leader, France has kept that madcap spirit in the centuries since its inception as a country. Despite the glimmering beautifications of its capital city and picturesque landscapes, France has always been a country with blood on its streets and hands. France as a country has been on the market, sold and packaged as an emblem of sophistication and free-thinking to the rest of the world. Within its borders, however, a different story unfolds. At the turn of the millennium, France was at a crossroads. The turmoil brewing within the country was becoming untenable. Police brutality, xenophobia, and riots were an everyday occurrence but few voices ever spoke out about the injustices outside of news reports. And even fewer of those voices were heard outside of France's borders. At the same time a movement was beginning in French cinema, one that would be named and derided by film programmer and writer James Quandt. New French Extremity was, as he declared, a "cinema suddenly determined to break every taboo, to wade in rivers of viscera and spumes of sperm, to fill each frame with flesh, nubile or gnarled, and subject it to all manner of penetration, mutilation, and defilement."[1] Referring to then-recent films by French auteurs such as Catherine Breillat, Claire Denis, Gaspar Noé, and Bruno Dumont among others, Quandt rages against his perceived disparity between the high art meant to be achieved by such filmmakers of promise and the viscera-ridden films that were being produced from this emerging subgenre. Unbeknown to Quandt, his piece, which appeared in *ArtForum* magazine, would create an umbrella under which a group of disparate but impassioned filmmakers would fall under creating vital, violent, and visceral films which would succeed in finding new ways to shock even the most hardened audiences out of their complacency. The films of New French Extremity are startling, unforgettable, troubling, and deeply French. They are not violent films but rather films about violence and its larger impact on the world. They are films about France; not the twee, kitsch-y films emblematic of the vision which France tried to create of itself to maintain its stature to the rest of the world, but rather an honest view of the problems and unrest that have existed in France since its inception. New French Extremity is extreme because it swings the pendulum in violent opposition to the France that represents its ideals but not reality. The films of New French Extremity deal in the terrifying reality of the current and forgotten historical past of France, challenging the country and audiences around the world to awaken from a deep, shared slumber.

Quandt brands New French Extremity as an art-house movement, which it was at the time he was writing. However, Quandt could not have predicted that the moniker would be taken up by horror films. Horror fans and journalists saw these films as an intellectual sibling to the emerging trend of Torture Porn which was becoming increasingly popular with films such as *Saw* (James Wan, 2004) and *Cabin Fever* (Eli Roth, 2002). Films of the New French Extremity movement such as *Martyrs*, *Inside*, and *High Tension* regularly top Best Of genre lists and are viewed as emblems of horror films that can be smart, traumatic, and transformative. The relationship between this movement from the art house to full-fledged horror films was a relatively smooth transition. Many of the filmmakers who spearheaded the movement with films such as Claire Denis's *Trouble Every Day* and Marina de Van's *In My Skin* were already making horror films, but within their aesthetics. This would push the directors who would go on to make outright horror films such as Alexandre Aja with *High Tension* and Xavier Gens with *Frontier(s)* to maintain their vision for their films in keeping with the idealism that began the movement. Once these horror films hit the North American market they were marked by their difference and sought out because of it.

Before New French Extremity, horror films were the bastard child of French cinema. The French not only invented and developed film-making technologies but were at the forefront of developing filmic language, from documentary cinema to narrative cinema. In doing so the French made the first-ever horror film *The Haunted Castle* (*Le Manoir du diable*) in 1896, directed by Georges Méliès. The French would go on to popularize through a metaphorical film language the horrific aftermath that World War II inflicted on their country with terrifying thrillers such as *Les Diaboliques* (Henri-Georges Clouzot, 1955) and *Eyes Without a Face* (*Les Yeux sans visage*, Georges Franju, 1960) which are both surreal, nightmarish horror films which deal in the deception of self and identity; two traits the French became adept at in the wake of World War II. In their introduction to the French section of their book *European Nightmares*, editors Patricia Allmer, Emily Brick, and David Huxley write:

> French cinema is often perceived as having a strong tradition of the fantastic, rather than of horror film per se.... Rather than a continual, interrelated horror tradition, French cinema has produced a series of outstanding individual horror films, normally by directors who did not specialize in the field.[2]

Some of these outstanding individual horror films of note from France are the works of Jean Rollin whose stylized and sexualized vampires were at once both alluring and frightening, *Blood and Roses* (Roger Vadim, 1960), *Shock Treatment* (*Traitement de chic*, Alain Jessua, 1973), and even Jean-Luc Godard's vicious black comedy *Weekend* (1967) has ties with the violent aspects of humanity. Lionel Delplanque's *Deep in the Woods* (*Promenons-nous dans les bois*, 2000) was a minor hit in France and abroad, functioning as a French *giallo* thriller in the style of Mario Bava and Dario Argento. It is slick, stylish, and sedate. One of the few French directors to specialize in horror, thanks to his film *High Tension* which in turn played a large part in helping New French Extremity find a North American audience, is Alexandre Aja, who said of the French film industry: "The problem with the French is that they don't trust their own language [when it comes to horror]. American horror movies do well, but in their own language, the French aren't interested."[3] The films of New French Extremity changed the way the film world looks at France. All of a sudden the perceived polish of austerity had been removed, with new and established French filmmakers getting their hands dirty.

The films of New French Extremity are an important cultural

touchstone because horror films reflect and refract the terrors that contemporary society faces. As film writer Jason Zinoman wrote in his book *Shock Value*, "[T]he modern horror movie has not only established a vocabulary for us to articulate our fears. It has taught us what to be scared of."[4] Horror films illustrate and explore what a society is scared of. The New French Extremity movement has shown what the French are afraid of, themselves. Throughout the films discussed in this book the overall theme that these films share outside of the aesthetic is the pliability of the self, how characters can be overtaken by circumstances beyond their control or even by themselves which irrevocably damages the world around them. The characters featured in these films grapple with interior struggles that inflict themselves on the outside world.

The French have a complicated relationship with their own history. Scholar Kristin Ross writes extensively on this topic in her book *Fast Cars, Clean Bodies: Decolonization and the Reordering of French Culture*. For Ross, post–World War II saw France unable and unwilling to acknowledge and accept the atrocities that had happened on their soil as a result of the Nazi occupation. Ross writes of France's desire for "cleanliness," a blank slate from which to start over. The French began to assume American culture and ideology as a means of forgetting their own past, but as horror films have shown time and again, the past has a nasty way of returning. The latter half of the 20th century in France was filled with political riots and tensions, unacknowledged wars and social unrest. France was stunted. They could not and would not allow for real change; they did not know what to be scared of.

In a sense, genre filmmaking in France at the turn of the millennium was in a similar situation as the American New Hollywood movement which saw the emergence of independent filmmaking in America in the late 1960s through the early 1980s. Filmmakers such as Arthur Penn, Brian De Palma, William Friedkin, Wes Craven, Martin Scorsese, and George Romero were making films that confronted their audience with filmic metaphors that dealt with their own sense of social tension and unease. The films of New French Extremity present what is uncomfortable, not talked about or forgotten and the horrifying implications of being forced to forget. This not only mirrors the sentiments of French history, which sought to forget the atrocities of the past, but also links it to the New Hollywood movement of the 1970s, when filmmaking shifted for a studio-controlled system to a system controlled by filmmakers who made films that reflected the atrocities that the public faced, which, in turn, was influenced by the auteur theory that emerged from French New Wave cinema. From the Charles Manson murders to the Vietnam War, little of the late 1960s and early 1970s made sense in America. The promise of the white picket fence had faded away and New Hollywood films such as *Rosemary's Baby* (Roman Polanski, 1968), *Texas Chainsaw Massacre* (Tobe Hooper, 1974), *The Last House on the Left* (Wes Craven, 1972) and *Night of the Living Dead* (George Romero, 1968) reflect those uncertain times. As film writer Peter Biskind wrote in his book *Easy Riders, Raging Bulls*:

> [T]he cultural convulsion that upended the film industry began a decade earlier, when the tectonic plates beneath the back lots began to shift, shattering the verities of the Cold War—the universal fear of the Soviet Union, the paranoia of the Red Scare, the menace of the bomb—freeing a new generation of filmmakers frozen in the ice of '50s conformity.[5]

Though directors discussed in this book made a cultural splash for their shocking work prior to New French Extremity (Catherine Breillat in particular), the importance of an overall movement cannot be understated. Viewed together, these films are in a perpetual dialogue with one another, critiquing the extremity of everyday life in France; from physical violence to sexual exploration. The movement from art-house films to full-fledged horror films is another important point when discussing New French Extremity. The art-house films which began this conversation such as *I Stand Alone*, *Sombre*, *Baise-moi*, and *Romance*, among others, began the horrific narratives; the latter half of the movement, with films like *Calvaire*, *Sheitan*, and *Martyrs*, continues many of those same conversations but within a genre that has a die-hard fan base that is always hungry for the next scare. And these films, all of them, deliver scares. Jump scares are rarely used, rather the knowledge that the events depicted in the films is all somehow real and present within our Western societies may be the most frightening scare of all. As sociologist and horror journalist Andrea Subissati wrote when discussing the importance of horror within culture, "[H]orror movies can be conceived as collective nightmares: complied representations of all the things that terrify and intrigue us at the same time."[6] With the films of New French Extremity, France's collective nightmare has finally been realized.

Antonin Artaud, a French theater practitioner who wrote the seminal theater treatise *The Theater and Its Double*, describes the Theater of

Cruelty, which would arguably become his most famous theorem. Artaud saw the Theater of Cruelty as a means of unleashing the subconscious, not turning it off with escapism but forcing it into a confrontation with reality. He believed a social veneer masked humanity's true desires and intention and that by removing theatrical artifice and having actors grunt and groan and react rather than simply act, the Theater of Cruelty would be a ritual rather than an act. Artaud believed that this kind of theater could enable an audience to live the experiences depicted rather than simply think about them. Artaud was never able to fully explore this theory during his lifetime. However, New French Extremity, with its emphasis on brutal humanity, experimental camera work and confronting its audience with taboos and violence, comes awfully closes.

New French Extremity is a movement that sees art-house and genre directors converge to mediate on the most horrific aspects of life and what remains after those social veneers are stripped away. While they do not offer moral lessons, they offer an unsettling catharsis. All the films discussed in this book have deep ties to France's land and history. The first chapter in the book explores France's history through the lens of violence. Violence is a common occurrence in the annals of history, but France's persistent conflict within its borders is notable. Every time a revolution was fought for, some gains were made but the status quo remained. Chapter 2 explores the French film industry, examining its history as well as looking at the use of France, Paris in particular, as a backdrop for American films and how that informs a worldwide understanding of France. The following chapters are grouped by filmmaker or themes within the films. These chapters are ordered so outside of the thematic groupings they can be viewed in close to chronological order in an attempt to ground the discussion in the progression in which the films were released. In the appendix of the book is a long-form interview with Colin Geddes, programmer of the Midnight Madness and Vanguard programs at the Toronto International Film Festival (TIFF). TIFF is a hugely important part of the history of New French Extremity, not only because James Quandt is a programmer there, but because when Geddes programmed *High Tension* in Midnight Madness at TIFF in 2003, it not only generated industry buzz from audience reactions at the screenings but yielded the sale of the film to LionsGate. Geddes programmed multiple films from New French Extremity, which has greatly aided in its emergence in North America. The latter half of the book deals with the unmistakable horror films of New French Extremity. While the art-house films played with horror elements and tropes, following Alexandre Aja's *High Tension* other French directors have fully embraced the horror tropes with which they had grown up but altering them to the point of near un-recognizability, creating something new and exciting within the subgenre. The final chapter looks at the American remakes that some of the New French Extremity directors participated in, to varying degrees of success. While J-Horror trend of the 2000s was waning, Aja and *Them* directors Xavier Palud and David Moreau attempted to inject the genre with new life. Perhaps the most interesting trend outside of the J-Horror movement is Aja's involvement with the remakes of seminal grindhouse films of the 1970s and 1980s *The Hills Have Eyes* (Wes Craven, 1977), *Piranha* (Joe Dante, 1978), and *Maniac* (William Lustig, 1980), in essence closing the circle for New French Extremity with their similarities to the New Hollywood movement.

The films of New French Extremity challenge an audience, forcing them to question their perception of the events unfolding in front of them and daring them to look away at the same time. These filmmakers show us that a new critical reading can emerge and engage with contemporary culture through a language of violence, pain, and cruelty. The extreme reality they depict had not been seen before these films. Their focus on transformation through violence and sexuality is truly exciting and engaging, allowing an audience to explore the most human of desires through the thin safety net of a screen. The filmmakers discussed in this book come from radically different backgrounds and have all gone on to do different things, yet the one commonality as they entered this new uncharted territory, is that they are French. The controlled, articulated burst of New French Extremity revels in its French-ness by those who know it the best; filmmakers searching to communicate a truth that had not been uttered before.

1

Vive la Révolution!
France's Bloody and Divided History

Man will never be free until the last king is strangled
with the entrails of the last priest.—*Denis Diderot*

For over a thousand years France has been a political, cultural, philosophical, and revolutionary mecca. The country has existed in the minds of many as an idyllic and idolized bastion of all that is beautiful, good, and true—as British writer Jonathan Romney would call France's cultural aesthetic "unthreatening upmarket heritage."[1] France often ranks highly among other international powerhouses in education, healthcare, and life expectancy, maintaining its desirable reputation, but unrest within its borders has bred a culture of uncertainty, violence, and mayhem. France is one of the world's most trampled battlegrounds. Wars have been fought in its streets and towns as well as their colonies abroad. It is a country where the tension of the divide between classes has always been simmering just below the surface. The longstanding, deep resentments between classes and communities continue to be a sources of civil unrest and political upheaval.

The land that would eventually become known as the Kingdom of France was first settled in the Iron Age by a Celtic people known as the Gauls. They were eventually conquered by the Romans, who maintained control over the region until 486 BC. The Germanic-Franks saw the land as desirable, raiding it and eventually settling there, establishing the Kingdom of France in 843. As France was being established under the rule of an absolute monarchy, they faced several substantial and long-lasting conflicts with the dynasty that controlled what was then known as the Kingdom of England, between 1337 and 1453, over what was, essentially, land disputes. These conflicts have become known as the Hundred Years' War, which saw the loss of substantive amounts of the French population, but resulted in a centralized government. England lost the land it had previously laid claim to, a great boon to France, which, in turn, established the idea of nationalism in the land and the beginnings of a French sense of identity and pride.

France's troubles were not over, as the 16th and 17th centuries saw many internal wars fueled by religion. The Catholics and Protestants were at war during this time, while the noble class also began to rise in stature. The rise of the nobility caused the monarch to oscillate between supporting the Catholics and the Protestants in order to secure their power and maintain peace. The wars came to an end, with the Catholics becoming a dominant religion in France while the Protestants still maintained a small presence.

Many of France's vast cultural achievements began at this time and continued to grow with the Renaissance. By the 18th century France was a world leader in culture and economics. It was a flourishing landscape that maintained a unified front to the rest of the world, bolstered by their national pride, which was fostered by their multiple war victories. Louis XIV, the king of France from 1643 to 1715, established French culture as a leader and taste maker. Ruling through absolutism, the idea that one person should hold all the power and influence, he also happened to be leader of the country as it faced massive financial debt from helping fund the American Revolution while several harsh hailstorms depleted their crops, causing food costs to rise dramatically. While the country was facing these external hardships, a more systemic problem would creep into the French way of life.

Every country depends on collecting taxes from its citizens to fund its initiatives and to keep it functioning. The leaders of France consisted of the Ancien Régime, who were made up of the nobility and clergy across the country. The Ancien Régime initially helped stabilize and centralize France after the Hundred Years' War by maintaining and controlling cities and towns in France before the 18th century; however, these regimes varied wildly throughout the country, particularly in the way taxes were collected. Those not in the Régime were taxed heavily and frequently during a time when France would need every last cent to continue to fight wars and keep the Ancien Régime in the kind of lifestyle to which they were accustomed without forcing them to contribute any of their wealth. The rest of the population was angry, hungry, and poor. Their king lived in the Palace of Versailles and seemed unconcerned with the struggle of his people; indeed, the opulence of the king's palace served only to antagonize the citizens further. While France was drowning in debt, Louis XIV did attempt to fix it by trying to democratize the Ancien Régime and consulted with various finance ministers, to little avail.

Much would change with the death of Louis XIV, in 1715. His death helped advance the Enlightenment in France, which was already underway in England. French philosophers would visit the neighboring country and return with radical, anti-establishment notions that would give rise to their own version of the Enlightenment. The people of France, who were ruled by a rotation of monarchy, nobility, and clergy, none of whom cared for their problems or way of life, looked for a way to change their status and end the disparity between classes. The philosophers of the French Enlightenment sought to end the nobility's rule over France by changing the way the population thought.

The French Enlightenment philosophers picked up on the idea of natural law from their British counterparts. A mixture of the science and philosophies of Isaac Newton and John Locke, the Enlightenment embraced the idea that every man had certain rights upon birth. The monarch maintained its grasp on power by asserting that their bloodline had been chosen by God, in His divine wisdom, to lead nations. The Enlightenment began to put an end to this idea in the hearts and minds of French citizens who began to look at themselves and others as equals, not superior or inferior. Citizens were equal to those who taxed them and the old ways of thinking and ruling were viewed as a hindrance to the nation's progress.

Louis XVI called a meeting of the Estates General in 1789, which brought together the clergy (the First Estate), the nobility (the Second Estate), and the peasants (the Third Estate), which had not met since 1614. The meeting was designed to provide solutions to France's struggling economy and societal discourse. However, the groups came to an impasse at their first agenda item—whether they should vote by group status, giving the First and Second Estates the advantage, or vote democratically, based on numbers, which would give the Third Estate the advantage. The First and Second States arrived to the meeting with approximately three hundred members each, while the Third Estate arrived with over six hundred members. After several deadlocked votes, the Third Estate declared that they would become their own National Assembly, which failed to please Louis XVI, who proceeded to have them locked out of the meeting during a break; this, he assumed, would prevent them from assembling, thereby rendering them meaningless. However, the new National Assembly met in an indoor tennis court and swore the now famous Tennis Court Oath, pledging not to stop until a constitution for France had been written despite that act being against the order of the monarchy. This oath put forth the idea that the people, who had assembled and organized in the largest numbers, held the power.

The king sent troops into Paris to quell the uprisings over the food shortages, but the politicized citizens saw this as an antagonistic act and responded by seizing the Bastille Prison on July 14. Idealistically, the storming of the Bastille was meant to free prisoners as a symbolic act but, in reality, was used to attain weaponry. On August 4, 1789, the National Assembly abolished the Ancien Régime, their privileges across the board were wiped out in the name of writing a new constitution. On August 26, the National Assembly proclaimed the Declaration of Rights of Man and the Citizen, which detailed the rights applied to every person that were made integral to the new constitution.

During this time, the monarchy was still ensconced in Versailles and it appeared as though they would become constitutional monarchs, which would allow them to keep their land but relinquish any real power. In October 1789 a rumor began to spread that Louis XVI's wife, Marie Antoinette, was hoarding grains, which led to the Women's March when peasant women stormed the palace and demanded that the king and queen move from their palace to Paris. While the ideas and politics of the French Revolution helped spur on the educated classes, for the peasants this was a revolution about access to the basic human necessities, such as food. The French Revolution was underway.

The turn began in the Revolution when the Jacobins, who were the more radical members of the Revolution, called for France to become a republic. They were subsequently shot at by the National Assembly, who wanted to reign in their more radical ideas. Marie Antoinette's brother King Leopold of Austria grew weary of the uprising in France, particularly the talk of establishing France as a republic, which would render the monarchy obsolete. Together with King William Frederick of Prussia, they issued the Declaration of Pilnitz, which looked to restore the monarchy in France. France, led by Louis XVI and the National Assembly, launched a war against Austria to steal their resources, including grain, restoring some of the revolutionary excitement which was becoming untrustworthy. However, the Prussians aided the Austrians in battle which Louis XVI encouraged, led the National Assembly to turn on the king. The Assembly then decided to suspend the monarchy and have elections in which men from every class could vote and create a new republican constitution. During this period, Louis XVI was put on trial and sentenced to death by guillotine. Ironically, the guillotine was invented as an egalitarian way to put someone to death, as the blade severing the neck from the head made no distinction between class, wealth, and gender, but it would put to death the most powerful man in France as voted by the common people. As historian Brian Moynahan wrote of the impact of this time:

> The intimidating mass demonstration has remained a French art form; it draws its legitimacy for the election of the Revolution in the national consciousness, and its potency is such that, as recently as 1968, some dreamy students seemed on the verge of chasing the elected president into exile. By then, of course, France was on her Fifth Republic, evidence of the strange instability that the Revolution injected into this otherwise brilliant and coherent country.[2]

Following the air of the change the Revolution had brought to France came the September massacre of 1792. This was the inverse of the revolutionary spirit and saw vigilante mobs murder the inmates in Paris's prisons rather than free them. It is estimated that the mobs dragged approximately twelve hundred prisoners into public courtyards and beat, stabbed, or burned them to death from September 2 to 7 based on fear from the Revolutionaries that the royalist armies would attack Paris and free the inmates to join the army in battle. Year 1 of the French Republic was declared on September 22, 1792. A constitution was presented at that time but carried with it a significant disclaimer, that it should be put into effect when peace was restored. The new Republic had no time to waste and, effectively, ignored the disclaimer. Louis XVI was executed in January 1793 and what followed became known as the Reign of Terror.

The Terror occurred from September 1793 until July of the following year and saw anyone deemed an enemy of the Revolution swiftly executed, usually by guillotine. Tens of thousands were executed across

France, with the majority in Paris. France then had its first emperor by way of Napoleon Bonaparte, a title which effectively gave him all the powers that previous kings had enjoyed. In many ways, the Revolution could be seen as a failure as it tore down a structure from which only the wealthy benefited, only to be replaced by another system of power eerily resembling that which had come before it. Napoleon managed to lead France to victory in the Revolutionary Wars and the Napoleonic Wars, eventually gaining control of continental Europe in the span of ten years (1804–14). He was also a leader socially and, during his leadership, abolished any remaining traces of feudalism, emancipated religious minorities, and moved political power away from the Church and towards the State. Napoleon's reign would come to a swift end after his defeat at the Battle of Waterloo in 1815. Royals returned to France, with Louis XVIII returning to take command before dying on the throne, the last French king to do so. Succeeded in 1824 by Charles X, who believed in the divine right to rule, worked to give power back to the Church, effectively undoing many of the political and social mores that Napoleon had put in place.

Six years after Charles X took the throne what would become known as the July Revolution, or French Revolution of 1830, took place. Due to Charles's decrees that any enemies of the Revolution would have their property and wealth restored and, making blasphemy punishable by death, many saw the new king as pandering to the Catholic church, thereby violating the decrees made in the constitution. It all came to a head on July 25, 1830, when Charles X signed into law the July Ordinances, which, among other things, restricted the press and removed the emerging middle class's right to vote in any upcoming elections. After three days of protests, Charles X abdicated from the throne and a constitutional monarchy, where the king or queen acts as a head of state rather than an entity with any political or social power, was instated with a distant cousin, Louis Philippe of the House of Orléans, agreeing to rule under the conditions.

The Revolution of 1848 began in February and continued through the rest of the year. Spurred by the outlawing of fundraising banquets (or politically minded dinner parties) and since any other political demonstrations or gathering were also outlawed at this time, Parisians took to the streets ignoring the criminalization of their right to politically demonstrate and took their anger out on the king and François

Guizot, the king's chief domestic and international advisor. Erecting barricades the protestor soon clashed with the Parisian municipal guards. Guizot resigned the next day and, when crowds gathered outside the Ministry of Foreign Affairs, a musket was believed to be accidentally discharged by a member of the guards, leading the other soldiers to open fire on the crowd, resulting in fifty-two deaths that day. While chaos consumed the streets of Paris, King Louis Philippe quietly fled to the United Kingdom. The Second Republic was born.

France's thrill of returning to a republic once more was short-lived. On May 15, 1848, feeling the new government was becoming too conservative, even in its infancy, a large crowd marched from the Bastille to the Palais Bourbon, where the newly elected chamber of the Second Republic sat. The National Guard swiftly broke up the march and the demonstrators turned violent. Troops were brought in from the provinces outside Paris, partially due to their particular dislike of the radical Parisians, to put a swift end to the emerging insurrection. Four thousand citizens were killed in six days.

Presidential elections were scheduled for December of 1848 and saw Louis Napoleon, nephew and heir to Napoleon, win in a decided victory over his opponents. While Louis failed to undo all the traumas of France in the 1840s, he did succeed in bringing the country up to date with industrialization and helped its economic expansion by way of banking and railroad industries. In December 1851 Louis Napoleon dissolved the National Assembly without any rights to do so, becoming the sole ruler of France, taking the title of Emperor Napoleon III. Louis Napoleon also restored universal suffrage (the universal right to vote, except for women) which, naturally, many in the Assembly feared as they believed the peasants would surely vote against them. This was the dawn of the Second Empire.

The Second Empire of France would be marked by victories in battle, freedom of the press, and continued economic expansion. The end of the Empire would be at the hands of the Prussians who had gained power in the 1860s. Napoleon declared war on Prussia after a deliberate provocation from Otto Von Bismarck, a conservative statesman who dominated European affairs during that time. The war began on July 1870, with France's 270,000 troops on the ground with double the amount of troops on Prussia's side and more arriving from their German counterparts. The French army surrendered on September 1, 1870.

The news of the surrender reached Paris on September 4, at which time a new government was formed. The fall of the Empire was declared and the Third Republic began.

This start of the Third Republic, however, did not see the end of the war with Prussia, during which the French lost territories, thereby contributing to the already brewing social unrest. A few days after learning of France's defeat to the Prussians and Napoleon III's surrender, the Prussians marched on Paris and saw the establishment of the German Empire as well as the Paris Commune. The Paris Commune was a brief but radical socialist government that ruled Paris from March 18 to May 28, 1871. When France's officials signed the armistice with Prussia they agreed to disarm their army but not the National Guard, which, in that time, had become radicalized and aided the Commune in coming to power. The Commune refused to accept the government's authority and was violently suppressed by the French army in what was called "The Bloody Week." The rule of the Paris Commune was short-lived but influenced similar uprisings in Moscow, Budapest, and Petrograd. The Commune was revered by communists for their radical leftist agenda and praised by Vladimir Lenin, among others. The Third Republic saw the reestablishment of a presidential head of state and additions to the French Colonial Empire as they acquired French Indochina, French Madagascar, French Polynesia, and large territories in West Africa.

At the end of the Prussian siege of Paris began *La Belle Époque* or the Beautiful Era. For the first time in living memory, France (and especially Paris) enjoyed a cultural revolution, during which the arts flourished and scientific innovations abounded. It was a time to celebrate the homeland and enjoy everything it had to offer before the early decades of the 20th century would become marred by war. Another proponent of this time was mass transport. As industrialization swept through France, more and more workers were required, necessitating more homes in populated urban areas—foreshadowing the Paris suburbs. The Paris Metro was built and worked, alongside buses and streetcars, to get the worker to and from their homes, in turn allowing the wealthy to remain in Paris and the poor/working class to occupy the suburbs, ensuring a physical distance between them.

The major point of political upheaval during this time was the Dreyfus affair, a political scandal in 1894. Alfred Dreyfus was an artillery officer of Jewish descent. Accused of passing French military secrets to the German embassy in Paris, Dreyfus was convicted and imprisoned on Devil's Island, in French Guiana. New evidence came to light in 1896 identifying a French Army major named Ferdinand Walsin Esterhazy as the true culprit. The evidence was suppressed by officials and more charges were levied against Dreyfus. Rumors began to circulate of Dreyfus's innocence and culminated in the writer Émile Zola's open letter, "*J'Accuse*," in the French newspaper *L'Aurore*, placing pressure on the government to reopen the case. Dreyfus was brought back to France to be tried; he was, ultimately, exonerated in 1906, when he was reinstated in the army. The Dreyfus Affair led to a deep divide between the pro–Army (and mainly Catholic) supporters and the pro-republican contingent known as the Dreyfusards, leading to an increased distrust of the government.

During this time, when every facet of art was flourishing, France would have its first taste of the mad and macabre when Le Théâtre du Grand-Guignol (or Theater of the Big Puppet) opened its doors in 1897. While the term has become synonymous with over-the-top bloody horror, the theater became a Parisian institution, taking inspiration from the violent plays of Elizabethan and Jacobean theater, including *Titus Andronicus* and *The Duchess of Malfi*. A former chapel, the theater was the smallest in Paris, but quickly packed the house with promises of death, destruction, and sex. Many argue that Paris's easy acceptance of the blood-filled splatter plays of the Grand-Guignol was simply a carryover and expression of the death and perversion that had been part of French culture since the advent of the guillotine and the Marquis de Sade, and even made the horrors of the past more palatable because they offered an entertaining catharsis and release.

> Most plays were usually taking place in dark spaces like mental asylums and prisons, which were a synonym for the deviant nature of human condition and a fertile ground for the development of the monstrous character. These places were claustrophobic, hopeless, with no chance of escape; suffocating, out of sight places where everything is possible, and where no one can hear the screams of souls tortured by their own morality and character. Themes of revenge, love, hate and the double nature of people were predominant on the stage of Grand-Guignol, in a way depicting the time and the horrors of World War I, which prevailed in the outside world.[3]

The decline of the Grand-Guignol took place after World War II, though the theater itself managed to survive until 1968. Many attribute the decline of the Grand-Guignol with Parisians unable or unwilling to face so much blood and horror after the trauma of World War II.

In the midst of the *Belle Époque*, World War I raged around France, from 1914 to 1918. France joined forces with the United Kingdom, the United States, Italy, Japan, and the Russian Empire, which came to be known as the Allied Forces. They faced what were known as the Central Powers made up of Germany, the Ottoman Empire, and Austria-Hungary. The war was mainly fought near, or on, French soil due to the shared border with Germany, which led the war. The French were already distrustful of the Germans, who taken the provinces of Lorrain and Alsace during the Franco-Prussian War of 1870. In 1914, France had a population of 40 million, with 1.1 million registered service men in army reserve. By 1918, France had managed to mobilize 8.6 million men to fight in the war, with 1.39 million dead and another 4.25 million wounded, resulting in the largest number of casualties of any of the major warring nations—double the number of soldiers lost in the British army in the same period, with a comparative population of 45 million. The French army faced huge losses at the battle of Verdun and during the failed Nivelle offensive on the Chemin des Dames ridge, in April 1917. Though World War I saw a great number on casualties on all sides (especially as this was the first war in which many modern technologies and tactics were introduced), France, being so geographically adjacent to Germany, felt a need for additional security following the war's conclusion in 1918. On June 28, 1919, the Treaty of Versailles was signed; this officially returned to France the provinces of Lorrain and Alsace. Another 166,000 civilians were lost from 1918 to 1919 due to an outbreak of Spanish Influenza; consequently, the birth rate decreased dramatically. The aftermath of World War I in France was not only a massive loss of life but also a failing economic structure, making any attempts at rebuilding the country and strengthening national morale nearly impossible. To compensate for the devastation in France, its citizens demanded increased security, with the possibility of a "buffer state," brought up by then-president Georges Clemenceau, in the Rhine region against the German border. Though Europe worked to essentially handicap Germany by reducing their armed forces and forcing them to pay restitution for the damages caused by the war, France never felt safe. During the 1920s, with the rise of right-wing politicians in Germany, France maintained a watchful eye on its neighbors.

France began to prosper once again. The economy recovered, and industry flourished. Due to the decreased population following the war,

France worked to attract immigrants to flesh out the population, particularly from Italy, Spain, and Poland. Financial stability was short-lived, however. Two years after the stock market crashed in America in 1929, France began to feel the effects. France's exports were no longer in demand, industry was slowing down, and unemployment was rising. Deaths were outnumbering births in France from the mid-thirties on, with their population in 1939 stalling at 41.3 million, barely over a million more than in 1914. Germany's population, however, had grown by tens of millions in the same time period. In 1933, Germany withdrew from the European council, the League of Nations, and introduced compulsory military service for all able-bodied men, beginning in 1935. Adolf Hitler rose to power, bolstering nationalism among the Germans and extolling the ideas of a "pure" race. Many in Europe and abroad began to worry about the Germany that was forming under Hitler, but France watched its neighbor, unwilling and unable to do anything to stop it.

In 1939, France offered incentives to employers to increase the forty-hour work week to forty-eight hours, aiding production and industry, bracing the economy as war with Germany, once again, seemed an inevitability. France and Britain had already declared war on Germany in 1939, which many dubbed the "phony war." The French generals assumed, incorrectly, that war would once again be fought in the trenches as it had in World War I and had not accounted for advances in technology and strategy. On May 10, 1940, the Germans attacked via the Ardennes forest, which the French military commanders had thought to be impassable for armies; by May 20, the Germans had the Allied forces surrounded. Northern France began to panic and approximately 10 million French citizens, including 2 million from Paris, fled their homeland. The French government was also on the run, fleeing their offices in Paris and settling in the spa town of Vichy. The Third Republic, known for its liberal leanings, was on its last legs, with an armistice between France and Germany taking place on June 25, 1940. The terms of the armistice stated that the French military was capped at 100,000, with 1.5 million remaining troops taken as German hostages. The Alsace and Lorrain province were taken back by Germany, with the Germans occupying the most valuable parts of France, the north and Atlantic coasts, with the South of France becoming what France's then-president, Philipe Petain, called the "French State."

The Vichy government began dolling out brutality to anyone refusing to bend to their will or were deemed as outsiders, including anyone in the Jewish population, as well as Freemasons and communists. The Vichy government was overall more right wing and more traditionally patriarchal than their predecessors who founded the Third Republic on the ideals of equality. The Catholic church became once again a large proponent of the government, which deemed it necessary to abolish labor strikes in order to increase capital and quashed freedom of speech and freedom of the press. Women were tasked with being mothers and homemakers to bolster the population and temper any notions of social progression. Petain felt that it was not only his duty to protect what remained of France from the horrors of the Nazis but also to return the population to a more traditional and controlled way of life, preaching the beliefs of the Catholic church, a doctrine that became embedded in the French family at that time. By 1942, the Nazis had occupied the south of France as well. As a way of ingratiating themselves to the new order, the Vichy government not only proclaimed their allegiance but also engaged in enthusiastic anti–Semitism, which had been part of France's tradition until 1789, at which time Napoleon emancipated the Jewish population. Many of the Jewish population who now resided in France had emigrated from Germany, fleeing Hitler's regime. Any remaining members of the Jewish population were then rounded up by order of the Vichy government and held in a sports stadium, which had been turned into a pseudo concentration camp, before they could be deported. The hatred was also spread to homosexuals and other minorities, many of whom were rounded up and deported as well. While the Vichy regime was kowtowing to the Nazis, a left-wing resistance began to form in the north of France. While the resistance was passionate, they were disorganized and lacked the proper means of communication. Ex-Junior War Minister Charles de Gaulle, who had fled to Britain at the beginning of the war, read his message of support for the resistance and continuation of the struggle against the oppressive regimes over the BBC airwaves, which made its way to France. De Gaulle worked on the side of the Allies, providing insight and information and generally making himself useful. On August 19 and 20, 1944, the French Resistance launched an insurrection against the Nazi occupiers, beginning the Nazi retreat. In August 1944, Allied forces landed in Province and were making their way through France, liberating cities from the Nazi regime as they went. On August 26, 1944, a triumphant procession, which included de Gaulle, marched on Paris and declared France liberated from the Nazis. This marked the dawn of the Fourth Republic. De Gaulle was instrumental in the idea that no "true" Frenchman had collaborated with the Nazis; those who did, however, were put on public trial—that is, if the mobs did not get them first.

"No serenity was possible," wrote Simone de Beauvoir of the postwar period in France. "The war was over: it remained on our hands like a great unwanted corpse, and there was no place on earth to bury it."[4] By the end of World War II, France, along with most of Europe and overseas, was celebrating. The French resistance fighters had been incorporated into the Allied forces that marched on Germany; this helped mend the broken French psyche: they were part of their liberation and the liberation of Europe. It was hard to forget, though, what role it had played by way of the Vichy regime that had played to the Nazis. France longed to forget and move forward to a brighter, more hopeful era, but the shadow of World War II would be cast over France for decades to come. Cultural theorist Kristin Ross writes of this time period in her book *Fast Cars, Clean Bodies*:

> In France the state-led modernization drive was extraordinarily concerted, and the desire for a new way of living after the war widespread.... The speed with which French society was transformed after the war from a rural, empire oriented, Catholic country into a fully industrialized, decolonized, and urban one meant that the things modernization needed—educated middle managers, for instance, or affordable automobiles and other "mature" consumer durables, or a set of social sciences that followed scientific, functionalist models or a work force of ex-colonial laborers—burst into a society that still cherished prewar outlooks with all the force, excitement, disruption, and horror of the genuinely new.[5]

In her book, Ross lays out the ways that technologies like film and television made these elements desirable and related and how such magazines as *Elle* preached the gospel of frivolity in the wake of wartime atrocities. It was a gamble that, in large, part paid off, allowing the citizens of France to forget the atrocities that occurred on their soil in favor of the clean slate modernity offered.

The Fourth Republic in France wound up resembling the Third, with a bent towards left-leaning politics as those who had led and aided the resistance played up their importance in postwar France. Power and control, however, shuffled between multiple prime ministers between the Communist, Socialist, and the progressive Catholic group known as the Mouvement Républicain Populaire (MRP). This moved politics in France towards the center to make concessions for the desires of the Right and Leftist parties. De Gaulle led the charge of the Right, but scared off much of the population with his mass demonstrations which resembled the early Nazi rallies in Germany that had been seen in France, via newsreels, in the prewar years.

As France continued to march forward with its mandate of Americanized modernization, they also moved towards decolonization. This led to the Indochina War (1946–1954), Morocco and Tunisia gaining their independence and the bloody Algerian War (1954–1962). "Colonialism itself," writes Kristin Ross, was

> made to seem like a dusty archaism, as though it had not transpired in the twentieth century and in the personal histories of many people living today, as though it played only a tiny role in France's national history, and no role in modern identity.[6]

De Gaulle came to power as president in 1958, marking the start of the Fifth Republic as a result of the turmoil that erupted during the Algerian War. The French identity was becoming confused and fractured. No one wanted to acknowledge the horrors of the Algerian War, which, until the 1990s, was called a "public order operation," and the French were not above using brutal torture to quell the uprising from the colony. The war came to France in the Paris Massacre of 1961 when Paris police attacked a demonstration by the Algerian National Liberation Front, a socialist political party which had bombed France in order to destabilize and ignite fear within the country. The French police officially reported forty protestors dead, but other estimates put the death count at over two hundred. Eventually, France withdrew from Algeria in 1962 as part of the Evian Accords, which allowed for Algeria's liberation though the accords unsuccessfully blocked by the Organisation de l'armée secrète (Organization of the Secret Army); this group had executed a series of bombings and an assassination attempt on de Gaulle in order to prevent the liberation.

The liberation of Algeria was particularly painful for France as it seemed to be their last hold on any claim to being a superpower that could stand among the world leaders. The tactics used in maintaining their futile hold on Algeria were even more frightening. As scholar Danielle Costa writes of that time: "Painfully aware that French troops were behaving like Nazis, [law enforcement] wanted at least to prevent the French people from being guilty, as the German people had been, of silent complicity with these crimes."[7] French philosopher Jean-Paul

Sartre would argue that colonization was an act of violence within the context of French history. The colonies were conquered and power maintained through violence. He argued that, through the act of colonizing these countries, the natives recognized violence as their only means of control and assertion, leading to escalating violence during the conflict with Algeria, which, as Sartre points out, is hardly the fault of the Algerians. Kristin Ross writes of the 1950s and early '60s:

> If the consolidation of the broad middle class more or less transpires during these years, it is also during these years that France distances itself from its (former) colonies … this is the moment of great cordoning off of the immigrants, their removal to the suburbs in a massive reworking of the social boundaries of Paris and other large cities. On the national level France retreats within the hexagon, withdraws from empire, retrenches within its borders…. The movement inwards … is a movement echoed on the level of everyday life by the withdrawal of the middle class to their newly comfortable domestic interiors, to the electric kitchens, to the enclosure of private automobiles, to the interior of a new vision of conjugality and an ideology of happiness built around the new unit of upper–middle class consumption…. [Once] modernization has run its course, then one is, quite simply, either French or not, modern or not: exclusion becomes radical or national in nature.[8]

During decolonization, French employers actively sought workers from the colonies and former colonies to contribute to the man-power needed for postwar reconstruction, which helped shape France into the multiethnic country it is today, though the workers who came over still faced their share of racism despite being an integral part of postwar France. As Ross writes:

> The immigration that haunts the collective fantasies of the French today is the old accomplice to the accelerated growth of French society in the 1950s and 1960s. With the labor of its ex-colonial immigrants, France would not have successfully "Americanized," nor competed in the post-war industrial contest. In the economic boom years, in other words, France made use of its colonies "one last time" in order to resurrect and maintain its national superiority over them—a superiority made all the more urgent by the ex-colonies' newly acquired nationhood.[9]

May 1968 saw virtually the whole of Paris brought to a standstill, with protests, demonstrations, and sit-ins across the city. At the beginning of the year the Communist and Socialist parties joined together in an effort to overthrow de Gaulle in the next elections. Political activists, students, and artists joined forces to sway France back to the Left rather than the Right Wing, in which France had seemed to once again become entrenched. By May it was the university students who first took decisive action as they found their schools unable to cope with the steadily increased student populations. Poor conditions at the Nantes campus of the Paris University ignited student action. The police became swiftly involved in the protests and, if anything had been established by the Paris Massacre of 1961, the police were not above using violent and brutal tactics to quell anything resembling an uprising. Soon, factory workers and unions joined the protestors, which then led to demonstrations and labor strikes across France. While the events began with the left-leaning population, the events of May 1968 became a kind of catch-all, with workers demanding more pay and more autonomy. Police brutality escalated, with truncheons and tear-gas used against protestors as well as bystanders. While the events of May 1968 disrupted a nation, the protestors were too divided to achieve any real success. De Gaulle announced that there would be no change in government or to policies; the protests and demonstrations soon died out. The government did, however, offer increased wages to those who qualified, which constituted just enough to get France back to work with the unified right-wing party the UDR (Union des Démocrates pour la République) garnering a decisive victory in the elections in June 1968. The left-wing group was left to lick its wounds.

Georges Pompidou would succeed de Gaulle and maintain the Right's control over France by propagating a steadfast infrastructure and appeasing the voters. Pompidou was instrumental in carrying on another of de Gaulle's projects, Paris as a site for the cultural elite. Begun in 1962, Paris's historical buildings were cleaned and refurbished while still maintaining their appeal to the elite.

The Left eventually returned to power from 1981 to 88, with the election of Francois Mitterrand as president. Mitterrand had worked for the Vichy government as a young man, but quickly joined the Resistance—a decision for which he was decorated. Mitterrand's tenure as president was marked by ups and downs and many lost elections, resulting in "cohabitation governments" led by Jacques Chirac (1986–88), and Édouard Balladur (1993–95,) with Chiraq becoming France's new president in 1988. Throughout the 1990s, one of the central controversies France faced was the banning of hijabs, a veil worn by some women of the Muslim faith, in French public schools. The controversy continues to this day, with no end in sight, as the French government feels it necessary to police Muslim and other immigrant communities in varying ways, citing different methodologies for their decisions.

As the Right rose once again in France in the 1990s, the fear and evidence of police brutality as well as conservative discourse sparked riots in Paris and its suburbs. The suburbs had been the site of multiple riots and political unrest for several decades, but the two-year period, beginning in 2005, marked its most violent and consistent outbursts. The flames of the riots were fanned by politician Nicholas Sarkozy, former minister of the interior, who was elected president in 2007. Leader of the Right, Sarkozy won on a platform of reform but spoke with increasing menace of his "path of brutality," which his opponents viewed as viciously unnecessary, socially conservative reform. During Sarkozy's rise to power, the streets of Paris and its suburbs were the site of deadly riots, pitting many young people from immigrant families against the police, marring Paris's beatific façade and tourist trade. The riots stemmed from police violence and led to Sarkozy's zero-tolerance policy, creating a state of fear and panic. Filmmaker Mathieu Kassovitz, whose 1995 film *La Haine* documented life in the Paris suburbs during a brutal riot, entered into a public debate in 2005 with then–Interior Minister Sarkozy when Kassovitz posted an open letter on his blog.

Kassovitz: If the suburbs are exploding once again today, it is not due to being generally fed up with the conditions of life that entire generations of "immigrants" must fight with every day. These burning cars are [in direct response to] the lack of respect the minister of the interior has shown towards their community. Sarkozy does not like this community. He wants to get rid of these "punks" with high-pressure water hoses, and he shouts it loud and clear right in the middle of a "hot" neighborhood at 11 in the evening. The response is in the streets. "Zero tolerance" works both ways. It is intolerable that a politician should allow himself to upset a situation made tense by years of ignorance and injustice, and openly threaten an entire segment of the French population.

Sarkozy: You seem to be acquainted with the suburbs well enough to know, deep inside you, that the situation has been tense there for many years and that the unrest is deep-rooted. Your film *La Haine*, shot in 1995, already showed this unease that right-wing and left-wing governments had to deal with, with varying results. To claim this crisis is down to the Minister of the Interior's sayings and doings is yet another way of missing the point. I attributed this to an untimely and quick-tempered reaction.

The second thing that shocked me is that you seem to clearly speak up for the minority, made of looters, rather than for the majority, made of families and young people who live in the suburbs too and who are sick of seeing the culture of violence and of power struggle undermine our legally constituted state. Why not speak up for those whose cars were burnt, and who are now deprived of a hard-earned tool, synonymous with work and freedom? Why not mention the young people whose gyms were burned down and the children whose schools were destroyed? Moreover, why not write a single word about the 110 injured policemen, the firemen hit by stones, the insulted doctors? Your emotional affinity with the suburban youths is understandable and respectable, but I feel that it leads you to accept the unacceptable. To make common cause with a minority whose actions are reprehensible, or even murderous in some cases, is not helping the situation in the suburbs. I even believe it has the reverse effect. To live in a working-class district or to be the son of immigrant parents or grandparents gives you no right to throw Molotov cocktails at the police and stones at firemen. To intimate the contrary is, in my opinion, to insult all those who behave as responsible citizens in similar living conditions.

Kassovitz: The brutal death of Malik Ousekine, followed by Charles Pasqua's (one of your predecessors) inhuman remarks, date from 20 years ago. The history of present-day France is stained with the blood of Makomé, shot down in cold blood in a police station of the 18th arrondissement, and of many other victims of the decline of the Republican values you defend. This history, full of injustice, fuels our present. I am only asking you not to forget, even if you are not directly responsible for this. We need to reeducate people, and not manipulate them. The dissension between forces of law and order and the suburbs' young people is a deep-rooted problem, which can only be solved by serious effort to educate both parties.

I am not opposed to the police; on the contrary, I am in favor of a better-respected, better-educated, and more human police…. A kind of police I can trust over my personal and my children's security, regardless of social condition, skin color, age, or belief…. When you mention a return to the Republican values, don't forget that you have to command respect before you can expect it in return. Since the police has lost the respect it should command, then once again you should ask yourself what the real problems are. You claim to be turned towards the future, yet your methods are repressive and obsolete. You panicked and voted the return of a military law dug out from some of the darkest days in the history of our country. The choice of this highly symbolic law is a disgrace to our country and its politicians. Yet, as usual, you are not responsible.

… We are French, and whatever our politics, we are rebels to the core, always ready to fight [for] a cause we deem honorable. Those are the values you defend through your acts; please try to understand that some other people do the same thing, even though their means might be inadequate and unjust. They are the only means for them to make themselves heard. The thousands of burning cars and the complete loss of political authority are more than simple explosions of violence—they are a symbol. Remain attentive. The future of a multicultural and antiracist France depends on that. The extreme right rhetoric is already echoing within your party. I am sure this makes you feel as sick as me.[10]

François Hollande, a left-wing politician, was elected president in 2012, though the fear and uncertainty in France has not ended with continued clashes between the police and the people. France has also been the site of numerous terrorist threats and attacks, such as the Charlie Hebdo shootings on January 7, 2015, and the November 13, 2015, rampage which would become the single deadliest terrorist attack in French history. Multiple shooting and grenade attacks occurred in a music venue, sports stadium, and several bar and restaurant terraces. *ISIS* claimed responsibility for the attacks.

Slovenian Marxist philosopher Slavoj Žižek has written extensively about the use of violence as a means of understanding public consciousness, citing the violence used in the French Revolution, the riots of 1968, and in the new millennium, which seemed to have no lasting impact but that of disruption. German philosopher Walter Benjamin, who wrote of "divine" and "mythic" violence in his essay *Critique of Violence*, identified "mythic" violence as state-founding violence which establishes and conserves laws, while "divine" violence breaks and disrupts the cycle of violence used to maintain order. Žižek applies this notion of "divine" violence to the French Revolution, and many other uprisings throughout the world, which served to destabilize those in power:

> [T]he opposition of mythic and divine violence is that between the means and the sign, that is, mythic violence is a means to establish the rule of Law (the legal social order), while divine violence serves no means, not even that of punishing the culprits and thus re-establishing the equilibrium of justice. It is a sign of the injustice of the world, of the world being ethically "out of joint."[11]

This notion of "divine" violence can be applied throughout France's history and extends to New French Extremity, which can be seen as an artistic representation of the idea. New French Extremity consistently and continually brings to light that which has been repressed and which the government feels is best forgotten. It is a demarcation in French cinema, a cinema of auteurs who tell the stories they see around them that merge history with the present. Violence in France has always been a given, not an anomaly.

France has been the site of revolution, art, and intellectualism. For all the accomplishments to which France can claim, they cannot ignore the sins of the past, which continue to revisit them. French political theorist and writer Alexis de Tocqueville (1805–1859) once described France as "the most brilliant and dangerous nation ... an object of admiration, hatred, pity or terror but never indifference."[12] For everything France has accomplished and contributed to the world, it has never truly grown up. From their demands of revolution in the 18th century to 1968 to 2005, France has failed to create change consistently demanded by its people. The government's use of fear caused its people to resort to anarchy, consistently destabilizing the country. The auteurs of New French Extremity may not offer solutions for which the masses have clamored, but they offer a vision of France, one that has not forgotten its history but confronts it.

2

Cinéma pour Tous
The Film Industry in France

I have always preferred the reflection of the life
to life itself.—*François Truffaut*

While France's history has been a tumultuous one, it has also been one of extensive innovation and artistry. France's film industry has been at the heart of its culture for over a century; it is not only the birthplace of film, but one of its leading producers. The French would use films not only to entertain and educate their people but to sedate them during times of uncertainty. There was a caustic and complicated relationship between the government which fought to control messaging in films, the auteurs who sought to make art in the emerging medium, and the audiences who went to the cinema.

The film industry truly began in France in the 1890s. In 1892, Léon Bouly had created the *Cinématographe Léon Bouly*, taking the term *cinématographe* from the Greek word meaning "writing in movement." Bouly, however, lacked the funds to properly develop the invention any further; neither could he afford to maintain the patent. He therefore sold the rights and name of the device to Auguste and Louis Lumière, who would become better known as the Lumière Brothers. The brothers continued to develop and build on Bouly's work and, in February 1895, patented their own version and shot footage with it for the first time on March 19, 1895. The subject of their experimental film was that of workers leaving the Lumière factory; this historic film bore the rather prosaic title, *Sortie des usines lumière à Lyon* (*Workers Leaving the Lumière Factory*). The Lumière Brothers held a makeshift film festival in the Salon Indien du Grand Café in Paris presenting the first ten films they had shot at the end of that year. The following year, 1896, saw the brothers take their invention on tour to Buenos Aires, Brussels, Bombay, London, Montreal, and New York City. The beginning of that year also saw the premiere of the most famous of their films *The Arrival of a Train at La Ciotat Station* (*L'Arrivée d'un train en gare de La Ciotat*). The film has gone down in popular lore as inducing mass panic among the first audiences who saw it. The film literally depicts a train coming into the station, with the train seemingly coming directly at the audience due to the camera's angle. Whether it caused the supposed panic or not, the film elicited a reaction by depicting an everyday event in an elevated and cinematic way, changing the audience's perception of a mundane event.

Through the dawn of the next century other filmmakers began to emerge, the most popular of which were Pathé Frères, the Gaumont Film Company, and the Georges Méliès company. Georges Méliès, a former magician and the cinema's first true artist, produced over five hundred imaginative short films, two hundred of which survive today. In 1896, he made cinema's first horror film, *The Haunted Castle* (*Le Manoir du diable*), which features bats, skeletons, witches, and demons present in the titular castle. He also made one of the most iconic silent films, widely regarded as the first science-fiction film, *A Trip to the Moon* (*Le Voyage dans la Lune*), in 1902. Both *The Haunted Castle* and *A Trip to the Moon* can be viewed in the context of the French literary tradition of the *fantasique* or fantasy genre, which would continue to evolve as cinema in France grew. Méliès's career went into decline beginning in 1908, when many felt his creative output was becoming repetitive. The year 1908 also saw American inventor Thomas Edison create the Motion Pictures Patent Company in an effort to control film production in America and abroad. The amalgamation of many prominent and emerging film companies under this banner required them to produce 1,000 feet of film per week. By the following year, Méliès had stopped making films due, in part, to his disappointment over the tepid reception to his most ambitious film, *Humanity Through the Ages*, a pessimistic retelling of humanity's lineage, and his frustration with Edison's monopoly over an industry that was still in its infancy. While presiding over the International Filmmakers Congress in Paris in 1909, Méliès articulated his concerns and the filmmakers present who decided not to sell their films outright but lease them for four-month periods, allowing the filmmakers to maintain some control over their product. Méliès would return to filmmaking to create some of his most fantastical films, including *The Conquest of the Pole* (1912) and *Cinderella, or the Glass Slipper* (1912). His later work failed to capture audiences' imagination; this has been attributed to his increasing reliance on classical narrative functions over the pure inventiveness of his early work. By the time the First World War came to France's doorstep, Méliès had all but given up the filmmaking trade and returned to his theatrical and illusionist roots, performing for the troops. During the war the French army confiscated over four hundred original prints from Mélièsir studio, melting them down to make, among other things, heels for soldiers' boots. At the Gaumont Film Company, onetime secretary Alice Guy was emerging as a prominent film director, overseeing more than a thousand films; she has also been credited as creating narrative cinema with *The Cabbage Fairy* (*La Fée aux Choux*), made a few months before Méliès's first fiction film. In 1908, Guy moved to America, where she founded The Solax Company, a motion picture studio, with her husband, Herbert Blaché, and George A. Magie. As the 20th century progressed into its teens, the film industry was proving to be a formidable rival to live theater.

The arrival of World War I saw a decline in the national French cinema. Resources were redirected to the war effort without consideration to the archiving of film (as was the case with Méliès's films) and during the period from 1914 to 1918 American films became *de rigeur* in the cinemas as they provided a virtually unending stream of content. One French film to break through the American films being shown was Louis Feuillade's *Les Vampires* (1915), a silent film told in a serial format, totaling an almost seven-hour running time, making it one of the longest films ever made. *Les Vampires* refers to the name of a group of criminals, rather than a literal vampire figure, and the film actually benefited from wartime, with Feuillade capturing eerie and unsettling shots of a deserted Paris. While the film was maligned by critics on its release due to its lack of morals and apparent lack of filmic techniques, it was nevertheless a hit with wartime audiences who responded to the scandalous and escapist subject matter. The film has influenced directors such as Fritz Lang and Alfred Hitchcock with its emerging thriller tropes and *avant-garde* cinema with its surreal images.

After the war, with resources still depleted, the film industry in France struggled to return to the momentum it had gained at the turn of the century. The audience's appetite did not fade, so the trend of importing American films continued in France and across Europe. To keep the film industry from completely collapsing in favor of the American product, France regulated a 1:7 import quota, meaning that for every seven foreign films imported France had to produce one film which would screen in cinemas. In the intervening years between the two World Wars, French cinema began to establish itself as an artistic counterpart to the narratively straight-forward American films as expressionist cinema flourished in the 1920s, and poetic realism, which favored a stylized recreation of life rather than a documentary-like format, became popular in the 1930s. One of the leaders of the French Impressionist Cinema was Jean Epstein, who is best remembered for his 1928 silent horror film, *The Fall of the House of Usher*. The film, which was co-written by Epstein and Luis Buñuel, focused on a stylistic interpretation of the Edgar Allan Poe story, creating fear and suspense out of atmosphere and imagery rather than plot, making it an emblem of the French *avant-garde* movement. The 1930s also saw the establishment of the Cannes Film Festival, which continues to this day to be highly influential in the industry, functioning as a buyer's market for international films and critical taste marker for both distributors and moviegoers.

When the German army crossed France's borders in 1940, the country's entire way of life would change. From June 1940 to August 1944, the Vichy regime governed France while the Nazis occupied it. The Vichy regime collaborated with the Nazis because they felt that it was easier than fighting and suffering the losses they endured in World War I. The cooperation with Nazis also allowed some of the French to indulge in their anti–Semitism and racism, which was a very poorly hidden secret. After the fall of France to the Nazis, artists faced the question of whether it was better to leave the country or stay and produce in the face of the Nazi regime, ensuring that French culture did not completely disintegrate at that time. There was a heavy split between the two decisions. Jean Renoir, Rene Clair, and Max Ophuls all escaped the country via the privately American-subsidized Emergency Rescue Committee (ERC). Other filmmakers stayed, sensing that they would have to adhere to whatever restrictions were imposed by the Nazis, but continued to make quality films.

Under the Nazis, French films were restricted from having any anti–Nazi or anti–German sentiment and were forbidden to utilize any contributions from the Jewish population. At the request of the Vichy regime, the Committee for the Organisation of the Cinematographic Industries (COIC) was established in Paris to ensure that French films continued to be produced and that the Nazis did not fully control the creative output of their people. American and British films were banned and German films were imported. Though the production of new films was significantly lower than in previous years, their popularity and profitability increased as audiences were hungry for the escapist nature of the new French films. That cinemas offered warmth and safety was an added bonus.

The creative output during this period was decidedly fantastical in nature, leading to the "vast mainstream of French productions indeed escaping censorship, thanks to the depth and fullness of their very creativity."[1] With the restrictions imposed by the Nazis, the French directors found it easier to turn to fairy tales, fables, and myths, with films such as Carne's *Les Visiteurs du soir* (1942) and *L'Eternal Retour* (1943), directed by Jean Delannoy. There was also the rise of what was dubbed the "woman's film" like Abel Gance's *La Fille du Venus aveugle* (*The Blind Venus*, 1940), Jean Gremillon's *Le Ciel est a vous* (*The Sky Is Yours*, 1943), and Pagnol's *La Fille du puisatier* (*The Well-Digger's Daughter*, 1942), all of which focused on female-driven plots wherein the women remained the idealized version of motherhood, domesticity, and servitude. Both these trends were in line with the conservative stance of the Vichy regime: encouraging women to stay at home and raise families and the fantastical trend in films was seen as being more purely French, of the land, without the influence of Hollywood or other external sources. As Rémi Fournier Lanzoni writes in his history of French cinema:

> Paradoxical as it may appear, French productions, unlike German and Italian national cinemas, never openly reflected any major theme of Vichy propaganda that was usually broadcast by Radio-Paris or by the Parisian press.... French audiences [during the occupation] were in large part ignoring the effort of [spreading] misinformation [in newsreels which played before films] (also found in the press, current affairs footage, and radio broadcasts).... As a matter of fact, the French people were known for their legendary, and self imposed *attentisme*, a "wait and see" state of mind.[2]

Despite all this, the films produced in France at this time were well-made crowd pleasers and more successful than the Nazi propaganda films. The French films upheld the Nazi ideology of purity and the motherland but dressed them up for popular consumption; eventually, the Nazis approved the distribution of these films to other Axis-controlled countries. One of the most popular films made during the period of Nazi occupation was *The Raven* (*Le Corbeau*, 1943), directed by Henri-Georges Clouzot. The plot deals with a small town in France where the local doctor starts receiving anonymous letters accusing him of having an affair. The letters begin to spread all over the town incriminating others, leading to a rash of suicides and murders. Several elements of this film are particularly forward thinking for their time: the protagonist doctor performs illegal abortions for women who request them; the doctor's lover is promiscuous and has a minor deformity; and the villain of the piece is revealed to be a highly educated and respected member of society. After France's liberation, the film was banned and those involved with its production were threatened with punishment and execution. Though the scenario is easily read as anti-authoritarian and anti-fascist, it was produced by Continental Films, a German film company established at the beginning of the war, which actually fired Clouzot before the film's release due its content. However, members of the Resistance felt that the film—along with every other title produced by Continental Films—was a symbol and reminder of the occupation and must be banned from public consumption.

Almost any film of this period can be read as anti-occupation, although this was never addressed directly at the time. Clouzot was banned from making films in France until 1947, although the director quickly returned to mass popularity with the release of such well-received films as *The Wages of Fear* (1952) and *Les Diaboliques* (1955). *Les Diaboliques* tells the story of a wife and mistress who murder the man who has been deceiving them both. The film is a chilling study of sanity, so suspenseful in its execution that it influenced directors for generations to come. Released in the United States as *Diabolique*, it was an international success, cementing Clouzot's status as one of the most entertaining directors of the 20th century.

Following the liberation of France, the *avant-garde* movement continued. Films such as Robert Bresson's *Diary of a Country Priest* (1951) contributed to the minimalist style of the time, and Jean Cocteau's *Beauty and the Beast* (*La Belle et la bête*, 1946) and *Orphée* (1950) pushed the boundaries of realism and surrealism with their dreamy atmosphere and camera tricks. The period also saw the birth of *Cahiers du Cinéma* (*Notebooks on Cinema*) in 1951. Founded by André Bazin, Jacques

Doniol-Valcroze, and Joseph-Marie Lo Duca, the film magazine developed out of *Revue du Cinéma* (*Review of the Cinema*) and involved the members of popular Paris cinema clubs, eventually giving rise to contemporary film analysis. The writers, under the watchful eye of Balzin, discusses contemporary and past works of emerging and established directors and eventually coined the term "auteur theory" (a term first used by critic Andrew Sarris in the early 1960s as a loose translation of the *politique des auteurs* notion, first promulgated in 1954 by François Truffaut), which views the director as the creative force behind the film. Among the writers at *Cahiers du Cinéma* were Jean-Luc Godard, François Truffaut, Claude Chabrol, Jacques Rivette, Éric Rohmer, and Truffaut, who would all go on, not only go on to direct, but to be labeled by the Paris press as the *Nouvelle Vague* (literally, New Wave). Lasting from the late 1950s to the early '60s, the French New Wave was not an officially organized or established movement, but the directors all congregated around the ideals of a less formalist approach to film, rejecting the tradition of adapting literary pieces to the screen in order to focus on more pressing issues and attitudes of the time. The directors embraced advancing technologies in cinema, using cameras that required little to no setup time, allowing them to shoot their films on the go. They also eschewed the formalist techniques of narrative films, instead embracing disjointed editing, handheld cameras, and including surrealist elements in naturalistic settings. These new techniques led to the films' ambiguous morals and outcomes, allowing the viewers to interpret and disseminate what they had just seen. The aesthetics of New Wave cinema have come to dominate the Western Cultural landscape rather than the ideas it espoused. As Richard Brody, film writer of *The New Yorker*, wrote of this effect:

> [I]t was a discerning passion for Hollywood movies that launched a young band of critics at *Cahiers du Cinéma* into notoriety and inspired them to make movies under the journalistic rubric of the New Wave—and it was the sudden rush of creation in the late fifties that led France's then Minister of Culture, André Malraux, to introduce a series of measures intended to promote the production and distribution of French movies not just as commercial ventures but as works of art that would be fundamental to France's cultural heritage. The New Wave directors, themselves at least in the early years, hardly benefited from this system, which, however, reinforced their critical legacy—that of the auteur, the individual creator, as the key element in movie production—as the image of French cinema as marketed to the world.... It's the art-film industry—or, all too often, some soft centered version of art films—that sustains the image of French films around the world, often less by way of the inventive artistry

than by a culturally-toned range of subject that substitutes genteel intellectualism and superficial politics for cinematic audacity.[3]

Through this and the coming decades, French cinema began an interesting relationship with the documentary format, particularly when dealing with the subject of the Holocaust perpetrated by the Nazis and aided by, among others, the Vichy regime in France during the occupation of World War II. The first images of the concentration camps were shown in cinemas in France in 1945 in the *Actualités Française* newsreel, *Les Camps de la mort*. Three documentaries would follow over the next few decades—Alain Resnais's *Nuit et brouillard* (1955), Marcel Ophüls's *Le Chagrin et la pitié* (1971) and Claude Lanzmann's *Shoah* (1985)— encouraging their French audience to remember the past and question their role in it. These films went against the mandates of the postwar period and Fifth Republic, established by Charles de Gaulle, which sought only to look forward and never back on the atrocities that had been committed on French soil. The Gaullist myth perpetuated the notion that the French people had never truly collaborated with the Nazis and were all working with the Resistance forces to oust them. Obviously, de Gaulle's notion of the *fantasique* was not confined solely to the screen. This trend of illuminating the travesties of history would continue into the 1990s, with *The War Without a Name* (*Le Guerre sans nom*, 1992), directed by Bertrand Tavernier and Patrick Rotman, which reexamined the decolonization of Algeria—hitherto unacknowledged as a war.

While the style of the day was decidedly New Wave attracting directors and actors from all over the country to work on this emerging trend, Georges Franju's lyrical nightmare *Eyes Without a Face* (*Les Yeux sans visage*) made a small impact in its 1960 release mostly because of the angrily dismissive reviews that preceded its release. Isabel Quigley, writing for the British newspaper *The Spectator*, called it "the sickest film since I started film criticism."[4] Roy Armes' history French Cinema published in 1966 describes Franju as belonging to "no school, group of generation and [paid] no heed to current fashions or trends."[5] Influenced by horror films of the late 1950s such as Terence Fisher's *Curse of Frankenstein* (1957) and *Horror of Dracula* (1958), Clouzot and his producers saw an opportunity to create a niche within the French market for horror films. Though *Eyes Without a Face* was unsuccessful on its initial release, it has become a cult-classic and a highly influence film in the horror genre. Much of the film's failure has been attributed to the French milieu of the time, fantastical films were *de rigueur* in the in industry but horror was seen as low-brow, at odds with the carefully crafted image for French cinema. Many critics felt confused that would-be auteur Franju would debase himself and his cinema with a low-brow tawdry horror film. Franju was best known for his documentary short *Blood of the Beasts* (*Le Sang des bêtes*) made in 1949 and co-founding the Cinémathèque Française in 1937. *Blood of the Beasts* features an in-depth look at the happenings within slaughter-houses contrasted with images of quiet and beatific scenes from the suburbs of Paris. In the film Franju creates a lyrical relationship between the brutality of murdering animals for their meat and the life that is allowed to flourish because of it.

Eyes Without a Face was based on the novel by Jean Redon. Franju was determined to update the story of a mad doctor whose daughter suffers a face disfiguring accident causing the doctor to kidnap, kill and remove the faces of young women in an effort to give his daughter a new face by bringing on the writing duo Pierre Boileau and Thomas Narcejac who wrote the novel *Elle qui n'était plus* (*She Who Was No More*) which *Les Diaboliques* was based on. The writers kept the basic plot of the novel but shifted the focus from the mad doctor to his daughter, Christiane. The hope was to draw empathy as well as fear from the audience in hopes of helping the film pass the watchful eye of the censors. Franju's film can be seen as a precursor to New French Extremity for blending gore with human frailty and tragedy. *Eyes Without a Face* embraced some aspects of the French Wave, especially the notions of vague morals and politics as the film ends on a bittersweet note and the violence that happens, happens out of love and familial ties. It has also been seen as formalistically made with each shot composed and formed, with little of the freedom which the New Wave espoused. It depicts brutal violence to multiple bodies while remaining beautiful, ethereal without explicit condemnation. The white, expressionless mask that Christiane wears throughout the film offers a physical manifestation of the blank slate that the audience is meant to project themselves onto, offering no answers.

Despite France's near-universal rejection of *Eyes Without a Face* as part of their national cinema, France's next horror auteur would follow a few years later. Jean Rollin's obsession with vampires was brought to the screen in the midst of riots of May 1968. Though not quite a hit,

Rollin's first feature film *The Rape of the Vampire* (*Le Viol du vampire*, 1968) established the tropes that would follow the director through his career; dreamlike disjointed narratives, beautiful nude women and bloodshed which would continue to permeate the frames of Rollin's cinema. While some disagree that Rollin even made horror films, it can be agreed that he made films outside the norm that were largely ignored if not reviled within his home country. Part of the beauty of the films that Rollin made (outside of their visual style) is that he brought all that was seen as low and tawdry such as nudity and sexuality and elevated them to the status of an art film through his filmic techniques. In his career Rollin directed more than 40 low-budget horror films becoming a popular cult director as his films found audiences outside of his native France. His films merged influences such as the French landscape, comic books and the work of surrealist artists to create erotic horror thrillers which have been unmatched even to this day.

The 1980s saw the emergence of *"cinéma du look,"* a term coined by French film critic Raphaël Bassan in the magazine *La Revue du Cinéma*. Cinéma du look is seen as favoring of past cinematic style and masters, with direct visual nods to past films particularly of the New Wave movement, utilizing new cinematic technologies which were being rapidly refined. Directors Luc Besson and Jean-Jacques Beineix made the populist films of cinéma du look and Leos Carax, a former writer for *Cahiers du Cinéma*, rounded out the movement with more intellectual films. Cinéma du look was repeatedly criticized for, just as its name suggests, valuing aesthetics over ideology and was often compared to "lower" forms of culture, such as the music video. As Guy Austin points out of the criticism of cinéma du look:

> [T]he absence of ideology [is] the central plank of attack [against Cinéma du look]—an absence which is seen to stem from the fading of Marxism in France (and indeed Europe), the electoral triumph of the Socialists in May 1981, and the growth of centrist "consensus politics" in the decade that followed. Equating "authentic cinema" with ideology, critics have tended to neglect the aesthetic importance of the Cinéma du look.[6]

Cinéma du look's longevity lies in its blending of populist (or "lower" aesthetics) with story lines that deal with the young generation in France who feel isolated and unsatisfied. The politics of their parents has failed to yield results that matter to them, leading to their feeling alienated by the culture they were meant to embrace. Cinéma du look brought

Hollywood-esque stylings to French cinema, making it more palatable and sleeker than the films which had come before it.

As France approached the new millennium, cinema was more important than ever. It was not only the major cultural output for the country, it was also a sign of the time. The French film industry flirted with classical French stories translated to film, thereby becoming part of popular culture. One example of this is Jean-Paul Rappeneau's *Cyrano de Bergerac* (1990), which won multiple César awards (the French Oscar) and was nominated for Best Foreign Language Film at the Academy Awards. The year 1990 also saw the release of Christian de Chalonge's *Docteur Petiot*, based on a real serial killer who operated in Paris during the Nazi occupation of World War II. Chalonge focuses on the double life of the titular character, a respectable doctor by day and murderer of members of the Jewish population by night. Film scholar Guy Austin views *Docteur Petiot* as the film that Jean Luc Goddard always thought was necessary to make about the Holocaust, quoting Goodard, "The only real film to make about them ... would be if a camp were filmed from the point of view of the torturers and their daily routine.... The really horrible thing about such scenes would not be their horror but their very ordinary everydayness."[7]

Cinéma du look director Luc Besson broke out from the pack with his international hit *Nikita*, also released in 1990. As with his previous film, Besson's slick style appealed to an international audience and his subsequent films, including *The Professional* (1994) and *The Fifth Element* (1997), created a international name for the French auteur, who combined European aesthetics with an American action sensibility. Besson would go on to produce and co-write the *Taken* franchise, which remains one of France's most profitable films. Besson would also be an ally to the films of New French Extremity, offering support and advice to such young directors as Alexandre Aja and Xavier Gens. Another emerging director of the 1990s was Jean-Pierre Jeunet, whose feature film debut was *Delicatessen*, in 1991. The plot follows a series of quirky characters in a post-apocalyptic world. The film was well-received in Hollywood as well, and in 1997 Jeunet directed the fourth entry in the Alien franchise, *Alien: Resurrection*, which was widely panned by critics and audiences alike. He returned to France and would go on to make one of the most iconic contemporary French films, *Amélie* (2001). Director, actor, editor Mathieu Kassovitz's *La Haine* was released in 1995 and was a star-making turn for actor Vincent Cassel. The film follows three friends who live in an impoverished multi-ethnic French housing project (a ZUP—*zone d'urbanisation prioritaire*) in the suburbs of Paris, in the aftermath of a riot. Kassovitz has stated that the inspiration for the film came from an incident when a young man from an immigrant family was killed while chained to a radiator in police custody. The film used footage of real riots that had taken place in and around Paris from 1986 to 1996, with actual riots occurring while the film was being shot on location. *La Haine* was a critical and financial success and opened a dialogue concerning the income disparities in and around Paris. The film made such an impact, in fact, that then–Prime Minister Alain Juppe organized a screening of the film which his fellow ministers were required to attend.

Kassovitz began the new millennium with the release of the bloody crime thriller *Crimson River*, which managed a respectable box office internationally, helping establish the star power of Vincent Cassel and Jean Reno (with whom American moviegoers were familiar from Besson's *The Professional*). The two actors would go on to have hugely successful careers in their home country and play supporting roles in American films such as *Mission: Impossible* (Reno) and *Ocean's Twelve* (Cassel). The year that saw the release of *Amélie*, 2001, also marked the premiere of Christopher Gans's *Brotherhood of the Wolf*, which blended France's historical past with kung fu and werewolf mythology and would go on to become another international sensation. American director Richard Linklater's beloved sequel to 1995's *Before Sunrise*, *Before Sunset* takes place in Paris, where two former lovers, Jesse (Ethan Hawke) and Celine (Julie Delpy), reconnect. While not a French film, the utilization of Paris as a backdrop propagated the notion of the City of Light as a place for lovers. Linklater presented Paris so lovingly that the city not only becomes, as the cliché goes, another character in the film, it might as well have been made by the tourist board of France.

During this time the emerging movement of New French Extremity would become a cultural crisis. While it had been bubbling under the surface of the French film industry—with films like *Sombre* (1998) and *Criminal Lovers* (1999)—it would come to a head with *Baise-moi* (2000) and *Irréversible* (2002), both of which ignited national, and even international, debate. France once again was part of the mainstream film conversation when, in 2008, due to Marion Cotillard's astonishing portrayal of Edith Piaf in Oliver Dahan's 2007 film, *La Vie en Rose* (initially released in France under the title, *La Môme*), for which she won the Academy Award for Best Actress. Cotillard's performance and acceptance speech at the Oscars charmed American audiences, allowing the actress to transition into roles in American films such as *Inception* (Christopher Nolan, 2010).

The second decade of the millennium would bring France's crowning achievement in the film industry in terms of international and critical recognition alongside a healthy box-office take. Michel Hazanavicius's 2011 film *The Artist*, a black-and-white silent film (and a crowd pleaser in the same vein as *Amélie*) continued France's path to Oscar gold, with the film nominated for ten Academy Awards and winning in the Best Picture, Best Director, and Best Actor categories. While the film was a critical darling; it failed to speak to any of the turbulence occurring in France; instead, it offers a charming, if milquetoast, look at old–Hollywood, with a helpful scrappy dog in a large supporting role. The American film industry's love affair with France continued that year, 2011, with the release of Woody Allen's *Midnight in Paris*. This comedy fantasy tells the story of an unfulfilled screenwriter who takes a vacation in Paris and is able to travel back in time to the *Belle Epoque*, discovering who he is and inspiring his love for writing once again. While the film was internationally financed, it is impossible to escape the Americanized, idealized view of France through Allen's lens. *Midnight in Paris*, like *Amélie* and *Before Sunset*, ignores any of the trials and tribulations of the country, utilizing it instead as a backdrop for the perfect French postcard.

3

Time Destroys All Things

Gaspar Noé's *Carne* (1991), *I Stand Alone* (1998) and *Irréversible* (2002)

> Violence is in life; it's part of human experience. I had problems with the French critics, because they don't like seeing France portrayed in this way.—*Gaspar Noé*

Described by *Vice Magazine* as "the most notorious punk rock auteur in cinema today,"[1] Gaspar Noé's journey as a filmmaker began when he first saw Stanley Kubrick's *2001: A Space Odyssey* at the age of seven. Born in Argentina in 1963, son of painter Luis Felipe Noé whose work was known for its tempestuous depiction of internal and eternal struggle, it is no surprise that in a handful of feature length, short films and music videos Noé has established himself as a pioneer of New French Extremity as well as one of the most controversial and *fêted* auteurs of his generation. When James Quandt returned to the subject of New French Extremity in his 2011 essay, "More Moralism from that 'Wordy Fuck'," Quandt addressed the criticisms that he did not comprehend Noé's *Irréversible*, a film about the darkest corners of Paris, by asking the reader: "Can one really claim that *Irréversible* marks any kind of advancement—aesthetic, political, social, sexual?"[2] In an attempt to answer that question, *Irréversible* must be examined in the context of Noé's first short, *Carne* (1991) and its feature-length sequel, *I Stand Alone* (*Seul Contre Tout*, 1998) whose character antihero, The Butcher, provides a prologue of sorts to *Irréversible* (2002). These three films can be seen as the spark that would set off the New French Extremity movement, which dares to ask the questions: Who lives and exists on the outskirts of society? how did they get there? and what happens when they take action against that society? The cinema of Noé is one of confrontation and disruption where the status quo is continually and violently challenged.

Carne marked the start not only of Noé's career but the beginning of *Les Cinémas de la zone*, his first partnership with his partner and fellow filmmaker, Lucile Hadzihalilovic. The forty-minute film tells the story of The Butcher (Philippe Nahon), who mistakes his autistic daughter's first period as the evidence of sexual assault and takes revenge on an innocent man, an action that sends him to jail. His daughter institutionalized, he finds work in a bar after his release from jail, sells his business, and gives up his apartment. The Butcher begins a carnal relationship with the female owner of the bar, who supports them both. The film ends with The Butcher leaving his daughter in the institution and leaving Paris with his now girlfriend for a quieter life in rural France. *Carne* introduces multiple tropes which Noé has continued to use, such as onscreen warnings and graphic, unexpected violence. The film also became notable for its opening scene, which features a brutal, albeit factual, depiction of a horse being slaughtered for its meat, reminiscent of Georges Franju's dream-like documentary *Blood of the Beasts* (*Le Sang des bêtes*, 1949), which also depicted the industrialized slaughtering of animals. Noé uses the scene to not only confront his audience but to show The Butcher's proximity to death. The Butcher consistently repeats that he is good at his job, but even that is questioned as he fails to butcher or kill the man he perceives to be his daughter's attacker. Upon his release from jail, he learns that the butcher who has taken over his position has a thriving business where he seemed to continually struggle. Throughout the film The Butcher narrates the proceedings with his internal monologue. He's content to blame the problems of the world on anyone outside of himself, but fails to accept or see his own faults. *Carne* ultimately brings together the notion of an unreliable narrator juxtaposing The Butcher's narration with the more truthful onscreen visuals. In the film, Noé creates a simple yet effective shorthand which exposes the hypocrisy and humanity of The Butcher. The film would go on to win the Best Short award at Cannes in 1991.

Despite Noé's initial success that led *Carne* to tour the international festival circuit, he could not acquire funding for a feature-length film. As Noé explained of that period: "Everybody said, no, do a normal movie. *Carne* was too violent, now you have to calm down, you have to grow up. Why don't you do a genre film?"[3] In the intervening years between *Carne* and its sequel *I Stand Alone*, Noé continued to play with and satirize standard filmic tropes—this time on television. In 1994 he made *Une Experience d'hypnose télévisuelle* for Canal+ Television, which sought to hypnotize the entire French nation. He then made a public service announcement against hunting and an explicit short championing the use of condoms. Through these jobs Noé was able to continue to develop his visual style while making connections which would eventually lead him to find financing for a feature film from Canal+ Television and French fashion designer Agnès B. *I Stand Alone* would take four years to finish. It is Noé's vision of France at the turn of the millennium. As Noé said at the film's 1998 premiere at the Edinburgh Festival: "A lot of people ask me if this is a racist movie, and I say, yes, it's an anti–French movie."[4]

I Stand Alone begins with a narrated prologue over static images (in a similar style used at the beginning of Jean-Pierre Jeunet's *Amélie*) which encapsulates the plot of *Carne*. The film picks up with The Butcher living in Lille with his girlfriend, the former bar owner who is now pregnant with The Butcher's child. He treats her and her mother, who lives with them, with outright contempt. A voiceover narration elaborates on how disgusting he finds them both. He finds menial work after his girlfriend, flush with profits after selling her bar, refuses to fund a butcher stall for him. A neighbor sees him walk an attractive colleague home; upon The Butcher's return to his own home his girlfriend berates him. He lashes out at her, punching her in her heavily pregnant stomach. He flees the house with three hundred francs to his name—and a gun. He hitchhikes back to Paris in the hopes that friends will help him and he'll be able to get back into his industry. His friends and the industry, however, have fallen on hard times, with little help available to him. He plots to shoot a former vendor who was not able to offer him an immediate job; he is also gunning for a bartender and his son for throwing him out of their bar after he verbally assaulted them. He decides to see his daughter one last time and takes her from the institution to a hotel. The screen flashes with a warning that the audience has 30 seconds to leave the theater before something shocking happens, a tactic used by horror impresario William Castle in 1961's *Homicidal*. While Castle used the tactic as a warning of violence and horror Noé uses it as a warning of an incestuous act. The Butcher, overcome with attraction to his daughter (first insinuated in *Carne*), wants to act on his feelings, as well as to kill her to free her from the suffering of life. The final act of *I Stand Alone* is shocking in its brutal honesty of a man on whom society has given up and who, in turn, has given up on society. Along with the onscreen warning, the moment is punctuated with a looming orchestral score and quick cuts that illustrate The Butcher's fractured mental state; the sound of gun shots can also be heard.

For the bleakness of the film's attitude to modern French society, Noé tells the man's story with an unmistakable energy, allowing The Butcher's fractured internal narrative to conflict with the onscreen events. The audience, which may sympathize with The Butcher on some level, is also held accountable for his actions by baring witness to them. The film also plays with character and moral interruptions with Noé's use of title cards that are used to distance the audience from The Butcher's state of mind. They function as a warning, indicating that society morals are opposed to those of The Butcher and, therefore, the individual's. The tension within the film stems from the audience's willing or unwilling allegiance to The Butcher. The title cards, at the very least, serve as a reminder of the world outside of The Butcher's perception. Noé utilizes this trope subversively, calling into question not only The Butcher's motives, which are shown to be reprehensible throughout, but also as a criticism of society's hand in the actions of the individual. As J. Hoberman wrote in his review of the film for *The Village Voice*:

> Noé's antihero may call France a "shithole of cheese and Nazi lovers," but like Céline's *Journey to the End of the Night*, *I Stand Alone* can be seen as bizarrely patriotic. However beleaguered his national culture, the miserable, martyred, misanthropic butcher of Paris will not go quietly into oblivion. I think therefore I am, the movie's antihero bellows, knowing that his ferocious diatribe has the power to amaze tout le monde—the whole world will hear this French dog bark.[5]

I Stand Alone (as well as *Irréversible*) has been criticized for homophobic and racist content, but as Noé described, his film is racist against France, a country which turned on immigrant and homosexual citizens, among others, in order to appease a right-wing fascist agenda that became part of everyday life during the Nazi occupation of World War II. Despite the goals of the French Resistance, such attitudes did not disappear but became embedded in the fabric of France. The conservative politicians told the citizens of France that immigrants were taking their jobs and failing to conform to the French way of life, a way of life thought to be the most desirable in the world. As Noé said in an interview at the time:

[I was attacked for being a fascist] because some people said, "well, why did this guy [The Butcher] stab this Arab?," and I said, "well, because workers in France are Arabs." They said, "well, because if you show a man stabbing an Arab in France it's because you're a fascist, you belong to the National Front," and they started talking about morals.... It was too much for me. I said, "well, if you want to talk about morals, in the next movie we'll talk about morals." If you just open your dictionary, "morality" is the sense that separates good from evil. And if you really want to see what evil is, it just says that "evil is the opposite of good." And if you ask, "Then what is 'good'?" it says that it's the opposite of evil. You can put whatever you want inside evil and good in morality. I think in life, people know what they want. They want to survive, they want to have a family. They want to procreate because it's in the genetic law. And in this case [of *Seul*], you have this man who has problems feeding himself— maybe he's too animalistic to behave in a clever way—so he doesn't find a clever way to survive and fulfill his own needs, and at the end of the movie well, at least there's the one need he can fulfill. It's his need of love ... in a very twisted way. There is an ending, because you identify with the character and when he comes to this end—not you, because you're very open-minded—but a lot of people are totally fucked up by the end of the movie. Because they say, "it's like a happy end, but it shouldn't be," and, "Where did you bring us to?!"... Most people feel aggressed by anything that is different from them. I think that in the American film industry—or even in the European cinema—movies are made not to disturb any kind of class or any kind of minority. And in fact, this is an aggressive movie but it's not aggressive towards any particular minority. It's aggressive to the whole world. And that's why the movie in French is called *Seul contre tous*. It means "alone against the world." And in fact it was translated as *I Stand Alone* because it's a much more common expression in English. In French you say, "I'm alone against the world" and that means, "I hate everybody and everybody's against me."[6]

I Stand Alone draws considerably from American cinema of the 1970s (or New Hollywood, so named for the rise of an independent sensibility in films), most notably Martin Scorsese's *Taxi Driver* (1976), as well as Sam Peckinpah's *Straw Dogs* (1971) and John Boorman's *Deliverance* (1972). While Noé has oscillated between claiming to have seen and not seen these films, their shared subject matter of violence that occurs on the outskirts of society speaks to a shared political climate. The early 1970s was a time of social change; there was a lack of trust in authority (particularly regarding the Nixon administration and the brewing Watergate scandal) and brutality at home, with demonstrations and riots (notably on college campuses, such as Kent State in 1970), as well as overseas instability and the atrocities committed during the Vietnam War. France was facing similar social and political upheaval from the

1990s through the new millennium, creating a dialogue between these films and countries. In The Butcher, Noé creates an antihero in the same vein as Travis Bickle in *Taxi Driver*, a disillusioned vigilante whose psyche corrupts the morals of the film. Both *Taxi Driver* and *I Stand Alone* end on ambiguous notes, indicating that the unresolved society offers no resolution for its characters. In *I Stand Alone*, The Butcher finds a brief respite from the world with his daughter. For the chaos throughout the film, this solace comes as something of a relief for the audience—that a man so disenfranchised could be appeased, but at the cost of the morals of a society.

In *I Stand Alone*, Noé mixes the brutality of one man against the brutality of society, challenging his audience to empathize while still remaining critical of his actions. Noé's film remains shocking to this day not simply because of the taboo subject matters of violence and incest but because he presents them as a dark comedy of errors. The film manages to keep its tongue firmly in its cheek defying audiences to question what they are seeing, relating to, and rejecting.

Noé's next film, *Irréversible*, would catapult the director into the international spotlight due to the film's brutal and unrelenting beginning. The film garnered notices as soon as it was announced by simply featuring French actor Vincent Cassel and his wife, Italian actress Monica Bellucci, who was garnering international press for appearing in the Matrix sequels. *Irréversible* tells the story of Alex (Bellucci), who learns she is pregnant with her boyfriend Marcus's (Vincent Cassel) child. The two head to a party with Alex's friend and former boyfriend Pierre (Albert Dupontel). Once there, Marcus begins behaving foolishly, flirting with women and taking drugs while Pierre begs him to spend time with Alex. Alex grows irritated with Marcus and leaves the party. Unable to catch a cab, she takes an underpass to try her luck on the other side of the street. While walking through the underpass, Alex encounters a pimp beating a prostitute. Scared, Alex cannot react, and the pimp turns his attention to her, resulting in an almost nine-minute anal rape scene that culminates in the pimp beating Alex. Pierre and Marcus leave the party and come across Alex being taken away in an ambulance. Marcus takes it upon himself to seek revenge on the perpetrator, tracking him down at a gay club called Rectum; all the while Pierre pleads with him to stop his search and go to the hospital to see Alex. Marcus thinks he has found the man who was been identified as Le Tenia (The Tapeworm) but misidentifies him, leading to a fight during which Marcus's arm is broken. Pierre, overcome with rage, takes a fire extinguisher and beats the man's head in while the other members of the club cheer him on and Le Tenia smiles. The film concludes with Marcus being taken away on a stretcher, and Pierre in handcuffs.

Irréversible lives up to its name and Noé's disposition of fracturing cinematic tropes by telling the film in twelve long takes, in reverse order, beginning with the end titles diagonally entering the screen and swirling camera movements that ultimately settle on The Butcher in an anonymous apartment as he laments his life and country. The camera swoops down to street-level, with Marcus being taken away on a stretcher and Pierre being led away in handcuffs. The film begins with violence and ends peacefully, with the characters, whom the audience has just witnessed being pushed to the extremes of humanity, seeming completely relatable. At its premiere at Cannes it was reported that several audience members left the screening due to the violence as well as the nausea-inducing camera movements and droning score, which contained a bass rumble recorded at 27 Hz, the frequency used by police to break up mobs or demonstrations as it frequency causes actual physical nausea. "I think people walk out not because they are bored but because they can't take it," said Noé of the film's controversy.

> I also think it makes a difference whether you see it in the afternoon or at night. Usually [walking out] happens more at night because you feel weaker at night. I walked out once during a rape scene in a movie, which came in the middle because I said, "Well if this is the middle of the movie, I don't want to see what happens next." I suppose in my movie a lot of people suspect that the end of my movie is going to be worse than the beginning because that's how the climax of the movie works. The fact is if they stay they will get something that will erase these first images.[7]

The fact that *Irréversible*'s most brutal scenes occur at the beginning codes it as a tragedy. As the film's scenes work backwards towards the beginning, the characters become more tragic because they become more human and the film's final scene (chronologically, its first) ends with Alex sitting in a park, in the daytime, reading a book, watching the children play as the camera swirls around, creating another nauseating and disorienting scene. The brief prologue that opens the film features The Butcher in a bedsit, admitting that he slept with his daughter and that they are separated once again. The Butcher remarks that "time destroys everything" to the anonymous man in his room, a line similar to the one in *I Stand Alone*: "No act is reversible." The line is the thematic spine of the whole film. While Noé's assertion that the end of the film will cleanse the audience's palate, the final scene in the park is what serves to make the film tragic. Though the film's denouement is comprised of the trio's metro ride to the party, during which they discuss sex, love, and life, and the final long scene between Marcus and Alex where they appear to be very much in love, those moments are all tainted because the characters do not know their fate but the audience, which has seen the film, does. These good people, who are not dissimilar to the majority of the audience, will face a night of unforeseen violence that will impact the rest of their lives.

Irréversible's time play is not only with its reverse story but with the mirror image that film shows of itself. The book Alex reads in the park is J.W. Dunne's *An Experiment with Time*. Dunne's thesis in the book is that there are two times running parallel to each other at all time: Time 1 is linear time and Time 2 is a subconscious time, which fuses past, present, and future.

> We must live before we can attain to either intelligence or control at all. We must sleep if we are not to find ourselves, at death, helplessly strange to the new conditions. And we must die before we can hope to advance to a broader understanding.[8]

Dunne's book explores the idea that, while humans are living, humanity's consciousness prevents us from thinking beyond the current actions and stimuli around us, to which we are in a continual state of responding. The only way to escape these limitations, Dunne theorizes, is to dream, during which we are not restricted by consciousness. The final long scene of *Irréversible* begins with Alex and Marcus asleep together; they are awakened by a phone call from Pierre, confirming their plans for that evening. Alex remarks that she's had a strange dream of walking down a red hallway while Marcus keeps shaking his arm which has fallen asleep, the same arm that will be broken later that night. In the scene, violent elements that will befall these characters are foreshadowed, such as when Marcus playfully spits at Alex, which La Tenia will do violently later that night, as well as this exchange:

MARCUS: I want to fuck your ass.
ALEX: I thought you were romantic.

Time 2, the subconscious time, is present throughout *Irréversible*, but the audience experiences the film through the lens of Time 1, where the characters are forced to react due to uncontrollable elements around them. The violent actions that take place at the beginning of the film force the viewer to react primally to them as they do not yet have a context for these characters. The concept of dreams issuing a kind of *déjà vu* or premonition is not explored until the final third of the film. Noé's use of these two times in shaping the audience's view of the characters forces viewers to experience the violence and trauma that takes place as though it were happening to them, with no time to rationalize or explain by means of conventional cinematic tropes. The violence in *Irréversible* is tangible because it is visceral and demands that the viewer experiences it in that way. It is only at the end of the film and, upon reflection, that the opening line, "Time destroys everything," becomes applicable as the audience understands that the characters' fates are inescapable, the timelines bleed into one another.

Along with camera tricks and disruption of cinematic conventions, Noé utilizes the plot trope of the wrongful avenger. In *Carne*, The Butcher's life begins to unravel when he attacks an innocent man; so, too, does Pierre's after he kills the wrong man. Working with his cinematographer, Benoît Debie, Noé's camera is almost reliably unstable as it swirls overhead, following characters through rooms and intruding on their most intimate moments without reproach. The only time the camera remains static is during the infamous rape scene, during which the camera seems to rest on the dirty pavement, keeping the viewer within the eye-line of Alex, who has been pushed to the ground. The majority of rape scenes in cinema are forced to edit portrayals of rape to maintain an "R" rating; in *Irréversible* the camera focuses on Alex's face, with La Tenia's body on top of her. While the rape is violent and aggressive, it is also the dialogue throughout the scene that increases the volatility, with La Tenia demanding that Alex call him "Daddy" (a potential reference to *I Stand Alone*) and calling her "upper-class swine." Because the camera has been in motion throughout the few scenes leading up to this, the lack of motion from it in this scene is almost unbearable. Noé, however, knows his audience and even the most hardened film fan may be tempted to look away, but that will not stop its brutality. The score with its hardened frequency, Alex's screams, and La Tenia's continual verbal debasement renders *Irréversible* as one of the most unrelenting and unforgiving films ever made.

Tim Palmer writes of *Irréversible* in his book *Brutal Intimacy: Analyzing Contemporary French Cinema*, wherein he labels it and films of its ilk not New French Extremity, but under his term of *cinéma du corps* (cinema of the body):

> Its stylistic conception and execution [has been] overlooked, as has the bravura means by which diegetic defamiliarization occurs, the contraction of social spaces that are apprehended in the context of such stark, atavistic, threateningly amoral case studies. This brutal intimacy template most profoundly extends to the actual viewer, a role that becomes highly unconventional, challenged overtly by the artful proximity of such formally and physically confrontational events.[9]

Nowhere is Palmer's concept of "brutal intimacy" more clearly visible than in the rape scene in *Irréversible*. The intimacy of this act, both the audience's proximity and violation perpetrated against Alex, is meant to explain the actions taken by Marcus, and eventually Pierre, even though they only witness the aftermath. In the trio's conversation on the metro, Alex explains to Pierre that "everything can't be explained … sometimes you fuck" in an effort to get him out of his own head as it is consistently implied that he overthinks everything. When Pierre finally attacks it is after an hour (or longer) chase through the underbelly of Paris, where Pierre tries to calm Marcus down, prevents him from attacking a transgender prostitute, and tries to stop him from destroying and innocent cab driver's taxi while Marcus hurls racial epithets at the driver. Pierre's rationality is destroyed, making his decency all the more tragic as he attempts to do the right thing throughout the proceedings. *Irréversible* depicts the corruption of the seemingly incorruptible.

Much has been made of *Irréversible*'s view of Paris, which is seen as crime-ridden and diseased, with a particular focus on the homosexual community, through prostitutes and the confrontations at the club Rectum. Writing for *Slate*, film critic David Edelstein said: "Noé's portrait of gays and their lifestyle makes *Cruising* (1980) look like *Philadelphia* (1993). *Irréversible* might be the most homophobic movie ever made."[10] The criticism of homophobia was continually lobbed at Noé throughout the film's festival circuit tour and eventual distribution. Noé himself responded to the accusations saying:

> In France [the gay community] love the movie. Gay people thought Vincent Cassel was so gorgeous and so sexy. There will always be people saying it's homophobic. But the reaction of the gay community was better than the straight community. People most offended are really heterosexual men. Male dominants have problems identifying with a woman who's raped…. The fear [of rape] disappears with men when you are 18 or 20. I wanted this movie to bring back men's old fear to show them how it is to be raped. Remember, Vincent's character almost gets raped, too. It's funny because you have to be in America to consider people as members of groups…. In France

people don't use the word "community." Even in France any sense of gay community is diluted. The whole ethnicity thing is much more mixed in France; no one says here you have the Arab community, the Asian community. Anyone can be racist when they get angry for the wrong reasons—the boyfriend [Cassel's character] was just finding a way to insult his Asian cabdriver. Before shooting that scene, Vincent asked me, "How far should I go?" I said, "You are angry. Say whatever your character would say to make him go faster." If you start taking care of all the communities in this world, you can never leave your house. Life is made of everything. The actors in my movie are not heroes, they're just human beings.[11]

As Noé stated while promoting *I Stand Alone*, adding racist and homophobic characters and elements to a film does not mean the directors or screenwriters are themselves racist and homophobic; they are merely presenting a view of the world. Although the depiction of homosexuals in *Irréversible* is indeed problematic, Noé implies that the problem stems from a deeper, systematic factor endemic to France.

Irréversible is a confrontational film, as Palmer implies, because it asks the audience to marry their perception of the characters at their worst with their best. It speaks to a Paris that is racist and homophobic, which Noé depicts unflinchingly. The fates of Alex, Marcus, and Pierre are all tied to one another, meaning that when one is threatened so are they all. When Quandt asked what kind of advancement *Irréversible* offered, the simple answer is presenting the audience with a view into a world they choose not to know, or avoid at all costs. In what is arguably the most chilling moment of the rape scene, a passerby enters the underpass then quickly runs away. The inclusion of this detail seems to indicate that they did nothing to help Alex, at least at the time. *Irréversible* is a confrontation with a typically passive audience who would rather not engage with the violence that exists around them.

Noé's follow-up to *Irréversible* was *Enter the Void* (2009), which the director dubs a "psychedelic melodrama"[12] about a young American drug dealer who is shot by police in Tokyo and narrates most of the film from an out-of-body experience. The film, a longtime passion project for the director, was hailed as a cinematic triumph, while others, like Edelstein, asked: "Did you ever wonder what it would be like to be strapped in front of a strobe light for two and a quarter hours? *Enter the Void* and wonder no more."[13] *Enter the Void* failed to recoup its budget at the box office, making it another six years before the premiere of Noé's next film, *Love* (2015), which American website *Indiewire* claimed had some of "the most hardcore onscreen sex ever to screen at the [Cannes] festival."[14]

4

Body Commodification
Romance (1999), *Pola X* (1999) and *Baise-moi* (2000)

If French is no longer the language of power, it can be
the language of a counter power.—*Lionel Jospin*

Intimacy is a term that is inextricable from New French Extremity.
Film scholar Tim Palmer utilizes the term not only in the title of his
book, *Brutal Intimacy: Analyzing Contemporary French Cinema*, but
throughout the text. The need and desire to be close to another person
can overtake logic and reason, creating an untenable and violent situation. The three films examined in this chapter see different directors
tackling the correlation between sexuality and destruction. Each film
deals with this desire in a different way, yet they all arrive at a similar
conclusion: the desire of an individual is almost always at odds with the
desire of society as a whole; the only way to overcome this disparity is
through violence.

In Catherine Breillat's 1999 film *Romance*, the writer and director
explores the notions of disconnection and the anxiety over these feelings
through the protagonist Marie (Caroline Ducey), an attractive young
school teacher whose boyfriend, Paul (Sagamore Stévenin), has lost all
interest in a physical relationship with her. Marie takes the rejection
personally, clinging to him, not letting him out of her sight. Her fears
and insecurity amplify the situation until she asserts control over it by
embarking on a series of provocative sexual adventures.

Marie's adventures take her to sexual encounters with a widower
(played by real-life porn star Rocco Siffredi), an older male colleague who

introduces her to the world of BDSM, and a man on the street who attempts to intimidate and harass her until she invites him back to her building. Between these encounters, Marie narrates her state of mind, sometimes full of self-doubt and loathing, other times on the verge of lashing out at society and the men in her life.

> *Marie:* Love is bloody stupid. It's a question of power. A guy, you're faithful to 'cause you love him, won't fuck you anymore. Betray him and he'll start fucking you again. It's as simple as that. Not because they suspect we might be unfaithful, but because they understand, that we're escaping out of their reach.

Romance is a cheeky title, at once examining our desire for intimacy and, at the same time, mocking it. Unlike Hollywood films which deny audiences the contorted and real climax of human desire, preferring to cut around and hint at it so as to assure a potentially commercial "R" rating, *Romance* leaves behind any concern for ratings in its first fifteen minutes. Catherine Breillat is no stranger to this kind of controversy, having built a reputation as an *enfant terrible* on the international film festival circuit in the 1970s. She made her first splash in cultural circles in France when her debut novel, *L'Homme facile* (*Easy Man*), was published in 1965 when she was seventeen, which the government promptly banned for readers under eighteen. Breillat made her first film, *A Real Young Girl*, based on her novel *Le Soupirail*, in 1976. The French government once again moved swiftly and banned the film until 1999.

Breillat's films deal in explicit sexuality and the trials that come along with an open and honest exploration of that topic. She utilizes her filmmaking traits, such as long takes and taboo subjects, to confront her audiences. When asked whom she felt *Romance* was intended, she replied:

> I don't really think about my audience very much. You can't totally anticipate what the film will be until it's finished, so how do you know who your audience is? To me, what's important is, first of all, to just make the movie … it all comes down to finding out something about myself. Before you can offer something to an audience, you have to know who you are, otherwise, what is it you are offering them? It doesn't know who it is anymore than you do—that's why an audience comes to the movies.[1]

Before *Romance*, Breillat made five films in the years between 1976 and 1999, all of which dealt with sexually explicit themes challenging a patriarchal order. It was not until *Romance* that Breillat became a name— albeit a controversial one—outside of art-house film circles.

After *Romance*'s initial success on the film festival circuit, it was picked up and distributed by Rézo Films in France and Trimark Pictures in the United States. It played in Europe with an unrated cut, but was edited for an "R" rating by the MPAA in the United States. Breillat said of the American criticism and the censoring of certain scenes:

> It seems like a serious problem. It basically forces people to censor themselves. It's a kind of self-flagellation. By hav[ing] the rating, people are no longer able to judge for themselves what is a movie for adults and what is really a pornographic movie that should be rated with the "X." This is very infantilizing, especially since what they call "adult" cinema should be the most noble and serious, but it seems like no one here grasps the meaning of this term. The moment something is an adult film—which my film seems to be in their eyes—it's considered to be the most degrading and off-limits. In France, the situation is not that different, since the "X" rating limited the film to people over 18.[2]

The film received a small edit (of an ejaculation shot) when released on home video in the UK. *Romance* was also the target of some controversy in Australia, where it was initially denied a release; it was ultimately given an "R18+" rating on appeal, which meant that unsimulated sex could have an official rating in Australia. The film garnered more controversy when released in Canada, where it was given an "A" (or Adult) rating, while, in Europe, several countries showed the film in its entirety on late-night television.

Many ratings boards saw Marie's journey as salacious and upsetting. As American film critic Roger Ebert wrote upon the film's release:

> Of course the film is French. It is said that for the French, wine takes the place of flirting, dining takes the place of seduction, smoking takes the place of foreplay and talking takes the place of sex. *Romance* is so analytical that you sometimes get the feeling Marie is putting herself through her sexual encounters simply to get material for her journal. These poor guys aren't lovers, they're case studies.[3]

Ducey's physical appearance feels particularly French with her angular features, lithe body, and minimalist yet chic clothing adding to the icy austerity of Marie. The audience can see her delve into her own thoughts, analyzing, criticizing, and memorializing her experiences, chronicling them, perhaps, to make them real to herself. She alternately asks herself, "What do women want?" and later remarks that "this face cannot possibly be connected to this cunt." Breillat herself has said that "this is not just a sex movie but a movie about sex."[4] Her statement seems to be the answer to the questions and concerns that plague Marie. Something within Marie drives her desire. Breillat shows us the multitude of stimuli that would push a person to the extremes, not only the desire to enjoy the physical and carnal pleasures of sex but also Marie's desire to be desired. It is not an intellectualized ideal of love, but physicalizing it offers stains of proof that she is desired.

The three main encounters that Marie experiences vary wildly, but all add to her understanding of her body and its limits. With the widower Paolo, they experience fairly normal heterosexual sex: two attractive, consenting adults participate in sex, resulting in his orgasm. This sex is unsimulated, with the actors actually engaging in sex onscreen, adding a strange intimacy to the scene, in which Paolo seems to long for a closeness to Marie that she rejects in the hopes that her boyfriend, Paul, will eventually want her again.

Marie then enters the world of BDSM through her colleague Robert (François Berléand), who also happens to be the headmaster of the school where she teaches. He subtly hints at his kink, as if testing the waters with Marie, which does not faze her. He invites her into his BDSM practice which she participates in and eventually breaks down, crying. She reveals that she is angry at herself, not because she participated in BDSM with Robert but because she feels that she reached her limit.

In one of the most complex and traumatic scenes in the film, Marie encounters a man on the street who says to her, "One hundred francs, I can eat your pussy." She brings him back to her apartment and, on the way up the stairs to her door in the building, he rapes her. Marie reaches yet another limit of her sexuality, crying out in fear, though, ultimately, she considers herself triumphant for having survived the ordeal.

Marie has reached the boundaries of sexuality when she finds out she is pregnant. After telling Paul, they have sex, and she feels that perhaps the relationship may be salvageable. Breillat cuts to months later. Marie is ignored by Paul once again and, while heavily pregnant, she kills him. Marie sought out and endured a sexual journey that cut across multiple spectrums. She arrived at the end to find she was pregnant and hoped that this would offer a final solution. She would be a mother and they would be a family. Marie's sexual journey is ended by pregnancy, which is seen as the end of sexuality in society. By allowing Marie's story to continue beyond Paul's acceptance of her pregnancy we are treated to a dark coda, one which shows that the making of a family is not the ending to insecurity and instability that society promises it will be. Doubt and fear remain. As film scholar Martine Beugnet summarizes:

Breillat's filmmaking directly addresses and demystifies not only the kind of clichéd perceptions of the feminine epitomized in pornography, but also conventional definitions of the female as object as well as stereotypical notions of femininity as mystery. In so doing, the film debunks such representations of the female body as familiar as they are contradictory: a series of holes to be filled, an idealized object of desire or a medical object to be investigated.[5]

There are two scenes in the final third of the film which offer a realistic look at the female body. For the majority of the film the audience has been privy to Marie's thoughts and actions—detailed examination of one woman's desire and her means at achieving her goals. Once she becomes pregnant, she begins to lose that agency. While she thinks she attains her ultimate goal of Paul's sexual affection, her pregnant body becomes society's. As Marie says, "People say, a woman is no woman, until she's given birth to a child," an indication of society's stake in femininity and its expectations thereof. Shortly after Marie and Paul's reconciliation, Marie goes for a gynecological appointment. Dressed in a hospital gown, her feet in stirrups and a white sheet covering her legs to keep the illusion of discretion, a doctor examines her to ensure that the baby is healthy and that there are no concerns. A group of younger doctors observe and then take turns examining her in the same way. Later, Marie's narration transforms into a dream sequence where women's bodies are separated at their waists by a wall. On the side of the wall with the faces, hearts, and brains, they are in a hospital delivery room; below the waists, they are glory holes in a brothel. Is it a metaphor for the desires of women by society? Women, after all, are always supposed to be sexually available to men but be ready and willing to be a mother and desexualized by undertaking that role. It is a shocking scene not because of the sex—the film has already shown plenty of that—but because it explicitly confronts society's expectations of women which Breillat shows the audience in all its absurdity; in order to become mothers, women must engage in sex; in order to engage in sex, women must be desirable or sexy, which a mother should never be.

The scene continues to subvert and shock the audience's expectations as a man is about to reach climax in the glory hole scene when Breillat cuts the scene to a baby's head emerging from Marie's vagina. Breillat challenges the audience, with the extremes of *Romance*, that sex, kink, and childbirth can all come from the same body.

Grainy black-and-white images show bombs falling from a great height. The planes revealed to be dropping bombs do so in uniform formations, destroying whatever lies below. Pop-punk music plays in the background, creating a heightened sensation as the audience bears witness to this destruction. Leos Carax begins his comeback film, *Pola X* (1999), with these images of the German Luftwaffe operations used on France to secure the Nazis' swift entrance into the country, focusing on the destruction of graveyards. In essence, a destruction of death.

Carax broke into the French film scene at the age of twenty-three with his film *Boy Meets Girl* (1984) and was hailed as part of the new, contemporary vision of French filmmaking, alongside director Luc Besson. Less than a decade later Carax released his third film, *The Lovers on the Bridge* (1991), which bankrupted three production companies during its filming and nearly ended Carax's career. *Pola X* was meant to be a return to form for the director who was still searching for his place in the industry. Adapting Herman Melville's 1952 novel, *Pierre; or, The Ambiguities*, Carax found in the author a spiritual brother of sorts. *Pola X* comes from the French title of the book *Pierre ou les ambiguïtés*, with the "X" representing the number 10—the number of drafts the script went through before shooting began, although the "X" has been used in various marketing materials to suggest the sexual nature of the film.

Melville's novel, his first published after *Moby Dick*, was met with harsh criticism from the literary community for depicting and implying incest and homosexuality in the book. As the starting point in the film, Carax utilizes Melville's basic premise of Pierre, a young well-to-do writer from the upper-classes, who encounters a strange woman claiming to be his half-sister. Pierre follows her, rejecting his comfortable lifestyle and, ultimately, succumbing to poverty and insanity.

Melville's novel ends with a pile of bodies, but Carax decides instead to focus on the sexual torment of his characters and their descent into another, foreign world. As the titles and documentary footage of the Nazi air raids come to an end, Carax fixates his camera on the bright and luxurious world of Pierre (Guillaume Depardieu), who lives with his mother, Marie (Catherine Deneuve), whom he calls his sister in Normandy. He is engaged to Lucie (Delphine Chuillot), who lives in a neighboring chateau and shares Pierre's sunny blond looks and rarefied position of privilege. Pierre has recently published a novel under a *nom de plume*, which has become a trendy best-seller. It is during this time that he meets Isabelle (Yekaterina Golubeva), who claims to be his long-lost half-sister. Intrigued, he follows her to Paris along with a mother and small daughter who appear to be vagrants. Rejected from the life he knows due to his new companions' non-existent social status, they take up residence in an immigrant commune. Paranoia, fear, and disillusionment consume Pierre, whose sheltered, privileged life comes crashing down around him as he attempts to write his follow-up novel.

Carax trains his camera steadily in the first third of the film as Pierre's life of complacency is established. Contributing to the false sense of a classical film, Carax does away with this technique in the scene when Pierre first meets and interacts with Isabelle. Passing her on the road, he sees her for a second time and goes to confront her. She flees into the forest. When he catches up with her, she gives a disconnectedly poetic monologue about her life. She walks ahead of Pierre as if talking to herself, while Pierre trails a few paces behind. The farther Isabelle walks, the deeper she descends into a literal darkness; indeed, as the film progresses, both characters continually move away from any sense of light or community. They are isolated in their obsession with each other. Isabelle's French is decidedly broken, but actress Yekaterina Golubeva gives it an ethereal nature. Carax clarifies that Isabelle is from Bosnia, casting a shadow on the film with the recent history of the Bosnian War, an international conflict which was part of the breakup of Yugoslavia and has become known for its terrifyingly vicious war crimes, including mass rapes and ethnic cleansing, in which all sides participated. As Carax says of the scene in the woods with Isabelle and Pierre:

> The reasons that men give for going to countries at war are often fairly shady ... but what happened in Bosnia coincided with the rebirth of the project. And Isabelle comes from that chaos. The implosion of all origins. All the elements that make up man. She is like one of the corpses in Abel Gance's "J'Accuse," standing up and walking towards us.
>
> From her first appearance she is linked to darkness. She is not really "living." She says: "Had I father, mother? I don't know...." In the novel there's a scene that's impossible to shoot but which really attracted me: Isabelle's monologue that fills two chapters in which she is apparently telling Pierre her life's story. But, in fact, she tells him nothing ... virtually nothing concrete. She starts with "I have no tongue to speak to thee, Pierre, my brother." And then, over the next 40 pages she evokes the experience of being alive ... her slow awakening to a consciousness of the world and herself in that world. These two chapters are extraordinary. It's as if the most beautiful cinema sequence already existed.[6]

Throughout the scene in Carax's film, Pierre and Isabelle grow darker, as if they are descending into death. The brightness with which Carax splashed his early scenes at the chateau is nearly forgotten. The darkness bleeds into every part of the screen, staining its characters as though marking them for what will follow. Pierre's sense of history is disrupted. His father, a famous diplomat, impregnated a woman, and then leaving her and their child in what was becoming a war zone. Suddenly, Pierre's embarrassment about his life and wealth overcomes him. His life seems faulty to him because he has not earned his sense of privilege and feels the need to absorb what has become of Isabelle to understand how two connected lives could veer in two diametrically opposed directions.

Pierre's follow-up book, which the viewer has seen him write passages of early in the film, becomes obsolete in his mind. "I'm another Pierre now," he says to Isabelle after her biographical monologue. "Thanks to you. Yes, I owe you everything. The ideas I had at home for a second novel make no sense now. What's in this? Sincerity? I was blind! Now, I need new tools, understand? Raging torrents, volcanoes ... the stuff for a true book! I want to see what's hidden and live my hidden life to the full." Carax says of the character at this state:

> Because a writer seen from behind always looks like a "great writer." ... But Pierre isn't ready for a great book Melville's irony concerning this is wonderful ... at one particular point, he even tracks forward over Pierre's shoulder to show what's he's writing; it's sincere but extremely naive and purloined from all the great masters. Pierre is a tragic character because he cannot meet his own expectations. But he's a proud hero because he wants to "do right" ... which leads to all these ambiguities.[7]

Pierre's new life is full of rejection from his former friends for abandoning his mother and fiancée. He is then turned away from hotels on sight due to the appearance of the rest of his party, who meekly follow him around when they arrive in Paris. In a cab ride to seek shelter at a friend's house, the cab driver admonishes Pierre for the state of his friends, refusing to take them any farther. Pulling over, the cab driver pepper-sprays Pierre and the police arrive on the scene and demand to see the cab driver's identification and registration. It is apparent that they can immediately identify the immigrant, while Pierre, Isabelle, and the others flee.

When Pierre and Isabelle settle into their migratory life on the outskirts of Paris, Pierre descends into madness, furiously scribbling pages for his new book, which he is sure will one day give them the money they need. What becomes concerning at this stage is not Isabelle's presence but her passiveness. After lighting a fire of confusion and uncertainty under Pierre, which he saw as a calling to change, she offers nothing but glances and worried looks as the sexual tension builds between them.

As Isabelle fills scenes with her passiveness, Carax allows his audience to question her motivations, although Pierre never does. Her silence becomes cavernous as she stares and watches as her supposed half-brother becomes increasingly isolated. The warehouse in which they take shelter is inhabited with many other transients, who increasingly take up arms and attack the Paris metro. The chaos and violence that surrounds Pierre and Isabelle never seems to touch them, but it does solidify their position as social outcasts. As film writer Trevor Link comments on this tension:

> If Carax's ethic of personal freedom becomes dangerously lawless here … it is because there is no value Carax holds above this freedom. No packaged prescription the attainment this freedom exists, no safe way to reap its benefits without any of its costs. Freedom punishes because the truly free man or woman will always be the enemy of society, as Pierre becomes when even his once dearly close friend Thibault rejects him. Moreover, as with Carax's cinema, true freedom is a weapon without precise aim. We cannot honestly seek freedom in some aspects of our lives while desiring constraint and normalcy in others. To pursue and attain freedom, we can only aim past it, inevitably overtaking it.[8]

Pierre's rejection of a society that valued him is at the core of the extremity of this film. By rejecting the values of a society that has cherished him he transgresses their expectations, rendering his existence as radical. Carax highlights this when Pierre and Isabelle make love. Already the audience has been given enough time to doubt the validity of Isabelle's story and wonder why Pierre was able to so easily turn his back on his life but in the moment when they give into their desires it does not seem to matter. While Pierre is happy to call his mother his sister and converse with her while she is in a bath as well as marry his cousin Lucie, there is a purity to those scenes, as though any sexual connotations could be read as superfluous. When Pierre and Isabelle have sex, it becomes not only intimate, with the camera lingering on their bodies, but animalistic, even violent. Carax keeps the camera focused on the lovers without judgment, rendering their physical passion acceptable by the camera's eye, if not society's. Carax said of the intercourse scene: "It's the relationship that seems to have become impossible. The reunion with part of yourself that you thought was lost for good or permanently hidden, Isabelle or Pierre, there's no difference."[9] Ultimately, Carax asks the audience to be a witness, not a judge, of Pierre's journey, allowing for sense and instinct to take over, questioning what the search for freedom actually entails in a contemporary society.

When a French film offers two possible translations of its title, the moviegoing public would likely assume that one interpretation would be correct and one would be wrong. In the case of Virginie Despentes and Coralie Trinh Thi's 2000 film, *Baise-moi* (which has two English translations, *Rape Me* and *Fuck Me*), it seems unfair to pick only one, hence the film becoming better known by its French title than an English one. Released a year after *Pola X* and *Romance*, *Baise-moi* incited a rage not commonly seen when in comes to films made in France. The film follows two lower-class sex workers, Nadine (Karen Bach) and Manu (Raffaëla Anderson), who meet by chance after separately committing murders. They embark on a road trip, not necessarily to escape the police, but to wreak havoc on the unsuspecting bourgeoisie French landscape.

Adapted from Despentes's 1993 novel of the same name, *Baise-moi*'s first literary incarnation created a sensation and was part of the 1990s movement of French female writers re-appropriating the noir genre. For Despentes, the noir genre revolved around a trauma to the female body which was then dealt with by the appropriate patriarchal force. In her novel, trauma still occurs to the female body, but the trauma causes a rejection of patriarchy, liberating the female characters. Before the book's release by the small publishing house Florent-Massot, Despentes had distributed proof copies among her friends and collaborators in the punk scene in France, which led to a lot of positive buzz and fifty thousand pre-sold copies. The book would eventually be translated into ten languages.

The film was shot on grainy digital video and both Bach and Anderson were well-known French porn actors, which allowed for an unsimulated sex scene, adding a sense of reality not only to the scenes where the characters have sex for fun, but when they have sex for money and when Manu and her friend are raped. The aesthetic has an art-house bent to due to its use of long takes, extreme close-ups, and lack of rigidity. When the audience is introduced to Nadine, the camera follows her in a long, shaky close-up. After a few seconds pass, the audience becomes aware of the performative aspect of a woman onscreen. As the seconds continue to pass, the audience is once again confronted by the fact that this woman is not famous, this is not a big-budget film, and this woman, who would normally be undeserving of screen time, is deserving of the audience's attention for reasons that will become clear. It is one of many moments in which *Baise-moi* challenges its viewer either to join these women or reject them. Helped by the fact that both Bach and Anderson are charismatic performers, they make it hard to look away. Of shooting the actual film, Despentes and Trinh Thi said:

> TRINH THI: The first part of the film, the rape scene in the tabac, that's all part of everyday France. After that, the film become much more like a cartoon, a comic strip. It's a fantasy, a rather joyful fantasy. There's a kind of irony in the choreographic death scenes…. In the end, it was much better that is was produced cheaply, with a "trash" aesthetic. Can you imagine trying to make such a film with Hollywood production values? Not only would it have been inappropriate, it would have taken forever.

> DESPENTES: It was difficult from the start to the end. People thought we would argue, so nobody wanted us to direct. Then they said Karen and Raffaela wouldn't be able to act, that it was a bad idea to use porn actresses, that it was a bad idea to show real sex, that it was a bad idea to shoot on DV [digital video] because it wasn't high enough quality, that it was wrong to use available light because nobody would be able to see anything, and so on and so on.

> TRINH THI: And the funniest thing is that after we made the movie, everyone said, "Oh of course it's so easy to shoot a low-budget movie on DV with no light and two ex-porn stars. Obviously it was going to work." In fact every single decision was a risk, every idea was dangerous, a step into unknown territory. Everything was a struggle, every idea had to be haggled over, because there was no money.[10]

When the film was released in France it initially received a "16+" rating, with a warning from the Ministry of Culture. Days after the decision was made and the film opened, far-right, pro-family groups, along with the right-wing National Front party, demanded that the rating be revised. The State Council offered a rating of "18+," which had been abolished in 1990, meaning that *Baise-moi* inadvertently received an "X" rating. This meant the film could not be seen by minors, only be shown in specially licensed outlets and receive no financial support from the government, rendering it nearly impossible to recoup any costs. Despentes and Trinh Thi, along with their producer Philippe Godeau, launched a campaign against the "X" rating. It soon became a national debate, with the far right decrying the film's antiestablishment-directed violence and sexuality, while the intellectual and artistic communities lobbied for freedom of expression and the cultural merits of the film. Soon *Baise-moi* had supporters such as Catherine Breillat, Claire Denis, and Jean-Luc Godard, culminating in a public demonstration on July 5, 2001. Succumbing to pressure from both sides, the French Minister of Culture came down on the side of both parties by reinstating the "18+" rating, which allowed *Baise-moi* to be legally released in cinemas in France. As Despentes says of that time:

We really took the brunt of a lot of prejudice and paranoia. We didn't realize how much fear and hatred it would arouse, but it definitely stoked up a lot of nasty stuff. Not least because it's about poor, non-white women. In France, there's a real conflict between the white majority and the Arabic population. Our two lead actresses both have African roots—one is half–Moroccan, the other is half–Algerian—and in France, don't harbor any illusions, it's visceral, [a] problem. A lot of people really don't want to see two North African women who have been raped, taking up arms and shooting European men. That's a little too close to historical reality.[11]

Many saw the film as a spiritual successor to a mainstream film like *Thelma and Louise* (1991), which features two women celebrating their independence on a slightly violent road trip, or a cult exploitation film like *I Spit on Your Grave* (1978), wherein a female writer retreats to the country to finish her book but is gang-raped by locals and seeks vengeance. However, both of those films are about transgressions for its female characters who are forced to step outside of societal expectations. In *Baise-moi*, Nadine and Manu are lower class and expect this violence in their lives. It is only because they meet and see each other as kindred spirits that they begin their crime spree.

It is this political dialogue which grounds [*Baise-moi*] in contemporary France. Unlike other films, Manu and her friend are raped not because they have climbed above their social order, but because they are already at the bottom of it. She says, "We're just girls. It is the natural order of things," challenging the "natural order" via the killing spree which is, for Manu, as much about class rage as male abuse.[12]

The catalyst for Manu's journey is the rape and her brother's rage when he finds out. Manu, however, accepts the altercation as expected. During the scene she is uncomfortable and pained but bears it while her friend screams out. Scenes such as these were inspired by real-life events, when an epidemic of gang-rape or *tournante* ("pass around") rose in France in the 1990s. Estimated that these cases made up 10 to 20 percent of serious crimes in French juvenile court in 1991, many saw it as disenfranchised young men on the outskirts of society turning their rage on weaker women of the social class.

The very DNA of *Baise-moi* could seen as lower class. From the grainy-digital video, to the actresses who have appeared in porn, to the explicit sex and violence that permeate the film, *Baise-moi* could have easily slipped through the cracks of popular consciousness as lowbrow exploitation. What could not be ignored is how the film succeeds in and of itself by engaging with the complicated past and present of the country in which it was made. In a society that grants neither Manu or

Nadine any agency, they take it back. Nadine's first killing is of her roommate who lashes out and aggressively chastises her; Manu's first killing is of her brother who, at first, seems concerned for her, but winds up berating her and treating her with a callousness she knows all too well. Freed from their respective constraints, Nadine and Manu meet in the tunnels of the metro and, without much conversation, agree to leave the city. Beginning their road trip with the murder of a seemingly upper-class white woman, Despentes and Trinh Thi prove that they have eschewed any plot that an audience might know. There is no vigilantism, only pure mayhem.

Baise-moi offers a critical view of classism, upward mobility, and capitalism by two characters with no access to any privilege or help. Having been successfully marginalized by a society who would prefer if they kept quiet, the two women lash out, demanding sex from men, killing indiscriminately, and decking themselves out in finery. This, of course, cannot last forever, and the authorities are soon on to them. In one of their many holdups for supplies, Nadine sits in their car, waiting for Manu to come out with the loot. In the holdup, Manu is shot and dies. Nadine drives away with her body and creates a funeral pyre for her friend, both memorializing and destroying her body so no one else can get hold of it. The two women attained what society told them they could not—fame, notoriety, and excess.

Part of the perceived danger of *Baise-Moi* is that it shows Nadine and Manu's violence-infused road trip with no commentary on their actions. There are no voices in the film other than Nadine, Manu, and a handful of their victims/conquests who do not have all that much to say. How could this film not strike fear into the right-leaning sections of France? What could have several influential groups so worried about this film? While many explore the notion of its political and social roots which have a significant resonance with many, *Baise-moi* is fiction, until it isn't. The sex is real, the plight of women in this class is real. Since few directors have showcased these stories without dripping them in sentiment, *Baise-moi* offers an honest resonance in the real world.

In the final scene the audience sees Nadine, alone. She stands on the edge of a body of water and prepares to take her own life. The police are closing in and she has lost her only ally. This moment of a final action against society is taken from her as the police arrive and arrest her. The audience loses the narrative of Nadine at the end—what becomes of her? Does she repent or stand resolute? The answers to these questions are not at the heart of *Baise-moi.* "*Baise-moi* derives is significance precisely from the refusal of a useful purpose."[13] For the seventy-seven minutes spent with Manu and Nadine, it is not about their transgressions, it is about their ability to live, to experience beyond what they were told they could have. *Baise-moi*'s legacy is in its ability to detail a vision of female desire, both sexual and social, and combat the critics who deemed this desire reprehensible and outrageous. The political and social scandal that erupted because of this film proved how out of touch many on the political right are.

> The scandal of *Baise-moi* was that it exposed the underlying logic of the abstract republican ideal of universalism, exploring some of the structural inequalities that are foundational to the French republic. The reception of the film revealed unresolved anxieties and concerns about ethnicity, citizenship, gender and sexuality that are played out in contemporary French society. The film was disturbing because it brought to the surface what should remain hidden: namely, the social salience of class, ethnic and gender differences in the context of new challenges to national identity by minority groups.[14]

The very existence of *Baise-moi* challenged everything France had fought to forget after World War II and decolonization. *Baise-moi* proved that France's pride over maintaining a quality of life and some semblance of international influence could be challenged, overtaken, and destroyed by two women, creating instability in the republic.

5

In Wolf's Clothing
Sombre (1998),
and *L'Humanité* (1999)

> To live without loving is to not really live.
> —*Molière*

France has endured a long history of serial killers wreaking terror on unsuspecting victims. One of the earliest on record was Gilles de Rais, one of the wealthiest men in France who has haunted the halls of history and literature since his death by hanging in 1440. He was Joan of Arc's personal bodyguard and was even appointed Marshall of France, a title he kept for four years before stepping down. After his withdrawal from public life he retreated into his castle where he killed approximately 140 children, either through ritual sacrifice to the Devil or a demon or through sheer sexual perversity. De Rais is believed to be the inspiration for *Bluebeard*, the story of a man who locks up his dead wives' bodies, though the Bluebeard story is, in some ways, more palatable than that a pedophile. Many other famous serial killers have followed in de Rais's fearsome footsteps but few have cast such a long shadow over history. At the beginning of New French Extremity, Philippe Grandrieux's *Sombre* (1998) and Bruno Dumont's *L'Humanité* (1999) emerged as two challengingly dark yet engaging films, dealing with the isolation and contamination of the French countryside by nihilistic forces and presences among the tourism-friendly landscapes.

The Tour de France began in 1903 as a publicity bid to sell more issues of the new sports newspaper *L'Auto*. The race was a success in gaining traction for the emerging newspaper and helped raise national pride, as cyclists peddled their way throughout the country. The tradition continued, though stopped for the two World Wars, and eventually became an international sporting event as the length of the race grew and spread to France's neighboring countries. It is still one of the foremost international sporting events and continues to aid France in the growth of its tourist trade by showing off its lush and idyllic landscape to the world.

When video artist Philippe Grandrieux premiered his first feature film, *Sombre*, it was met with the scorn that accompanied many films in the New French Extremity movement. Simply put, *Sombre* is the tale of Jean (Marc Barbé), a traveling children's puppeteer who works his way through France laconically following the Tour de France (perhaps intentionally, perhaps not), touring his puppet show while also raping and murdering women. Jean meets his foil in Claire (Elina Löwensohn), a virgin whom he helps after her car stalls on her way to meet her sister, by offering to give her a lift. Unexpectedly, Jean delivers Claire to her sister unharmed and the threesome begins to travel the countryside together. Jean soon reveals his true nature as he assaults Claire's sister and subjects Claire to a night out, plying her with liquor and men. Claire sees Jean's darkness and falls in love with him.

The plot in *Sombre* is secondary to the sensation of the film. *Sombre* is notable for establishing Grandrieux's directorial style, which is reliant on handheld camera work, disorientation, varying film speeds and intensified sound. James Quandt, in his rallying cry against New French Extremity, derided *Sombre* as

> a disorienting plunge into the consciousness of a compulsive rapist/murderer. The first half hour of *Sombre* is taken up by a vertiginous transcription of a road tour of carnage, as the killer casually dispatches women in the French countryside. Underlit, indeterminate images, flickering, unfocused, and flash cuts, summon a sense of menace and illegible dread.[1]

While Quandt accurately describes the unfocused qualities of *Sombre*, he fails to capture the pure essence of the film, that of a sensory descent into both the mind of a serial killer and the woman who falls in love with him. Grandrieux offers many clues as to his inspiration for the sensory reception of the film: children. The opening scene tracks along stretches of road as the sun sets. The roads are rural and lined with trees, with little indication of any kind of nearby population. Grandrieux sets his camera at the eye level of a driver, immediately suggesting that the viewer is already locked within the camera's subjective gaze. The establishing shots echo those in Stanley Kubrick's *The Shining* (1980), which show Jack Torrance (Jack Nicholson) on his way to an interview at the haunted Overlook Hotel. The bird's-eye view of Jack's car traversing the Colorado Mountains suggests an omnipotent being watching over the proceedings. Ominous music over the shots make it clear that whatever is watching Jack is truly malevolent. In contrast, Grandrieux's eye-level shots of the road indicate that someone is driving and in control of the car and, rather than a musical score, Grandrieux layers in white noise that grows in intensity until it feels as though the film will break. There is a quick cut to children madly screaming at a puppet performance, either warning against action or demanding violence from the puppets onstage. The cut from an almost blinding white noise to a faction of children's screams creates an unsettling and immersive effect. As film theorist Martine Beugnet writes of Grandrieux's introduction to the film:

> Grandrieux's images refer to the lost pleasure of the complete rapture often experienced in childhood. There is a sinister undercurrent to the sequence in *Sombre*, however, an ominous sense of threat, carried by the vibrations, that appear to permeate the frame from the outer field. In effect, the main character of this enigmatic crime film, the puppet master Jean, is a murderer whose journeys are punctuated by brutal and apparently random killings of women. We do not know this at this stage—indeed kept off frame, both the puppeteer and his show remain invisible for the duration of the early scenes. The sequence could offer a familiar, endearing sight; yet it creates an unsettling feeling, as if something vampiric was at work in these shots drained of light and images, the distortion of the picture and sound emphasizing the ambiguous mix of pleasure and abysmal fear of the children's reactions.[2]

Already in *Sombre*, Grandrieux has established that the relationship between the audience and film is about what is being watched, that the camera is predator, not prey. This disruption of the narrative breaks many audience expectations, allowing Grandrieux to facilitate a sensory experience within a common thriller narrative. *Sombre* goes beyond the typical slasher point-of-view shots, however. Made famous by Michael Powell's *Peeping Tom* (1960) and John Carpenter's *Halloween* (1978), the camera was placed as the killer's viewpoint for short periods of time and utilized intermittently throughout the film, creating the sense that the viewer is complicit in the actions of the murderer, while also granting knowledge over the story's victims, creating a tense power struggle. In *Sombre*, Grandrieux creates a sensory landscape, where nothing is ever fully viewed but everything is felt. Grandrieux works to evoke the sense, often editing the film between textures (skin, fur, leather) and submerging the images in darkness only to provoke the audience by illuminating a body briefly but poignantly, intermixing moments of silence with heavy breathing. The effect is uncomfortable, and intentional. Grandrieux continually challenges viewers to distance themselves from the proceedings flickering on the screen in front of them. He merges moments of brutal violence with tender looks and caresses. As Grandrieux himself says of the cinematic experience:

> You film with a history behind you. It's hard to film as if Dreyer, Murnau and Lang had never existed. But I never think of antecedents as I film a shot; I couldn't. I don't have a cinephile background. My cinematic culture was formed late. When I was eighteen, nineteen, I'd only seen regular films like *The Guns of Navarone* (1961)—which, by the way, I liked a lot! But I had an urge to make films and, in the course of my studies at INSAS in Brussels, I discovered three films a day, seeing things that I had no idea existed. I remember *Moses and Aaron* (1975) by Jean-Marie Straub and Danièle Huillet, that was a blow, an aesthetic and political shock. I still recall it today. Suddenly—cinema. And what came through bodies, fragmented bodies, legs, the extremely flat earth, the sunlight at its zenith, the brutality of the shots. All of that struck me. I was motivated. My cinephilia has constructed itself in a fragmentary way, but it's not like there is cinema on one side, and literature and philosophy on the other. All of it is part of the same question, the same attentiveness, the same enterprise.[3]

The film oscillates between Jean and Claire's view of the proceedings. The more Claire falls in love with Jean, the more of the world we see through her as she succumbs to the darkness. Throughout the film, Grandrieux teases out parts of the puppet show that Jean travels the countryside performing, which seems to be "Little Red Riding Hood." The tale of the wolf that follows a little girl into the countryside to consume her and her grandmother has multiple endings: the wolf dies at the hands of Little Red Riding Hood; the wolf dies at the hands of a hunter; or the wolf eats Little Red and her grandmother. As with other pieces of folklore and fairy tales, the stories have generated multiple interpretations and endings based on their own internal history. While the audience does not see the full scope of Jean's puppet play, snippets are shown. The children reacting to it in the opening scenes and, later, Jean's manipulation of the puppets, which Grandrieux shoots from beneath, illuminating Jean's face and displaying his focus and concentration while animating the puppets, makes the children's delight palpable and Jean's attention to detail intertwine with the children's joy. Jean also brings with him a full wolf costume, which the viewer never witnesses him wearing in performance. The audience sees it when Claire sneaks into Jean's room and looks through his suitcases. The puppets are of little interest to her but, when she finds the wolf costume, she strokes its fur and puts it on, giggling to herself as she does so. Just then, Jean enters and hurriedly removes the costume. Grandrieux is careful to show little of Jean's interaction with the outside world. As the audience never sees the puppet show, Grandrieux never allows the audience to view the rest of his day-to-day life. What the audience sees is his view of the countryside, the murder and rape of multiple women, and his orchestrating of a children's puppet show. In essence, Grandrieux creates Jean as a myth not unlike Gilles de Rais, a cataclysmic view of a sideshow murderer. He is the bogeyman, with no interior, a long-standing myth that casts his shadow across the country landscape, creating fear. As Grandrieux says of *Sombre*:

> [T]he film is a fairy tale. The character Jean, who is archetypal, has no psychological refinement: he is presented as a block of childhood, a block of sensation cut off from other men. From this point onward, it is no longer a question of morality. Is there a question of morality in *Red Riding Hood* or *Bluebeard*? As a human being I carry with me a definitive social condemnation of murder. But I didn't place this film within a social framework, but rather on the level of the unconscious. *Sombre* invokes the most archaic of impulses. Hearing and sight, two senses which ground us from the very first moments. The film combines the question of form and grounds through these senses, and only through these senses.[4]

The camera's unfocused gaze throughout the film creates not only an eerie, but otherworldly, quality. What Quandt describes as "illegible dread" could also be read as an obscuring of narrative. A focus on the viewpoint that Jean's mythological bogeyman conjures as he spreads fear and menace.

The figure of Claire would normally illuminate the monstrous character in a more mainstream film, but in *Sombre* she only serves to cast Jean further into darkness. Claire is introduced as normal, attractive young woman who succumbs to Jean's perversions, indicating some darkness already within her. When her sister reveals that Claire is a virgin, Jean seems taken aback. Claire's childish nature and the passion of her love for Jean cannot save him, even as she offers him her body. Claire's body represents the pure and untouched; Jean's illusion and destruction. Jean is the predator but cannot prey on Claire because, to him, she represents an immersion into a society in which he remains on the outskirts. While Jean's other victims have been prostitutes or women on the outskirts of society, Claire's familial bonds render her safe from Jean's predilections.

> Bodies are objects in Grandrieux's films; things are done to them just as they stubbornly refuse to be recognized as human. In *Sombre*, Jean is the figure who manipulated pliant women's bodies as if they were the puppets he carries in his bags; in each of the six murder scenes, he pushed his fingers into the mouths of his victims in an obviously erotically charged act of penetration. The act also represents the locus of life and death; in breaking the skulls of the women through their mouths, Jean's gesture is a ritual, life-annihilating one—a gesture of command but also a gesture of death.[5]

Jean's purest inclinations come through his movements. Whether hunched over, working with the puppets, twirling in his hotel room, or destroying women's bodies, those movements offer an understanding of his desire and intent. While *Sombre* comes close to being a silent film, Jean's conversational interactions are all commands or short statements; everyone else who speaks in the film is rendered obsolete. What they offer is unimportant, or a lie. Grandrieux conflates human interaction through speaking as untrue and manipulative, while Jean's urges and desires are often the most direct parts in the scenes where he interacts with others. While the audience begins to realize that human language is codified in manipulation, Jean's methods seem oddly quaint, and somewhat childlike. A child asks and demands, having not yet learned the ins and outs of a socially contracted interaction; Jean relies on his senses and gives in to his impulses.

> Grandrieux talks about the imminence of his work and wanting to return to a state of early years where all the sensations are deep and primal. When the world is understood through the senses, rather than as a world of decoded experience. Grandrieux's work seems to work at a semiotic antithesis where there are no signs or symbols to decode just febrile physical experiences to endure and experience. His images seem to come from within the audience [and] from their darkest psychic recesses. Sex, violence, wild spaces and urban desolation. The images of descent into inner madness.[6]

In essence, Grandrieux paints his bogeyman simply as a man who has not been socialized out of his primal urges, suggesting that those impulses reside within everyone at all times. The end of the film sees Jean chase Claire away as a way of saving her. She drives away with a widower and seemingly to safety, though she tells the woman of her relationship with Jean, revealing an elaborate inner fantasy that may indicate a deeper psychological crack. The last shot of Claire is of her face—peaceful, her eyes closed against a darkening sky as the camera slowly pans up. Is Claire imaging Jean? Longing for him? Absolving him? Or psychically leaving him? The film then cuts to Jean tearing through a wooded area, returning to his wolf-like animalistic longings, leaving behind any sense of humanity that Claire brought to his life. The final extended shot of the film is of the crowd watching the Tour de France. The camera pans by at eye-level, looking at the crowds passively watching the proceedings. The camera has let go of its hold of Jean and Claire. As Grandrieux describes:

> The final traveling shot of the Tour de France is like the absolute reverse shot of the entire film. The exterior world exists: we find it again when we leave the film behind us, and me, I am caught up in this—I do not feel the least bit distanced from these people for whom I have no contempt whatsoever.... We are these people—they are us. A little bit abandoned by the side of the road, we watch, it passes by us, we are dazzled by it, and then it has already disappeared.[7]

As the camera casts its eye back into the untroubled and untouched world, the figure of Jean still looms and lurks in the shadows of the audience's mind—a frightening reminder of what could be out there in the woods.

Echoing Grandrieux's filmic aesthetics, filmmaker Bruno Dumont says:

> What interests me is life, people, the small things. Cinema is for the body, for the emotions. It needs to be restored among the ordinary people, who don't speak a lot, but who experience an incredible intensity of joy, emotion, suffering, sympathy in death. They don't speak, speaking is not important. What's important is the emotions. It is for the spectator to make these things conscious, it is not for me to do it.... The power of the cinema lies in the return of man to the body, to the heart, to the truth. The man of the people has a truth that the man of the city, the intellectual has lost.[8]

Bruno Dumont's *L'Humanité* was derided by many critics because it received three awards from the Cannes Film Festival jury in 1999. Led by filmmaker David Cronenberg, the awards for Best Actor Emmanuel Schotté and Best Actress Séverine Caneele, who tied with Émilie Dequenne for *Rosetta*. This was seen as particularly offensive to certain sensibilities as Schotté and Dequenne were non-actors, which caused some critics to question the validity of giving them such a prestigious award. Upon its release in North America, *Entertainment Weekly* critic Owen Gleiberman placed *L'Humanité* in his Five Worst Films of the Year, while other critics in Europe and America called the film "anti-audience," citing the lack of narrative action in the film.

Dumont sets *L'Humanité* in the small French village of Bailleul, where he was raised and continues to live. The film begins with the rape and murder of an eleven-year-old girl and follows Pharaon De Winter (Schotté), a police superintendent who is tasked with solving the case. De Winter, however, seems neither interested nor able to solve the murder. He spends his time quietly tending to his lot in a garden, with his only friend and neighbor Domino (Caneele), to whom he is attracted but weary of since she is in a relationship with a local bus driver. The characters in the small town all feel deeply isolated and alone, and Dumont shoots their solitude with reverence. While the film is framed around a traumatic murder, little of the film is actually affected by it. The threat and presence of a brutal crime seems to be all too normal in the small town.

The trope of the police procedural film has been one of the most popular in contemporary cinema, with directors the world over looking for new ways to reflect and engage their audience. Dumont, however, approaches this subgenre in an entirely new way. A film revolving around a crime depends on how characters react, attempting to right the wrong caused by the crime. Dumont trains his camera on De Winter, an isolated and ambiguous character, depicting what happens when a character does *not* react. While many grizzled detectives in other films sit under flickering lights trying to piece together clues, De Winter goes to the sea, plays his electric keyboard, and attempts to deal with the local factory workers, including Domino, threatening to go on strike. Dumont challenges his audience to accept that a crime can exist and life continues on around it.

The opening of the films sees De Winter traversing the rural French landscape by running back and forth across it, disturbing the landscape shot which Dumont places before the audience. De Winter then runs through the mud, falling in it, and eventually makes his way back to his police car, where he receives the call to come to a crime scene. He then sits quietly in his car listening to Bach's *Brandenberg Concertos*, as if reorienting himself before entering a world of social construct. Dumont then cuts to the crime and focuses his camera on the young girl's vagina which, with Dumont's framing, recalls the painting *L'Origine du monde* by Gustave Courbet. The shock which the audience receives from this explicit image does not cause De Winter to react; in fact, the rest of the film sees him amble through life with only the slightest hints at his inner workings. At one point Domino mentions that he lost his girlfriend and baby, but no more is made of that. He lives an insular life of his choosing, which Dumont, as a filmmaker, also acknowledges without forcing a narrative on him; rather, he lets De Winter simply exist in this world.

Shortly after De Winter arrives at the crime scene, he returns to his home and tells Domino of the murder. Her boyfriend, Joseph, arrives and they go into Domino's house and begin to have sex, at which point De Winter follows them, observing them. De Winter's face remains blank and the audience follows his gaze as he watches Domino and Joseph give in to their desires. At once both erotic and absurd, the scene can be viewed by its audience on their own terms. It is at once the most human instinct to fornicate and, at the same time, off-putting. Dumont allows the judgment to be the audience's, not his and not De Winter's.

Dumont situates the film within a historical context by having De Winter be the grandson of the famous painter of the same name; on the wall of his bedroom hangs one of his grandfather's paintings, which he later donates to a local museum. In a way, the protagonist of *L'Humanité* is himself a painter—taking in the rural landscape, marking it, remembering it, memorializing it rather than attempting to solve the case he encounters in the way film audiences have come to expect. De Winter acts as a stand-in for all of humanity; the film's other characters and their acts reflect upon him, allowing them to see themselves. When Domino finally offers her body to him, she does so while to pleasuring herself in front of him. His reaction, at first, is one of silence. He then rejects her because the offering seems crude, animalistic, and unromantic. She berates him and lies on her bed, crying. Dumont cuts to a simple head-on shot of her vagina, not only mirroring the earlier shot of the crime scene and Courbet's painting but also implying that her tears stem from her worry that all she has to offer is her body.

L'Humanité focuses on De Winter's chosen isolation. In one of the moments that elevate the film beyond a simple *cinéma vérité* look at a small-town murder, De Winter, working in his plot in the community garden, looks up and begins to levitate between the flowers. Whether or not this moment is real within the story of the film is irrelevant. It is in this moment that the audience chooses to accept or reject the filter of the film, told through De Winter's perception rather than an omniscient narrator. His levitation could be seen as Christ-like, or at least extraordinary. He literally rises above the ground, indicating that Dumont views De Winter's silence and awkwardness not as a weakness but as emblematic of an evolved being.

In the final moments of the film, when De Winter has been all but officially removed from the case, he finds out that the bus driver Joseph, Domino's boyfriend, was arrested for the murder of the girl. De Winter sits with him under the guise of guarding him until his bosses' return, then embraces him and eventually kisses him on the mouth. It is a moment of pure tenderness and resolve seemingly borne out of Joseph's fear, as it is clear he has been crying. The scene is reminiscent of an earlier moment in the film, when De Winter interrogates an Algerian who admits to dealing drugs, an admission De Winter reacts to by placing his hands on his face, almost as an act of absolution. Dumont has implied through the film that Joseph is capable of such acts of violence after an outburst at a restaurant and the aggressive, passionate coitus in which he and Domino engage. The kiss between De Winter and Joseph lasts several seconds and ends abruptly when De Winter pushes Joseph back in to his seat, treating him as a prisoner and walking out the door. In the next scene we see De Winter collecting flowers from his garden and then comforting Domino as she cries. The final moment of the film has sparked impassioned speculative debate. There is a cut from De Winter and Domino together to De Winter facing away from the camera, sitting silently in the interrogation room, wearing handcuffs. Was *he* the killer? Or is Dumont indicating that De Winter is indeed a Christ-like figure and has absorbed Joseph's guilt through their embrace?

> Dumont's filmmaking pushes the banality, and the banality of horror, to its limits; his camera investigates the concrete surface of things relentlessly, the long take extending the possible meaning of images well beyond their denotive and connotative functions, to the point of total defamiliarization, where the categories are upturned and the banal turns into the repulsive and the uncanny, and more rarely, the repulsive into the absorbing and moving.[9]

All are possibilities in the world that Dumont has created. No matter who was truly the killer in the story, Dumont indicates that the sins of one affect all. In the final scenes of *L'Humanité*, the audience bears witness to the main characters struggling for comprehension, understanding, and absolution. Dumont shows us, without words, how deeply our emotions can be felt and that humanity comes in many different forms.

Sombre and *L'Humanité* offer a treatise on the deafening silence of rural life. While other films in New French Extremity place the violence and terror in an urban landscape, both *Sombre* and *L'Humanité* explore the banality of evil, the evil that exists in every community, which may not be as obvious as a murder or assault. These films deal with the quiet terror and dread that exist throughout France, where the figures of the rich and powerful, who can be as evil as they are wealthy, extend their nihilism and fear beyond their lifetime.

6

Fine Young Cannibals

Trouble Every Day (2001) and *In My Skin* (2002)

All true language is incomprehensible, like the chatter
of a beggar's teeth.—*Antonin Artaud*

Film scholar Tim Palmer offered an alternative name to New French
Extremity, *cinéma du corps*, or cinema of the body. Playing on past trends
in French films, such as the 1980s movement of *cinéma du look*, Palmer's
cinéma du corps easily fits into the New French Extremity definition, but
it is an important distinction to understand within this subgenre. Palmer
defines this movement in his book *Brutal Intimacy: Analyzing Contemporary French Cinema* as "a cinema profoundly centered on the body,
dwelling on the visceral aspects of corporeal acts, from body crimes to
self-mutilations, often savage behaviors derived from unchecked sexual
and carnal desires."[1] While many films discussed in this book contain
elements of Palmers's *cinéma du corps*, no two films capture its essence
as well as Claire Denis's *Trouble Every Day* (2001) and Marina de Van's
In My Skin (2002). Both films isolate the acute sensation of consumption
which, in turn, breeds isolation. The films explore these notions which
have become increasingly prevalent in modern society—consumption
is a byproduct of a capitalist system, we consume to survive and to pleas-
urable excess, while technology allows a society to connect while becoming increasingly isolated. *Trouble Every Day* and *In My Skin* explore
these themes, pushing their characters to their physical limits while
challenging the audience to see a relatable extremity in these characters.
For Palmer, the audience has a special relationship with the films of

cinéma du corps, a role "that becomes highly unconventional, challenged overtly by the artful proximity of such formally and physically confrontational events."[2]

Antonin Artaud was a playwright, actor, and drama theorist who espoused the virtues of confronting an audience. Born in 1896 in Marseille, he was a sickly child with a nervous temperament, causing his parents to send him to a sanatorium for long-term care. He was eventually discharged in 1919 and given a prescription of laudanum (a medicalized version of opium), which would lead him to a life-long dependence on that and other opiates. Moving to Paris after his discharge, he pursued a career as a writer, which eventually led him to the bourgeoning *avant-garde* theater movement. He soon became a well-known essayist, poet, and theater practitioner. Paris was a thriving epicenter of the arts at this time, not only influenced by the artists and political movements within its borders but also by touring performances and traveling luminaries.

In 1938, Artaud published his seminal collection of essays, *The Theater and Its Double*. The essays called for a revolution in theater, to do away with staid notions of expressions and challenge an audience's expectations of what they hope to see when the lights went down. One of the most influential sections of *The Theatre and Its Double* is the chapter on "The Theatre of Cruelty." For the purposes of the chapter, Artaud defined cruelty as showing an audience reality, not just confirming their moral beliefs. He believed that theater should be about the journey the characters undertake rather than the moral outcome. Theater, in this period, usually offered depictions of morality, confirming that what the audience believed to be morally good was good, and what was bad was very bad. In order to confirm this for an audience, a play would offer a resolute, moral ending in which bad characters were punished, and good characters were saved. This was beginning to change at the end of the 19th century with plays like Henrik Ibsen's *A Doll's House* (1879), which ended on a challenging and ambiguous final note, igniting controversy wherever it toured. Artaud believed that the Theatre of Cruelty could be achieved by new acting and directing practices which would be based more on movement and sound to shock the audience. This, he believed, would force them to pay attention, triggering their subconscious and primal reactions and, ultimately, eliciting a true reaction to the work.

Many of Artaud's theories have been used across the world by many experimental theater practitioners, such as British director Peter Brook.

Clair Denis's infamous 2001 film *Trouble Every Day* could also be seen to follow in the Theater of Cruelty's footsteps by tearing down an audience's notions of humanity while causing a panic in the art-house world on its release.

Trouble Every Day tells two parallel stories which constantly threaten to meet. Dr. Shane Brown (Vincent Gallo) and his new bride, June (Tricia Vessey), fly to Paris for what June believes to be their honeymoon. In fact, Shane is only interested in hunting down a former colleague, Dr. Léo Sémeneau (Alex Descas), and his wife, Coré (Béatrice Dalle). Léo was once a well-regarded neuroscientist but left his practice to become a general practitioner so he could monitor Coré who, when sexually aroused, becomes filled with a murderous, cannibalistic desire. Shane seems to be suffering from this malady as well.

On its release, *Trouble Every Day* became known as a *film maudit*, a cursed film, flying in the face of Denis's previous well-received films *Chocolat* (1988) and *Beau Travail* (1999). At the Cannes Film Festival, *Trouble Every Day* screened out of competition and was met with boos and walkouts. Much of the anger surrounding *Trouble Every Day* concerned the fact that Denis, a respected and revered filmmaker, had made a horror film. But what is love, contagion, and carnal desire if not horrific?

Unlike the labels critics like to slap on films, Denis's *Trouble Every Day* (like most films in the New French Extremity movement) rejects a rigid definition. There are horrific and disturbing elements, but there are also moments of tenderness and understanding, followed by moments that blend those elements together, creating something new and visceral. The film veers wildly between moments of true horror and quiet containment. Ordinary objects silhouetted against the sky and the iconic Parisian backdrop take on an eerie or malevolent presence, making the familiar unfamiliar, which is at the very heart of *Trouble Every Day*.

When the characters do speak to each other, particularly Shane and June, June resists the knowledge that something is truly wrong with her husband, rendering their conversations stagnant and unconvincing. It is a show of artifice. The weight of the film is given to the physicality of Coré, who slinks through scenes and watches her prey like a predator about to strike. Denis follows Coré's serpentine actions with dreamy, cinematic camera moves that indicate reality, elevating those scenes above the benign normality of Shane and June. When Léo locks up his wife every day before he leaves for work, he locks up desire and passion because he has seen what has happened when it is unleashed. As Laura McMahon writes:

> Denis' techniques of tactile filming in *Trouble Every Day* work to "touch" and contaminate the viewer, spoiling the hygiene of a distanced viewing. An emphasis on the surface of images seems to replace the importance of narrative and dialogue: the contagious bodies of Coré and Shane are cut adrift from any expository structure and left to circulate as volatile, tactile intensities through the film. Here Denis departs from the conventions of the horror genre, whereby the viewer agrees to be terrified of the film in return for a clear unfolding of the plot. By removing the sterility of a structured narrative, Denis leaves the viewer dangling, exposed to these contagious intensities in a realm of dread without guidance.[3]

Denis provides just enough narrative through the film to ensure that the audience has enough to hold onto, to guide them through a world that seems just familiar enough. The film, as McMahon points out, becomes unsafe as Denis sets us adrift with the two most dangerous characters, Coré and Shane. The audience understands from the opening of the film that Coré has succumbed to the disease and that, while her husband's hopes for finding a cure are valiant, they are almost sure to fail. Any scene with Coré in *Trouble Every Day* defies audiences' expectations, creating an unstable and unexpected film experience by letting the characters take over.

At the climax of the film, young robbers break into Léo and Coré's home. In any other film the audience would be worried for the woman's safety. In *Trouble Every Day* the audience is worried for the safety of the robbers. While Coré's disease has been hinted at, it is in this scene that it is finally on show and experienced. One of the young men discovers Coré locked away and, after several sexually charged glances back and forth, he begins to tear down the wall that separates them. As they begin to have sex her appetite reveals itself and her kisses turn into bites; his screams can be heard as his flesh is torn away from his body. Coré never speaks in the film, so it is unclear if the disease has caused her to regress to a primal state where she cannot control herself, or if she has actually evolved beyond the niceties of humanity, claiming what she wants. Denis challenges her audience through the film by making the narrative and expository scenes feel fake, rehearsed, and inherently "unreal." The scene in which Coré seduces and kills the young man feels like the most honest one in the film, not only because the character has given into her desires but because of its visceral, authentic quality. Much of *Trouble Every Day* lacks a narrative cohesion, even the scenes which offer some sort of explanation or motivation come out of order. It is only in the violent attack scenes which bear the weight of importance and confirm the characters' objectives, if not their motivations.

After the young man is killed and partially eaten by Coré, the camera stays with her, contemplating her from afar like a caged animal. In whatever time has passed, Coré has remained in her white dress, stained with blood, as are the walls surrounding her. She is free from her prison and, with the camera trained on her, the audience is able to contemplate the carnage she has wrought. Shane enters the house after finally figuring out where they live, but before he is able to talk or reason with Coré about the disease that is taking hold of him, she lights the house on fire and dies within it. Shane, meanwhile, escapes.

From there, *Trouble Every Day* becomes Shane's narrative. The disease, which the audience has witnessed in its full force, grows within Shane. He tries to play husband for his wife, but cannot bear it. While trying to have sex with her he feels that he cannot climax, so he retreats and masturbates. He goes for long walks, leaving her alone. Eventually he adopts a puppy in hopes of placating June, which seems to work. Throughout the film, June is presented with enough information to glean that something medically is wrong with her husband, yet she chooses to look away. Is it because the clues point to something too fantastical to be believed, or does she feel that her version of femininity has failed him? As a bookend to Coré's scene with the robber, Shane has sex with a maid at the hotel where he and June are staying. It mirrors the roughness and directness of Coré's scene but with a man in control and, from what we know, diseased. This scene is even more threatening than the first due to the sheer brute force Shane is able to muster. In the final violent act of the film, Shane's disease overtakes him during coitus with the maid, whom he kills while consuming her. While Coré's scene feels like a fitting reversal, with the potential victim in a robbery becoming the attacker, Shane's scene feels terrifying in its normality. While there seems, at first, to be trepidatious consent from the maid, Shane's actions soon become frightening and violent. This is the form of masculinity that society fears: angry, violent, and uncontrollable. Now the audience knows what it takes for Shane to climax.

Trouble Every Day was derided by critics for its excessive use of horror genre tropes, graphic violence, and explicit sexuality. By looking considerately at the film, *Trouble Every Day* does not offer blood and semen for the sake of titillation, it offers it to the audience to implicate them with these acts. It plays on the audience's fears of sexuality, linking it not only to desire but to humanity's animalistic nature. Through Coré and Shane, the audience experiences a breathless desire for a tactile and violent sexuality, one that has been bred out of society in hopes of normalization and sustainment of the species. Léo and June are two characters helplessly out of step with their partners' desire, who will continually try to save them. Rather than invest time in the normalcy of Léo and June, Denis tempts the audience with Coré and Shane. When Coré finally gets her way and is able to consume the flesh of the robber the camera cuts between their bodies and skin, both covered in blood, soon becoming indistinguishable from each other. The audience is part of Coré's desire and hunger. Denis also implicates the audience in the assault and death of the maid who appears briefly throughout the film, tidying up Shane and June's hotel room. The camera lingers on her, follows her, much like Shane's gaze. She has become an object of desire. When Shane finally attacks, the audience receives the payoff that has been hinted at throughout the film. When it finally comes, however, the audience is forced to bear witness to an attack in which they are now implicated.

Early in the film, as the newly married couple is about to touch down in Paris, Shane whispers to June, "I will never hurt you." At the end of the film, that feels like a promise. While Coré and Shane may never hurt their spouses, that promise comes at the price of other lives. At the end of the film, June walks into their hotel room, where Shane is showering off the blood following his attack on the maid. As June joins Shane in the shower, he wipes the blood on the shower curtain. He tells June that he would like to go home, back to America. They embrace as June replies, "Okay." There is a shot of a few blood droplets streaking down the shower curtain; the film then cuts back to June's eyes blankly absorbing the embrace and agreeing to an uncertain future.

Marina de Van's feature film debut, *In My Skin*, could be described as a meditation on body horror. Since the 1970s, Canadian filmmaker David Cronenberg has long carried the torch of what was deemed "body horror"—a cinematic study of the decomposition and deterioration of the human body occurring either naturally, supernaturally, or by force. In Cronenberg's films the body is seen as a temporal item which wears down and declines. At the dawn of the new millennium, as society became more attached to technology than to one another, body horror returned with a vengeance.

> I felt no sense of panic, no pain, even though I should have passed out. I saw my leg as just another object, a deformed object ... a scrap.... Later, at school my scars became a kind of game. My friends and I amused ourselves by sticking them with needles, because my skin had become numb there. I felt proud, but at the same time this insensitivity was frightening.[4]

Filmmaker Marina De Van recalled this story in the French press about the moment in her childhood when a car ran over her leg. The incident would not have been out of place in one of Cronenberg's films, which are replete with spurting blood and protruding bones. However, de Van's lack of reaction to the incident which, as she says, became a schoolyard game of sorts, stoked an idea within her, one which would eventually become *In My Skin*.

In My Skin follows Esther (played by de Van), a young woman who seems to have it all. She has a good job, is up for a promotion, and has a loving boyfriend. She has attained, or is on the cusp of, everything society has impressed upon her to achieve. One night while at a house party, Esther steps outside and cuts her leg on some industrial supplies strewn outside the house. While she does not immediately notice the cut or feel pain, she eventually sees the blood and dutifully goes to the hospital for treatment. The doctor playfully admonishes her for not feeling anything from the injury; he then bandages her up and sends her on her way, assuring her that the scarring will be minimal if she takes care of it.

When she returns to work, Esther is asked by her superior to fix a mistake she made. Feeling the pressure of a looming promotion, she goes to the supply closet in her office and, finding the first sharp object, cuts into her skin, offering a release. Soon, her friend and boyfriend begin to notice the additional cuts and question her about them; she simply laughs it off. The film becomes increasing abstract and disjointed as Esther's need to inflict wounds on her skin grows. She withdraws from her loved ones and work, turning increasingly inward, spurred on by the need to self-mutilate.

Nearly everything surrounding Esther's success is based on the surface metaphor. She is a healthy, attractive young woman with a healthy, attractive boyfriend. Her job is with a company that specializes in consumer surveys, requiring that she be subordinate to the opinions of others. When she and her boyfriend make plans to move into a better apartment, she gets her promotion, assuring them of this goal. It is not until her skin is pierced and disfigured that Esther turns her gaze inward. Lying to her boyfriend, friends, work associates, and downplaying her injuries, she continues her journey into a meditative self-destruction. On the problematic nature of her chosen subject matter for her debut feature, de Van responds:

> There was the obvious visual problem in showing, or not showing, or deciding how much to show of her actions. But I can't get excited about something which doesn't present some kind of great difficulty. I'm not excited unless I'm really afraid to fail.... I was drawn to the subject because of the feeling that the body could become a stranger, that there might be a distance between consciousness and the life of body. And there was the idea that the main character, this girl, could try to investigate these sensations. So the challenging aspect was one of my main motivations, the key.[5]

De Van's sequences with herself, as Esther, cutting into her flesh, tasting it, examining it, are slow and laconic, become hypnotizing. When she is alone it is a journey of self-discovery, of understanding one's self. When she is confronted or must act quickly, the act is quick and violent. But on her own, it is an act of pleasure. When her boyfriend confronts her about the increasing number of cuts on her body, Esther simply says, "I did it without thinking. It came over me." When Esther's gaze is forced onto her body after the initial accident, she reconnects with a part of herself and becomes fascinated by it. Speaking on Esther's self-mutilation, de Van remarked:

> I really wanted the audience to be affected strongly.... What was most important for me was the emotion of her curiosity, of the anguish you can feel at your body's disconnect from you. It's a very human emotion.... Because my subject was the material of my body I couldn't hide the blood. I couldn't hide the gestures, but even in scenes of incision, or cutting, I systematically avoided filming the knife coming down, evoking violence that way. On the contrary, in scenes like the one where Esther licks at her cuts, I aimed for a kind of sensuality ... while there was something very desperate in Esther's condition, there was also something very childish and childlike, especially in how she uses her mouth. At many of the screenings I attended, I did feel that the audience was moved, but not in a negative or aggressive way ... they had sympathy for her not as a sick person, but because they identified with her curiosity ... that her nature was neither hysterical nor destructive.[6]

When Esther cuts into herself, de Van's camera shows the destruction and decay of her body, yet Esther's face always remains neutral and unflinching, as if she has fully turned inward, and, without the glare of her loved ones and co-workers, she is simply being rather than performing for them.

In the tensest scene in the film, Esther has just received the promotion she desires and is at a dinner, meeting her boss and clients. They drink and smoke and talk about the Japanese market, remarking how foreign it is to them and how different their cultures are. As the conversation continues to idle, Esther loses focus on her fellow diners and begins to focus on her own body. From the quick shots of those seated around the table and Esther's own flesh, it becomes clear that she longs to cut herself. Whether it is to relieve tension or pain, the audience is not sure, but the desire is palpable. What is clear from de Van's direction is that Esther can focus on nothing else. The scene crescendos when Esther loses control of her left arm, which begins to grab at the food still remaining on her plate. She manages to get her hand under control until her left forearm detaches from her body. Esther sits in shocked silence while her colleagues blithely continue their conversation. As Esther becomes detached from the conversation, so does her own body detach from her. A waiter arrives to clear her plate which still contains most of her meal, but she informs him that she is not finished. The surreal moment continues as Esther, calmly but firmly, reattaches her arm under the table. Seizing a steak knife, she begins to cut into her skin. The cuts are not deep, but they manage to draw blood. Esther tentatively touches the cuts and brings her fingers to her mouth to taste blood; for a moment, she is satiated. De Van then simultaneously shows Esther cutting herself and the other diners cutting into the meat on their plates, highlighting the tearing of flesh, the red juice that emerges from a rare steak. The consumption around Esther is not that different from Esther's desires, but hers are seen as taboo. Esther's desire increases as she tears at her pantyhose, determined to touch and damage her own flesh. De Van connects the dinner conversation with Esther's hallucinations while maintaining a removed banality towards the whole affair. If what the audience gasps at is Esther's desire to pierce her skin, is it not just as horrifying to cut into the flesh of an animal? Esther's desire is to consume herself rather than a foreign object. The staid evening comes alive for the audience when Esther's body begins to react to itself, creating a more dynamic conversation with Esther's own body than the one occurring at the table.

After the dinner, Esther's needs grow as she rents a hotel room to cut herself, uninterrupted. She even stages a car crash to explain her growing wounds to her boyfriend. While de Van has eschewed many political interpretations of her film, preferring to look at the film as an anomaly in a normal woman's life, the filmmaker sets up many scenes to showcase Esther's healthy and normal lifestyle. In order for Esther to gain any kind of satisfaction or feeling, she is forced to remove herself from society. The more Esther tears into her own body, the more she removes herself from the outside world.

Esther's removal of herself from society, exemplified by the booking of the hotel room, removes her from the systems that society puts in place to safeguard its citizens. Esther's cool neutrality allows her to move between the outside world and her growing interior world. As Palmer points out:

> This anxiety about absent or fragmented communities in some ways reflects contemporary France, which has become increasingly marked by social solitude. National census data confirms that in the early twenty-first century 31 percent of all French households now consist of a man or woman living alone, 18.5 female versus 12.5 percent male. Nearly a third of France's domiciles are now not cohabited.[7]

For a society to function, safeguards must be in place, one of the most obvious being significant others who serve to monitor and care for their partners. In a world where solitude is becoming the norm, who can help when a member of the society is in crisis? As film scholar Martine Beugnet concludes:

> Esther commits the ultimate transgression—she mutilates, disfigures and thus renders dysfunctional a body that had been shaped to fit, represent and entirely contribute to the perpetuation of a specific socio-economic system. Yet by the same token, she performs a process of self-reappropriation, and through the grotesque horror of it, reaches for that archaic dimension of the sovereign that ... a society entirely given to reason cannot tolerate.[8]

Esther's boyfriend, Vincent (Laurent Lucas), is the most consistent voice of concern in the film, worrying about her well-being and chastising her at the same time. His concern for her seems almost suffocating, forcing Esther to take increasingly extreme measures to commit the acts she so desperately wants to do. As has been noted, romantic cohabitation is vital not only to the procreation of the species, it is also the stability of a society where families are formed and relationships made. As Kristin Ross notes of the modernization of the French couple in the post–World War II period:

> The construction of the new French couple is not only a class necessity but a national necessity as well, linked to the state-led modernization effort. Called upon to lead France into the future, these couples are the class whose very way of life is based on

the wish to make the world futureless and at that price buy security. The French urban techno-couple feels itself to be fictive not only because it is historically contingent and historically new but because it is produced, materially and aesthetically, in its depths and surfaces, elsewhere—and yet it must *be* France.[9]

De Van mirrors Esther's sentiment in her own filmmaking process and ideology, reflecting her valuing of isolation and individuality. When asked about how she feels about the growing number of female filmmakers, she replied:

> I always think of myself as an individual, as different from another woman or another man. Maybe in real life I have more links with women, but as an artist I don't feel a connection, especially. I don't identify with the term "women's cinema" or "feminine cinema." It can be a way of treating certain artists as a minority, or marginalizing them.[10]

As Esther continues to withdraw from society, the film loses any sense of the linear narrative with which it started. De Van employs a split-screen technique to escalate the sensory reaction to Esther's mutilation. The cut down the middle of the screen mirrors Esther's cuts into her body. Esther's desire has overtaken the film as she is able to derive both pain and pleasure from herself. The audience is under the command of this desire, a desire that seems alien from contemporary society. De Van denies the connection between the body and sexuality, a link which Cronenberg made with his film *Crash* (1996), which de Van has cited as an inspiration for *In My Skin*. As the camera glides over her increasingly destroyed skin, the audience understands that these acts of violence are for her and no one else. As the film progresses, the damage spreads from her leg, to her arm and, ultimately, to her face—a final defiant act by a beautiful woman. As the film ends, the camera remains focused on Esther's face, which stares blankly into the lens.

Both *Trouble Every Day* and *In My Skin* reject the classic notions of what society has deemed appropriate and acceptable. They reject it with the blood of their characters causing what some deem horrific to become truly transgressive and confrontational. In *Trouble Every Day* it is the trappings of marriage that are shown to be deadly to the innocent characters onscreen. Léo and June are forced into their caretaker roles out of love and commitment. They are bound to each other at the cost of their safety and the safety of others, covering their tracks while they go. The utilization of marriage as a tool of integration and acceptance into society is the very thing that keeps them separate from the rest of the world. *In My Skin* sees a healthy and able body destroyed as the filmmaker challenges the audience to empathize with the main character. While the characters in both films attempt to engage in normalcy, they are incapable of it. Denis and de Van so clearly articulate the artifice and tedium of both normal filmmaking plotting and techniques, as well as societal standards, that the audience cannot help but gaze back and feel empathy for these characters who, willingly and with increasing necessity, turn their backs on a society that has no place for them. *Trouble Every Day* sees its diseased characters, Coré and Shane, arguably the most powerful characters in the film, act with increased recklessness, while Denis never reveals their ultimate fates. De Van ends *In My Skin* with the camera focusing on Esther's damaged skin, an unblinking portrait of defiance and desire. Both films utilize extreme acts upon the body as a form of longing. Filled with conflicting emotions and changing alliances, these films demand that the viewer not look away.

7

Lovers in a Dangerous Time

Criminal Lovers (1999) and *Twentynine Palms* (2003)

It is easy to hate and it is difficult to love. This is how the scheme of things works. All good things are difficult to achieve; and bad things are easy to get.—*Rene Descartes*

The French are perceived to have a monopoly on love. From the term "french kiss" to the Pont des Arts bridge in Paris where lovers from all over the world travel to place a lock on the fence by the bridge symbolizing their eternal love, the French have long been associated with suave romanticism. As has been discussed in previous chapters, love and sex figure heavily in the films of New French Extremity. The passion and desire for connection drives violence, both emotionally and physically. In François Ozon's *Criminal Lovers* (1999) and Bruno Dumont's *Twentynine Palms* (2003), couples are at the forefront. They are the stand-ins for all of humanity, symbolizing the most intimate relationships which are chosen rather than familial. The damage these couples inflict upon each other is almost as brutal as the violence visited upon them from outside forces. They are Hansel and Gretel and Adam and Eve; unaware and dangerously curious.

François Ozon was quick to become a sensation in French cinema and even quicker to take up the mantle of *enfant terrible*. After graduating from La Fémis, a prestigious film school in Paris where Ozon met his sometimes collaborator and fellow director Marina de Van, Ozon made several shorts and his feature debut, *Sitcom* (1998), was well

93

received by both critics and audiences. The following year he released *Criminal Lovers* (*Les Amants criminels*), which merges the anti-hero figures of Bonnie and Clyde with a fairy tale gone awry, when two would-be criminals get lost in the woods while making their escape. The marketing for the film played up the lost-in-the-country aspect by invoking the big genre film hit of 1999, *The Blair Witch Project*, when the film was released in the U.S. The film, however, functions more as a retelling of the Adam and Eve or Hansel and Gretel tales than it does with a malevolent witch inflicting malice on poor lost souls.

The film follows Alice (Natacha Régnier) and her boyfriend, Luc (Jérémie Renier), as Alice has Luc kill their high school classmate Saïd (Salim Kechiouche). The pair then flees the town, committing robberies along the way for food and money, all the while bickering with each other. They drive deep into the forest to bury Saïd's body, only to lose their way and be taken hostage by a hermit who lives in the woods (Miki Manojlovic). As the pair plots their escape, Luc is seduced into a homosexual relationship with the hermit, further complicating his already strained relationship with Alice. The film relies on flashbacks to illuminate the killing of Saïd, as well as revealing more about Luc and Alice. Ozon places the flashbacks throughout the latter half of the film and while they serve to inform the plot, they do not add up to a concrete resolution, instead allowing the film to spiral out into multiple interpretations. As Ozon says of this ambiguity:

> The criminal act is presented as it is in all its mysterious and frightening brutality, without any psychological explanation or sociological context. One rarely knows the real reasons why someone commits an act. That's what interests me, to try and get closer to that obscure moment of the murderous impulse. In fact, it seems to me that Alice doesn't desire Luc, but actually desires Saïd. She doesn't assume her sexuality. She isn't ready to have a real love relationship with the young Arab. She sticks to fantasy and provocation. She turns him on…. She then has the object of her desire killed so as not to respond to that desire. The decision to act, this delight in killing, is her manner of attaining orgasm.[1]

Indeed, Ozon suggests that both Alice and Luc are not who they appear to be; that is, healthy and attractive high school students. In the opening scenes the audience witnesses Alice's seduction of Saïd before Luc enters, stabbing him to death. In a flashback, it is revealed that Alice coerced Luc into murdering Saïd by telling him that Saïd's friends raped her and that Saïd has photos of the assault. Alice tells Luc that if she relents and has sex with him, Saïd will turn the photos over to her. Later in the film, in another flashback moments after the murder, Luc looks for the photos among Saïd's belongings and finds none. Alice then casually informs Luc that there are no photos and, therefore, there was no rape. Through the flashbacks the audience also learns that Luc is constantly teased in school about being a virgin, and Alice complains that he never gets an erection. Ozon's calling card as a director has been taking common tropes in film and queering them, providing a homosexual element that, at first, might distance the audience, yet endears them at the same time as they are drawn into the story. When Alice and Luc are locked in the Hermit's cellar, the Hermit allows Luc upstairs, feeds him, and allows him to bathe. As Luc and the Hermit lie next to each other in bed, the Hermit fondles Luc, which he allows, and he eventually climaxes. Upon Luc's return to the cellar, a nonplussed Alice remarks that she is happy he came. Luc then rejoins the Hermit, having agreed with Alice that he will steal the keys and free them. The Hermit and Luc engage in consensual sex in a tender scene, indicating that Alice's rejection of Saïd may have been an act of social guilt and implying that Luc is suffering from the same impulses. It is implied that Alice's initial attraction to Saïd was complicated due to their different ethnicities, while Luc fears the stigma of his burgeoning homosexuality. The fairy tale that Ozon creates in *Criminal Lovers* is continually complicated as it overtly examines the sexual impulses that the protagonists (Alice and Luc) share with their captor, the Hermit. As Luc is discovering his sexual desires, Alice is reliving hers through the flashbacks to which the audience is privy.

As the Hermit takes Alice and Luc prisoner, he forces them into the cellar of his house, only allowing Luc upstairs. The Hermit also uses this time to find the body of Saïd, dig it up from the shallow grave that Luc and Alice prepared, and bring it back to his home—all without Alice and Luc's knowledge. As Luc is set free from the cellar he has a chain put around his neck and his first act is to help bathe the Hermit, who stands resplendently naked before him. Luc is then offered the same courtesy as he is allowed to wash himself. The Hermit feeds him various meats, from rabbit to Saïd, whose body the Hermit has cut up and cooked. The Hermit generally keeps Luc in good stead while he behaves. Alice, meanwhile, is forced to stay in the cellar, without food or water. Her power and status is significantly weakened during her imprisonment in the cellar and she must depend on the generosity and weakness of

Luc as she succumbs to dehydration and hunger. As Ozon says of the structure of the film:

> The idea of this story came to me from a passion for both crime stories and fairy tales. I wanted to combine two genres: a crime film inspired by headlines mixed with the fairy tale, mostly a literary genre. Normally they oppose one another. One is rooted in reality and the other in a fantastic and symbolic universe. Nevertheless, they both have the same dark side, often the same themes—murder, abandonment, incest, suicide…. Fairy tales arouse the same kind of fascination in both adults and children. These stories, real or imaginary, speak to us intimately about our doubts, our fears and our worries. Furthermore, everyone has his or her favorite fairy tale, which says something about the individual's personality. In my favorite fairy tale, "Hansel and Gretel," the parents are forced to abandon their children in a forest because they don't have enough food to feed them. This is followed with the determination to escape in the symbolic sense. The ogre, the witch or whatever kind of animal involved, all have specific functions. I found it interesting to make the portrait of two adolescents based on a news headline and then slips little by little into the fairy tale world. For me, more interesting than just using the structure of naturalism and the classic justifications of social commentary cinema.[2]

Luc and Alice manage to escape from the Hermit, whom Luc does not harm, though Alice chides him to. Ozon is careful to show the Hermit witnessing the couple's departure and letting them go without giving chase. It is heavily implied through the camera's focus on the Hermit's face that Luc's escape saddens him. At the climax of the film Alice and Luc run through the forest, though it is apparent they do not know in which direction they are going. They stop by a waterfall and begin to have sex. As Luc is about to climax they hear footsteps coming closer, and begin to run. Luc's leg is caught in a hunter's trap, and Alice runs on. The police capture Luc and manage to corner Alice. As she turns, she reaches for a gun she has stolen from the Hermit, causing the police to open fire on her with a hail of bullets, a scene reminiscent of Arthur Penn's final moments of *Bonnie and Clyde* (1967). A smile crosses Alice's face as she dies. As Luc is hauled away in a van, he sees the Hermit being detained and hit by the police. Luc screams that the Hermit did not do anything. It is only outside of Alice's watchful and intrusive relationship with Luc that he is able to discover his true feelings and desires. Ozon casts Alice as a femme fatale, manipulating the men around by any means necessary, with no true allegiance but to herself.

Early in the film, Alice attempts to seduce Luc by undressing for him while he's blindfolded. She asks him which items to take off next, and then moves the fabric to sound as though she's removing those items. She produces a camera while Luc is still blindfolded, hoping to take a photos of him in a compromising situation. When Luc hears the click and whir of the camera he removes his blindfold and she reveals that there is no film in the camera. As she fails to seduce him, she reminds him of the power she wields over him. The use of photos, or rather, the absence of photos, is a source of power for Alice. It is at this moment that she tells him about the rape photos Saïd supposedly has of her. The fear, the threat of evidence, and exposing of sexuality is what Alice uses to manipulate Luc, who has no reason to distrust her. Alice uses this tactic again once they are trapped in the Hermit's cellar. She is able to hear and see into the room enough to deduce what is going on between the two men. Her seemingly offhanded remark that she is happy that Luc was able to finally climax comes across as both nonchalant and potential ammunition.

Ozon presents his lovers as both innocent and hardened—hardened because they feel little remorse for their actions; innocent because they seem so inexperienced. The murder occurs as the result of their mutually repressed sexuality, and their criminal scheme involves little to no forethought. Their bickering is a result of having robbed a jewelry store rather than a bakery and of only having chocolate bars on them instead of more substantive food. Fairy tales deal with the transition from childhood to adulthood, as does *Criminal Lovers*. As Ozon says of the final moments of the film:

> Fairy tales serve in acting as catalysts for the worries of children. And also by trying to solve them. I think that cinema can have the same function as the fairy tale. Everyone has violent impulses, murderous thoughts. Seeing these impulses acted upon on screen can be liberating. Fritz Lang said: "If I hadn't made films, I might have become a criminal." Everything is in the point of view of the director. I don't think that my film is indulgent, but there's above all a loss of reference points that is destabilizing.... I filmed [the final shot] on instinct. During the shot, I abruptly asked actor Jérémie Rénier to look at me. I needed that. The spectator can interpret it how he or she feels like. All of a sudden, we're confronted with the expression of this boy who lived through this experience. It's as if he's saying to us, "I gave you my story.... What will you do with me now? Will you abandon me?" Some might take it as an accusatory look, others as an imploring one.... Luc is in tears, then suddenly he stops crying. Those are perhaps his last tears of childhood.... Alice smiles before dying. She's achieved her fantasy. She refused to become an adult. Luc, with his expression, becomes a man.[3]

Criminal Lovers reveals the implications of crime, the moments when lies and actions become insurmountable. Luc becomes far more aware of himself and his desires through his experiences. The intimacy and tenderness between him and Hermit is real, while Alice's manipulations are a source of lies. While Alice and Luc worried about the Hermit's intentions for them, he kept them safe and hid Saïd's body alongside them in the cellar. The world within the Hermit's house was a safe haven, allowing Luc to self-realize, and de-powering Alice. Luc begins to understand, far too late, who his true self is, without the trappings of school (a microcosm of society) or Alice standing over him. Alice is able to live out her fantasies, without ever having to realize the consequences of her actions. Hers is a winning death, as she escapes while living out a fantasy. Ozon's film is both a condemnation and celebration of youth, the revelations and euphoric certitude that derive from believing in the power of beauty and sexuality.

For some, Bruno Dumont's *Twentynine Palms* can be seen as the starting point for critical discourse on New French Extremity. It is with this film, Dumont's third after *La Vie de Jésus* (1997) and *L'Humanité* (1999), in which the director physically leaves his home town of Bailleul (also the setting of his first two films) and ventures as far afield as one can get from picturesque rural France, to the desert setting of Twentynine Palms, in California. While Dumont has always fixated his directorial view on larger stories while pinpointing the minutiae of human interaction, *Twentynine Palms* departs from this view by focusing exclusively on two characters, Katia (Yekaterina Golubeva, who also appeared as the seductive half-sister in *Pola X*) and David (David Wissak). David, a photographer, is heard on the phone in the opening scene remarking that he is on his way to the Joshua Tree National Park to scout locations. He is in a car with his girlfriend, Katia, in the backseat, idly watching other cars pass them. Once they have reached their destination they settle into a routine: driving out to the desert, walking around, having sex, eating, and bickering. Unlike Dumont's previous films, *Twentynine Palms* falls very much into the tropes of a road-trip film, by way of an art-house aesthetic. Dumont devotes many shots to the couple in slight variations of the same backdrops, always implying that they continue to search for something. Whether the search is for a perfect shot, a new start, or anything else, the audience is never made aware, but the routine of searching for David and Katia continues. The camera often cuts between close-ups of their bodies, followed by long shots of the same images. The effect is at once distancing and intimate, much like their relationship. The two often go long stretches without speaking, as David is American; Katia, Russian. They both share a delicate understanding of the French language and use that as a way to communicate, with the occasional slips into English. Their long stretches of silence are often marked with fornication, sometimes violently, but always viscerally. Should the film have ended with David and Katia driving into the sunset, still barely speaking but managing to co-exist, New French Extremity might never have been named by film programmer and critic James Quandt.

In the final thirty minutes of the film, David and Katia are once again driving through the desert, when they notice they are being followed by a white truck. The white truck draws closer and closer and David and Katia are eventually forced off the dirt road. Frightened, they are attacked and beaten by the truck's male occupants, and David is sodomized. The men eventually drive away and David and Katia return to their motel room. Afraid and embarrassed, David sends Katia to get food. When she returns, he emerges from the bathroom with his head crudely shaven and attacks Katia, stabbing her multiple times until she dies. The film then cuts to an overhead shot of David's naked body lying face down in the desert, dead, a few steps away from the red Hummer the couple has been driving throughout the film. A police officer on the scene radios for backup.

When James Quandt wrote his article "Flesh and Blood: Sex and Violence in Recent French Cinema," he was particularly dismissive of *Twentynine Palms*, having been a fan of Dumont's previous films.

> The convulsive violence of Bruno Dumont's new film *Twentynine Palms*—a truck ramming and savage male rape, a descent into madness followed by a frenzied knifing and suicide, all crammed into the movie's last half-hour after a long, somnolent buildup —has dismayed many, particularly those who greeted Dumont's first two features, *The Life of Jesus* and *L'humanité*, as the work of a true heir to Bresson. Whether *Palms'* paroxysm of violation and death signals that Dumont is borrowing the codes of Hollywood horror films to further his exploration of the body and landscape or whether it merely marks a natural intensification of the raw, dauntless corporeality of his previous films, it nevertheless elicits an unintentional anxiety that Dumont, once imperiously impervious to fashion, has succumbed to the growing vogue for shock tactics in French cinema over the past decade.[4]

Quandt begins his article with the above passage and then examines the effects of *Baise-moi* and Gaspar Noé's films, among others. At the conclusion of his article he once again returns to *Twentynine Palms*:

> Asked why he set out to disturb his audience in *Twentynine Palms*, Dumont responded: "Because people are way too set in their ways, they are asleep. They have to be woken

up…. You can never definitively say you are human, you have to regularly be confronted by something, to remind you that you still have a lot to do as a human being, you have to be reawakened." Awakened, though, to what? What new or important truth does Dumont proffer that his audience needs to be slapped and slammed out of its sleepwalk into apprehending?[5]

Quandt—and many other critics—could not get past the violent final act. To many it seems to be an extreme and unnecessary jump scare, which has no place in Dumont's film or, indeed, his already beloved oeuvre. In *Twentynine Palms*, David and Katia venture out into the Wild West on a road trip. Already pulling from several tropes that cast a long shadow in mainstream cinema, Dumont is determined to examine the effects of these situations on two seemingly normal people. Film scholar Martine Beugnet has written of how Dumont's filmmaking pushes the banality, and the banality of horror, to its limits,[6] and in *Twentynine Palms* there is nary an aspect of David and Katia's relationship that is not lingeringly examined. The entire film, especially the final moments, is devoid of cinematic trickery or coercion; they are events, sometimes artistically, unfolding in front of an audience.

David's issues with anger and ambivalence are some of the few moments that mark *Twentynine Palms* with more traditional dramatic tension. In a truly upsetting scene, David and Katia sit on their motel bed watching *The Jerry Springer Show*, where a father admits to sexually abusing his daughter.

"Poor thing," mummers Katia.

"Who?" replies David.

The chilling coldness of the scene mars the rest of their relationship, creating an uneasy tension between David, Katia, and the viewer. In another scene David allows Katia to drive his Hummer which she accidentally scratches. When David nearly convulses with rage, eliciting laughter from Katia which dehumanizes and alienates him, the audience is once again privy to an unnerving side of David, one that can flare up at a moment's notice. David's flashes of rage and unsympathetic outlook overshadows their relationship. He is protective of his belongings, one of which, he believes, is Katia. At another point the couple passes a uniformed military man with a shaved head. David asks Katia if she would like it if he did that; she replies that if he did, she'd leave him. She then admits that she finds the Marines very attractive, which launches David into a fit about their lack of real communication. David's killing of Katia occurs when he emerges from their bathroom after he has attempted to transform himself by shaving his own head. In a twisted way, David has become the man Katia views as attractive. David's purging of his hair causes a break in his psychosis, rendering him nearly unrecognizable and a tool for destruction, much like those enlisted in the Army. As Dumont says of David and Katia's relationship:

> Good and evil are polar concepts—one can't exist without the other. If there was no evil … the couple is in the primordial human condition of sexual bliss, but with this threat of disaster that can spring from any quarter without reason or cause…. It's about the banality of the couple. About boredom, anticipation, anger, reconciliation. All the so-called trivia, the details of a relationship, I made those the focus. I wanted to reduce the importance of the subject matter and change the figure-ground relationship. Have two tiny little figures against a vast backdrop. The best parallel I can think of is the transition from figurative of abstract painting.[7]

Dumont's view of Katia and David's relationship casts them as insignificant in the larger scope of the world; they affect no one else but each other. Their love and violence is only inflicted on each other, as long as the camera is with them. Even in the final moments the audience has few clues as to David's death. A few paces away from his beloved car lies his naked body, face down. An inverted image of the two lovers' post-coital joy, David's body is now no longer part of a whole, but a fractured piece.

Twentynine Palms reads as an American film, viewed by an outsider. It may seem shocking that a French director, known for his relationship to his homeland, would make a film about a country he has little experience with, but, as he says in an interview with *Indiewire*, *Twentynine Palms* is more about an outsider's perception of a country that has the power and means to influence the world.

INDIEWIRE: Had you wanted to make a horror film before you went out west?

BRUNO DUMONT: No. I decided to because of what I felt when I got there. I'd never been to a desert before and I had this profoundly metaphysical experience of fear.

IW: Not even the Sahara?

BD: No.

IW: Were you there at night?

BD: No, just in the daytime. But I knew I was in the USA, where anything can happen.

IW: Well, in Europe too.

BD: Yes, but … no no no no no. There's a longstanding myth about the United States that is still very prevalent in Europe [despite recent developments]. Historically the "America" of this myth is an incredible human adventure and experiment in political democracy. But at the same time, or so we're told, it's the land of extremes where the worst can happen.[8]

Dumont's view of America is thoroughly unromanticized. While the characters in his two previous films are given a weight of importance and grace, David and Katia are shown to be disposable elements in an ever-changing world. Their adherence to an artistic aesthetic, alongside a journey into a deserted landscape, causes the audience to view them as unimportant to society. Their actions show little impact other than contributing to the American economy by eating at restaurants. Dumont's view of America through the scope of *Twentynine Palms* is that of a wasteland that all too easily swallows its inhabitants.

Throughout the film, David amasses all the elements available to him of American masculinity. He drives a Hummer, redefines the former military landscape of the desert through an artistic lens, and engages in rough, and sometimes violent, sex with his partner. When an outside force disrupts and literally enters him, he breaks. The final violent imagery is Dumont's commentary that the audience's coded understanding of masculinity, femininity, and relationships are all false. In a post–9/11 America, the notion of an eye for an eye became all too prevalent, eventually inciting a "war on terror" under false pretenses. In *Twentynine Palms*, Dumont challenges those vary notions of protecting oneself through violence, by showing David not tracking and taking revenge on the men who attacked him and Katia, but taking revenge on the person closest to him. All of the symbols and actions taken earlier by the two only serve to mask their primal nature. When those masks are removed everyone becomes the "savages" that the cowboys fought against in Western films from a bygone era. Earlier in the film, when David and Katia scale a small mountain, make love, and, finally, lie naked on a flat rock, the camera stares at them from high above, rendering them, in the audience's collective imagination, as Adam and Eve reborn. The camera stays trained on them for longer than is necessary, guiding the viewer's mind as filmgoers to question Dumont's motive. Is something about to happen? Nothing happens in that scene, except David and Katia catching their breath. The audience's trust and training as a cinematic audience leaves them to believe that something traumatic is bound for these two, and that assertion is not wrong. The fear and uncertainty felt by Dumont's audience, in the earlier post-coital scene, is answered in the final scene: the only thing left to fear is ourselves.

Both *Criminal Lovers* and *Twentynine Palms* deal with the trauma of intimate relationships, when trust is placed in another human being who is as flawed and uncertain as anyone else. The terrains both couples must navigate are foreign and unfamiliar. They belong nowhere and to no one, not even each other. The films revel in the uncertainty of the audience's allegiances, which change throughout the course of both films. These films assert a very real fear of intimacy, where it is not only the lovers who cannot be trusted but the world outside of them.

8

Without Borders

Intimacy (2001), *Demonlover* (2002)
and *Ma Mère* (2004)

Those who can make you believe absurdities can
make you commit atrocities.—*Voltaire*

Love, sex, and intimacy have driven some to commit unthinkable
acts. Bodies have been used to facilitate attainment. These acts are not
uncommon in history or in New French Extremity, which continues to
pit intimacy and romance against the absurdity of the world and other
human beings. There can be no love without trust, but as New French
Extremity is quick to point out, who is there to trust? Each of the films
discussed in this chapter examines the fluidity of intimate relations, how
their rules change frequently and for varying reasons. Each of these
films offers a glimpse into romance and desire and, ultimately, the damage they inflict on everyone who comes into contact with the burgeoning
relationships. Taboos are broken unrelentingly, giving way to the brutal
aspects of the most personal of relationships.

A dingy London flat offers the gateway into Patrice Chéreau's film
Intimacy. A co-production between French, German, British, and Spanish companies, *Intimacy* garnered immediate reactions upon its release
for its heavy use of unsimulated sex between the two leads. The film
begins with a nameless woman (Kerry Fox) entering the home of Jay
(Mark Rylance), a failed musician. She comments on the state of the
apartment as the camera glides over its messy interior; without comment, the two characters who seem to be almost at odds with each other
then engage in passionate sex which is as real as its presented on screen.

The woman leaves without a word, returning every Wednesday afternoon for the same arrangement. Jay's curiosity gets the best of him and he soon begins to follow her. He learns her name (Claire), that she is an amateur theater actress and drama teacher with a husband, Andy (Timothy Spall), and a young son, Luke (Joe Prospero). Jay becomes entangled in their lives and must figure out a way to separate himself before their affair destroys the family.

The film is based on an autobiographical novel of the same name and two short stories, *The Wednesday Woman* and *Nightlight* by acclaimed British writer Hanif Kureishi. "I felt somehow that Patrice had made a sequel to [my book] *Intimacy*," said Kureishi in an interview:

> [That] he had moved on what happens to us when the most significant relationships in our lives breakdown. People use sex to do stuff with somebody else that they can't say to them. I guess we were interested in middle-aged people trying to find some kind of meaning in the body of somebody else, because they can't find it anywhere else.[1]

The wordless, primal sex in which Jay and Claire engage becomes the truest part of the film, as everything else becomes a sort of lie. Claire's stage career, though embarrassingly earnest, brings her joy because it allows her to become someone else, to live out another life. Jay, who has given up on music and his family, now makes his living as a bartender. He serves drinks to people who want to forget, and complains of the other bar staff that they are all actors and musicians waiting for something better to come along. He could not handle being a family man, so he left, and his new life is as transient as the co-workers he complains about. The commotion that surrounds the lives of both Jay and Claire is an illusion; the only truth they know is their physical nakedness with each other.

Marxist philosopher and cultural critic Slavoj Žižek remarked in his film *A Pervert's Guide to Cinema*:

> All too often, when we love somebody, we don't accept him or her as what the person effectively is. We accept him or her insofar as this person fits the co-ordinates of our fantasy. We misidentify, wrongly identify him or her, which is why, when we discover that we were wrong, love can quickly turn into violence. There is nothing more dangerous, more lethal for the loved person than to be loved, as it were, for not what he or she is, but for fitting the ideal.

Claire seeks to remove her identity from Jay by not revealing it; therefore, she can never become an ideal. She remains only a body that gives and receives pleasure every Wednesday afternoon—in short, defining her own ideal by keeping to her rules. It is not until Jay seeks her out and discovers her outside life that not only complicates Claire's other existence but also his own, forcing him to reconcile his own desires with the chance that he might destroy a second family. In the flashbacks that reveal Jay's previous life, it is revealed that his wife did not touch him, causing him to withdraw from the marriage and his two young sons. Claire, it would seem, is the missing puzzle piece to Jay's desire. But Jay's desire soon cannot be satiated with just sex; he desires a connection, something that brings the two of them together beyond what they share physically. Interestingly, what they share physically does not infer a passionate relationship, but one built on confusion and desperation. Jay and Claire's sex is awkward, with the two bodies fumbling with each other to create a connection.

At the beginning of the film, the audience shares a view of Claire through Jay's eyes: she is mysterious and sexy. When Jay discovers the rest of her life—the cheap theater and unsatisfactory marriage—Claire becomes less of an enigma and more of a contemporary to his own problems. As the film progresses and Jay begins to manipulate Claire's husband, Andy, the focus splits. Chéreau shows the interactions and confrontations between Claire and Andy, which culminates in Andy telling Claire that she is a bad actress, the implication being that she could not hide her affair and hide her desire. To Jay and Andy, Claire has failed at being an eternally sexual entity and at being a wholesome entity, bringing into question that nature of expectation on the ideal partner.

While *Intimacy* focuses on Jay's plight and his obsession with Claire, it is ultimately Claire who remains steadfast in her resolve. Her affair with Jay was supposed to make her marriage more palatable, while her marriage was meant to create stability. Neither Jay nor Andy seems able to accept the roles in which Claire has placed them. The sex scenes in the film fill the void of connection between characters and offer a look into the world after marriage has been obtained and a child has been produced. Claire does not want to shatter the illusion of familial bliss, but she cannot ignore her desires.

Intimacy was branded as a scandalous entry into European cinema at the turn of the millennium. Much of the press surrounding the film focused on the sexual aspects, which incite the events of the film but do not resolve the issues created by Claire and Jay's relationship. *Intimacy* offers an unflinching look at what the body desires versus what it can accept.

As Kristin Ross wrote in *Fast Cars, Clean Bodies*:

Once modernization has run its course, then one is, quite simply, either French or not, modern or not: exclusion becomes racial or national in nature.[2]

Olivier Assayas's 2002 film *Demonlover* extends the extremity which France found in the new millennium beyond its borders. Assayas frames his film as cyber-thriller, bringing into question the very nature of the capitalistic class system of which Ross writes. Ross's writing deals with the post–World War II period and the decolonization of France, for which the country relied on its very French-ness to bolster its national pride, winning the hearts and minds of its citizens in the process. Assayas breaks down the notion of a national identity in *Demonlover* by placing his characters at the center of an international business deal that relies on the commodification and production of desire.

Assayas seems to have made *Demonlover* "against" his previous films. *Les Destinées* was almost a caricature of a French super production, set in the past with period costumes and decors, inspired by a novel by Jacques Chardonne [former president of France]. François Mitterrand's favorite writer, Chardonne possessed a superb but highly classical style and a very conservative "tied to the land" vision of France, anchored in the French tradition of historical psychology, and literary cinema—in short, so very French.[3]

Indeed, *Les Destinées* plays like a film that could have been made during the Nazi occupation of France, when French filmmakers made escapist and historical films highlighting the country's past glories. *Demonlover* offers no home or respite for its characters: they are locked in a series of endless flights, business trips, meetings, and espionage. The reception to *Demonlover* was poor-to-mixed, with a disastrous showing at Cannes followed by a poor box-office take in France. The film gained traction when it received a limited release in the United States, where it received generally positive reviews; it even found an audience in France when it was release on home video and DVD. Says Assayas of *Demonlover*'s screening at Cannes:

Cannes was not a pleasant experience. For a long time I'd been making films within a framework I'd designed myself, which was part Bressonian, part modern, with an awareness of what would be accepted. I decided to move on from that with Irma Vep, and the reaction to the weirdest stuff in that was generally positive, which gave me confidence in the capacity of the audience to follow me into unknown areas. That was the first time I was dealing with a fantasy world, with the subconscious, and usually the reaction is that people are grateful that you are trying to do things other filmmakers don't do. But at Cannes people were angry I didn't make a conventional thriller.[4]

Assayas frames his film as a corporate thriller. *Demonlover* opens with the camera gliding through the first-class section of a plane. Its occupants are international passengers, most of whom sleep soundly and comfortably in the darkened plane cabin while violent images play on the screens surrounding them. The camera settles on Diane (Connie Nielsen), a member of the Volf Corporation, taking notes while her boss speaks of a nondescript business deal. The camera follows Diane as she takes her colleague Karen's (Dominique Reymond) hermitically sealed cup of Evian water and doses it with a drug. The opening five minutes of the film infuse it with an aura of suspicion and intrigue. Assayas keeps any form of resolution from the audience for the majority of the film, prompting more questions than it answers. In essence, Assayas sets *Demonlover* up as "a simple update and reinvention of the classic spy drama or war movie."[5] The drug takes effect and Karen is assaulted by men who follow her through the airport upon their landing, stealing a briefcase she had handcuffed to her arm. Diane is then put in charge of the deal on which they all have been working.

Flying with her colleague Hervé (Charles Berling), the mysterious deal is revealed: the Volf Corporation is finalizing a lucrative distribution agreement with TokyoAnime, the leading producers of sexualized anime or *hentai*. Once the deal is in place, Diane and Hervé attempt to make a deal with Dreamlover, an American company. Headed by Elaine (Gina Gershon), Demonlover not only distributes hentai but also runs a mysterious site called the Hellfire Club, an interactive torture website dealing with extreme sadomasochism, broadcast in real-time. Elaine mentions that their main competitor is a company called Mangatronics, but with their new initiatives, Demonlover believes they can render Mangatronics obsolete. Shortly after the meeting it is revealed that Diane is a double-agent who works for Mangatronics and passes information to her superiors.

The world of *Demonlover* begins to narratively disintegrate as Diane is blackmailed, more double-agents are revealed, and the Hellfire Club increases in presence. Many critics derided *Demonlover*, citing the first half of the film as watchable but the second half is a convoluted mess. While the narrative of the film does seem to disintegrate before the audience's eyes, it is that aesthetic which eventually helped find the film a dedicated following and a place among the emerging trend film that deals with the invasion of technology on the personal and private sphere. *Demonlover*, as a film, is very much a product of its time in that it is consumed and manipulated by the very technology it inhabits. The film evolves like a computer virus, slowly breaking down and corrupting the data. The break in narrative occurs when Diane murders Elaine in her hotel; Diane is then knocked out, and slowly recovers consciousness. Elaine's body, and the attendant blood, have been cleared away, with Diane seemingly free to go. Double-crosses become triple-crosses; motivations are revealed, but it is unclear if they are real or not. Assayas says of his process in plotting the film:

> I just started writing and somehow the characters took shape really quickly in a rough form, and I was sucked into it, moving from one scene I was really excited by to another and not allowing myself to be stopped by moments of explanation or logic. To me this is old stuff which audiences don't care about anymore, for good and bad reasons, in the sense that American films give them narratives that require five-minute attention spans. I thought, why not take advantage of that and experiment?[6]

The use of sex in the film exists mainly on screens the characters use. The audience sees animated depictions of sex and a pixelated version of the Hellfire Club over Diane's shoulder while she watches the computer screen. Assayas guides his camera through the world built by technology, a world that seems to be wholly comprised of sterilized spaces, reflective surfaces, and every amenity anyone could desire. It is a world of excess. Once these characters have satiated their desires, how much further must they go to attain pleasure and release? Assayas carefully utilizes the camera and editing to ensure that the audience bears witness to what the characters are watching, as well as watching the characters watching. A comment on humanity's newfound dependence on communication reaching us through a backlit screen rather than person-to-person illustrates the lack of trust in the spoken word in *Demonlover*; what the characters say to each other seemingly contradicts the majority of their actions, while the impulses and reactions to what happens on the screens in front of them cannot be ignored.

> As a powerful sensory composition that questions the impact of perception on our consciousness, *Demonlover* becomes an experience of cinema as a "body that thinks"—in this case, a body progressively "contaminated" by the visual material it explores, brought close to hallucination by a saturation of the sensory affects, and nevertheless traversed by a thought-provoking sense of disquiet and repellence.[7]

109

Demonlover explicitly shows the darker sides of sexuality in the brief glimpses of hentai which Diane and Hervé view at TokyoAnime (which had to be heavily pixelated to acquire an American release) and then, of course, Diane's viewing of the Hellfire Club, where the audience sees women in SM gear at the mercy of the demands of online participants. At the climax of the film, Diane goes on a date with Hervé after a long flirtation. Hervé uses the date with the reclusive Diane to reveal that he works with Demonlover and, by association, the Hellfire Club. They return to his home (one of the few homes we see in the film, which is as nondescript as the rest of the locations) where Hervé becomes aggressive, raping Diane twice. During the second rape, Diane retrieves a gun from her purse and kills Hervé. Diane is then kidnapped and wakes up in a PVC catsuit and a wig with an image of the actress Diana Rigg as Emma Peel in the 1960s British television series *The Avengers* next to her. The catsuit is reminiscent of one that Rigg wore in an episode of *The Avengers* entitled "The Hellfire Club," which was banned from American televisions due to the provocative nature of Rigg's ensemble. Diane is able to break free from the room, attempting to escape, but she is soon caught. The film then changes locations to a leafy, upper-class suburban street in America. A man arrives home and his son steals his credit card so he can access The Hellfire Club. But the young man is called away from his computer before he can finish detailing his fantasy; the camera then closes in on the screen, on which we see a blank-faced Diane. The boy returns to his science homework while Diane's gaze continues to penetrate the screen.

Demonlover functions as a cautionary capitalist fairy tale—work hard and be rewarded. While the film features sexuality in abundance, it is also a sterilized world. The fetishizing of luxury (the consistent commentary on Karen's new car, for example) idealizes the notion of acquisition. Whether it is acquiring a deal with a company, or the finest objects they can afford, the characters fall prey to the promise of capitalism. Detailing Diane's descent into Hell(fire Club), the audience witnesses her fall from a powerful and resourceful double-agent to a plaything on the Internet, offering a condemnation of overreaching for power. Even in the first half of the film the characters employed at the Volf Corporation are as anonymous and nondescript as savvy internet users who "are denied all spatial and temporal anchorage, as if they themselves exist in the digital realm."[8] As Assayas said of the incorporation of porn and sadomasochism culture:

I do believe that today's obsession with sado-masochistic sexuality is to do with the power games within the corporate system, which find a distorted mirror in S&M. In my earlier films the point was to describe believable characters having believable emotions that we could share. In *Demonlover* the characters are always hiding their emotions, and when they use language it's usually to deceive. It's about people within a system in which they have to hide their reality because that's the only way to survive. They have to pretend they are cynical and ruthless.[9]

The violence which the characters inflict on each other is cold and repressed, existing mainly in their minds. They maintain their coolly austere veneers while dealing with the business of sex, which they intend to sell through any means necessary to ensure their own survival. As with Ross's dominating theory in *Fast Cars, Clean Bodies*—that technology of the moment can erase the past—so do the characters in *Demonlover* they can live in their repressed world, content with their social status and ability to attain. It is, however, a veneer that only works when everyone agrees to the rules of the game. Diane violates these rules, first with the bloody murder of Elaine, and by devolving into a violent attacker and killing Hervé, thereby breaking the unspoken rules of modernity created in *Demonlover*.

Christophe Honoré's *Ma Mère* deals with the breaking of sexual taboos and caused a sensation upon its release not only because of its subject matter but because of its seeming legitimization with the casting of French star Isabelle Huppert as Hélène, the titular mother. Adapted by Honoré from the posthumously released novel by Georges Bataille, *Ma Mère* represents some of the more graphic elements of New French Extremity.

Bataille has been one of the most oft-cited influences of the extremity in French cinema as the majority of his works deal in transgression and sexuality as a function of society. Bataille began his career as a novelist with *Story of the Eye* (*Histoire de l'oeil*), published in 1928, which he wrote under the pseudonym Lord Auch (Lord Shithouse). Some read the novel as pure pornography (the story deals with perverse sexuality within a teenage relationship), while others viewed it as a mature work. During the 1920s and '30s he developed his concept of base materialism in opposition to materialism, the notion that there is no soul or higher consciousness, that life is solely defined by the act of collecting material goods. Bataille seeks to undermine traditional materialism by making the body, filth, and such things that society deems "base," seem normal and, therefore, acceptable. His works have been cited as an influence on filmmakers such as Catherine Breillat and Gaspar Noé by putting forth the notion that the act of sex in all its iterations is, in itself, a defiant act.

After Bataille's death in 1962, the pages of an incomplete manuscript entitled "*Ma Mère*" were found among the author's papers. In 1966, it was published, and almost forty years later—in 2004—was adapted for the screen by Christophe Honoré. Explains Honoré:

> I grew up with the writings of Bataille, with his conviction that literature exists to give something to the world that it wouldn't have otherwise. That literature is essential to the world, that writing is along the lines of meditation. And also the expression of Evil. Bataille wrote that a sharp form of Evil of which literature is an expression "has for us sovereign value. But this conception doesn't require the absence of morality, but demands a hyper morality." ... Adapting Bataille was about trying out his radicalness in cinema.[10]

Ma Mère begins with the reunion of seventeen-year-old Pierre, a pious Catholic, returning from boarding school to his parents' home in the Canary Islands. Shortly after his arrival, Pierre's promiscuous forty-three-year-old mother, Hélène (Isabelle Huppert), reveals that both she and Pierre's father have been unfaithful in their marriage, and that she feels no shame for this. The following day Hélène and Pierre receive news that Pierre's father has died in an accident, leading to the mother and son's descent into hedonism, drugs, and alcohol consumption. Hélène leaves Pierre in the hands of Hansi (Emma de Caunes), a beautiful young woman with a penchant for sadism, and eventually returns to aid Pierre's transition into adulthood by consummating their relationship.

Honoré remains largely faithful to Bataille's vision, with a few subtle but important changes. Hansi's maid and sex slave, Loulou (Jean-Baptiste Montagut), becomes a man in the film, exploring the gender relations in a sexually domineering relationship. At one point Loulou regales Pierre with the tale of a dominant/submissive relationship, in which the dominant partner overfed the submissive, causing him to gain weight; she then bled him and turned him into meat. (The exploits detailed in this fictional relationship seem like the plot of a particularly brutal 1970s slasher, but, in Honoré's film, the story is just another step toward sexual maturity.) Loulou appears several times in the film, waiting on Hansi in explicit ways, which irks Pierre; his discomfort, though, is dismissed by Hansi, who sees Pierre as being repressed. By the time Loulou makes her first appearance, Pierre has engaged in an orgy with two women. In his first sexual encounter with Loulou, his approach is aggressive; hers, subservient. This causes a discrepancy between the two males, which seems to trouble Pierre but seems normal to everyone else. "Loulou is a false maid who is whipped by her mistress," explains Honoré:

> I thought it would be exciting to transform her into a boy, to break the slightly systematic side of the masculine character in Bataille's work, surrounded only by women. Loulou is a backup for Pierre, who's no longer the only man who lives out a sexuality both put into danger and awakened by life.... He's an adolescent whose absolute passivity is a virtue, a threat to him and the people around him. Contrary to Pierre, who is so much at the mercy of the urges of his mother and [her friend] Rea. Pierre resists, he doesn't give himself up right away. There's a progression.[11]

Indeed, Pierre's so-called virtue remains intact through the first third of the film, which delves into his repulsion and confusion at his own sexual desires. After his father dies, Hélène asks him to throw out what is locked away in his father's office and to only keep what is of interest to him. Pierre obliges and discovers a closet full of porn and sex toys. He begins to masturbate furiously and ends the session by urinating on the pornography, making it as physically unclean as he ideologically sees them. As Pierre embraces and gives in to his sexual desires, Honoré presents the sex, and the discussion of sex, in an intimate way. The camera is almost always in close-up, characters' breath pulses on the soundtrack, creating an immersive, tangible—as opposed to voyeuristic—experience. While on the surface the sexual acts seem explicit and taboo, Honoré never treats them as such. "Personally, I don't demarcate well perversion from goodness," he said.

> I refuse to judge my characters. But I hope it's drawn through the direction and the way I present fiction, the "hyper-morality" which Bataille spoke of. Meaning a morality which isn't subservient to the one which governs our society. At the end of the film, I would like people to say these characters are never monstrous, nor more perverse than ourselves, but that they're simply more free, more fully alive.[12]

While Honoré explores the characters' sexual intimacy, it is never hidden from society. He transports the happenings in Bataille's book from 20th century Paris to the Canary Islands in Spain, a source of industrial tourism. Honoré explores the complexities of the landscape by utilizing two main settings, the family's house which is open-concept, with large windows and a terrace and pool overlooking the ocean. There is virtually no place to hide inside such a house. After his father dies, Pierre attempts to hide by taping paper over his windows, which serves only to diffuse the light still illuminating his body and his unhappiness. The paper is torn down when Pierre is tasked with going through his father's things, the beginning of his sexual awakening. Sex is engaged in freely in the house on a large bed shared by multiple people. Yet it is when Pierre loses his virginity that proves to be the most shockingly overt scene. Hélène tasks her friend Rea (Joana Preiss) with taking her son's virginity as they are somewhat close in age and Rea is a free spirit. The trio go out one night to Yumba, an entertainment complex with restaurants, clubs, and stores; Rea teases Pierre the entire evening. Hélène and Rea then abandon him, and he embraces the free-flowing alcohol. The two women later find him passed out in the concourse, at which point Rea decides to have sex with him. Pierre and Rea engage in awkward sex on the cement as passersby ignore them. While Rea and Pierre laugh about this, it creates an interesting dichotomy of the notion of anonymity in a place designed to attract tourists. The sense of the fleeting temporal self, with the hope for explicit freedom while on vacation, permeates this scene. There is no reason to believe that anyone would care about the two people having sex in this place, nor is there a reason from interrupting the two lovers during coitus. *Ma Mère* does not offer a treatise on sex as a political action, it offers it as freedom to these characters who engage in the act, seemingly without a care. The political comment comes from the sheer opposition to what is acceptable in most societies and what it means to live outside of one in the temporal space of the Canary Islands. Says Honoré of the locations:

> It seemed to me like a location where it's easy to recognize the emblematic changes regarding the relationship between the body and sexuality in Western society. The Canary Islands are an industrial tourism spot that gets kind of scary with all those English and German chartered groups. They go there for a week to consume sun, alcohol and sex. They go wild for a short period then go back to "normal" life. I wanted to see how Bataille's characters would hold up against this background of industrial tourism. They could have resembled those tourists, in their addiction to alcohol and sex.[13]

While Bataille's characters have been transplanted to the Canary Islands, it seems that a destination which trades on anonymity is the only place this family could exist.

It is this same anonymity that necessitates the climax of the film. When Hélène and Pierre finally give in to their carnal desires for each other and, as Pierre climaxes, Helene slits her own throat and dies. In *Ma Mère* Honoré conflates transgression with the temporal. The nature of human desire is still not accepted by humanity on a social and societal level so it must exist in fleeting moments. Pierre's sexual conquests all have the ability to be transient if he so chooses, the only one that cannot is Hélène, as they are tied to each other by blood. Hélène knows this, so her final act of love for her son is to kill herself in order to protect him. While Honoré situates Bataille's novel in contemporary times, the characters are still forced to live on the outskirts of society, with no interaction with those whose objections would render them nonexistent.

In *Demonlover* and *Ma Mére*, the characters' true desires come at a cost of their status. Claire could lose her family, Diane could lose her life and autonomy, and Pierre loses what remains of his family. They have been forced to give up that which they have attained due to risk and their individual predilections. Their objectives forced them out of the society which they knew, making them obsolete to the lives they knew before. Cast out of their respective homes, they search for a new acceptance, though none seems to be on offer.

9

I Won't Let Anyone Come Between Us

High Tension (2003)

A strange shadow approaching nearer and nearer, was spreading little by little over men, over things, over ideas; a shadow which came from indignations and from systems.—*Victor Hugo*

At the dawn of the new millennium, horror films were in flux. The reflexive teen slasher genre that began with Wes Craven's *Scream* (1996) had fallen victim to its own punchlines by the time *Scream 3* rolled around in 2000, effectively ending the trend. In 1999, *The Blair Witch Project* terrified audiences and had major film studios shaking in their boots that a film with almost no budget reaped a massive worldwide box-office take. The early 2000s saw the rise of American J-Horror, or Asian horror remakes, and with that, horror fans began to look internationally for their next scares.

After the release of *Trouble Every Day* (2001) and *Irréversible* (2002), audiences had gotten a sense of the kind of brutality that the French could produce. The release of *High Tension* (a.k.a. *Haute Tension*, a.k.a. *Switchblade Romance*) in 2003 saw international audiences acquire a taste for horror with a European bent. With *High Tension*, director Alexandre Aja took the brutality and metaphors of the early films of the New French Extremity movement—which stemmed from art-house films—and placed them within the context of the North American slasher film, thereby creating a new fusion of style and gore that remained accessible to horror fans.

The slasher film rose to prominence with films like *The Texas Chainsaw Massacre* (1974), *Black Christmas* (1974), and *Halloween* (1978). Slashers take a simple frame of a story and change the iteration of tropes within it, resulting in countless derivations. Most slasher films take place in a small town, or some remote location, and begin when an evil presence (either a person or a supernatural force) descends and begins killing a targeted group of young adults. Emerging from that group is a young woman who film scholar Carol Clover identifies in her book *Men, Women and Chainsaws* as the Final Girl. The Final Girl does not usually partake in the questionable activities (i.e., sex, drugs) of her friends which wind up putting them in danger. She is level-headed, assured, and, ultimately, brave. In slashers, the most prominent figure often becomes the villain, which led to the rise in cultural prominence of figures like Freddy Krueger from *A Nightmare on Elm Street* (Wes Craven, 1984) and Jason Voorhees from *Friday the 13th* (Sean S. Cunningham, 1980). With the popularity of *Scream* (Wes Craven, 1996), the slasher trend changed the figure of the Final Girl, making her increasingly important to the storyline. Due, in part, to the casting of successful young television actresses, such as Neve Campbell from the television show *Party of Five* in *Scream*, and Jennifer Love Hewitt, also from *Party of Five*, in *I Know What You Did Last Summer* (Jim Gillespie, 1997), the Final Girl came into her own as the heroine of these franchises. The killers would change throughout the series, but the Final Girl remained a constant.

Slasher films have their roots in many different social and filmic trends. They contain elements of urban legends and the *Giallo* films, from Italy, which feature black-gloved killers stalking victims, utilizing a POV shot. Films like George Archainbaud's *Thirteen Women* (1932), Michael Powell's *Peeping Tom* (1960), and Alfred Hitchcock's *Psycho* (1960), among others, have all been mentioned as precursors and influences on the slasher genre, but if anything is clear it's that slashers have drawn their inspiration from multiple sources in order to create highly entertaining, gripping thrillers that engage audiences and yield a substantial box-office return.

This brief overview of slashers does not take into account the fandom and creativity that went into these films, particularly in the 1980s. Fans all over the world still view slashers from the 1970s and 1980s as touchstones of their childhood and adolescence. As CGI effects become the norm, slashers represent a time when tactile creativity reached its peak with the unbridled enthusiasm of the effects team that created elaborate set and gore pieces.

Until 2003, slashers were an almost exclusively North American product. They had gained popularity all over the world, but they represented a particular brand of Americana, one that was a comment on the American way of life that had been promised and fed to its citizens but never delivered on. The American way of life was changing and slashers became a reaction to that change. The thrust of these films hinged on a group of young people discovering a terrible secret or event (i.e., a murder) that had been covered up in some way. This discovery represented the lies and cover-ups that had been sold to generations of Americans. France, too, has consistently fought with its own image. While touting Paris as the City of Light and Love, it has also been the scene of terrorist attacks and riots. From the French Revolution to the Nazi occupation of World War II, France has been at odds with its own history, desperately trying to forget it.

With *High Tension*, Alexandre Aja successfully fused what had begun with Gaspar Noé and Claire Denis, among others, with the commercially proven formula of the slasher. *High Tension* has become one of the most influential horror films of the new millennium and continues to divide fans based on its infamous final twist. The film follows Marie (Cécile De France), a college student driving with her friend Alex (Maïwenn) to Alex's family country house for a weekend of quiet studying. Once there, Marie is introduced to Alex's family, given a quick tour of the house, and settles in for the night. While this very ordinary setup is taking place, the film intercuts with a character only credited as Le Tueur, or Killer (Philippe Nahon), whom the audience first encounters as he manipulates a severed head into fellating him. This is also intercut with Marie masturbating while thinking about Alex; it is at this point that chaos descends on the quiet home. The doorbell rings, and when Alex's father goes to answer it, he is brutally slaughtered. From there the viewer enters a nightmarish world of death and destruction. Le Tueur stalks and kills Alex's family, abducts Alex, ties her up, and transports her in a van. Throughout all this Marie avoids detection as she simultaneously hides and follows Le Tueur and Alex in hopes of saving her friend and, perhaps, bringing them together in the process. In the film's climax it is revealed that the Le Tueur and Marie are the same person and that Marie has killed Alex's family in hopes of never being separated from Alex again.

Alexandre Aja burst on to the international film scene with *High Tension*, having directed a few smaller films—*Over the Rainbow* (1997), which was nominated for Best Short at the Cannes Film Festival, and *Furia* (1999), a post-apocalyptic genre film. While a number of horror films have emerged from Europe, they have never been as successful and as accepted as those made in North America. In an interview, Aja seeks to explain this anomaly.

> [In] Europe there is no horror movie. It's very hard to make a slasher or gory movie. There is no audience for that. I think the main difference between Europe and the U.S. is that there is a kind of freedom. We don't have this Puritanism problem. We don't have this stupid, silly problem with nudity. On the other hand we have this problem with violence. It's very hard to get very far. A movie like *The House on the Left* [*sic*] would be very hard to do in Europe. Like *High Tension* was. It was not very easy to do and find money to make the movie because it was so violent. We don't have a nudity problem, the only problem we have is too much violence. To give you an example, *The Devil's Rejects*, which I saw before leaving for L.A. It's a great movie. It's an amazing movie. But it'd be very hard to do in Europe because it's very violent and sometimes you are on the side of the killers and that'd be something they'd have a problem with.[1]

High Tension has been read through a variety of lenses that all lead to the moment in which Marie's personality splits as she is about to climax while thinking of Alex. Unable to cope with her homoerotic desires, Marie manifests a hulking male figure to carry out her secret desires of destroying everything and everyone that could possibly keep her and Alex apart. Film scholar Matthias Hurst writes in his essay on *High Tension* that "the frightening male representation of her lesbian desire and the related phallic aggression turn Marie into an impure and interstitial perpetrator with confused gender aspects. Consequently, her fury affects men and women alike; the terror works in both directions."[2] The psychotic fantasy is stopped when Alex escapes her confines and makes a run for it. The audience now clearly understands that Marie has been, in their minds, both the Final Girl and Monster. But Marie never experiences transference; the spell is never broken. It is Alex who transfers from victim to Final Girl, breaking the aforementioned spell by violently stabbing Marie, not to release her, but to put an end to the madness. Marie remains a victim to her delusion, the ultimate unreliable narrator.

The film ends with Marie institutionalized and eerily reaching out towards Alex, who is supposedly not visible to her. Through this ending, the audience understands that balance has not been restored. For the majority of the film, the audience has been in Marie's shoes; only at the end do they realize that the girl's diseased mind has overtaken the film. The person the audience believed to be the Final Girl (Marie) is revealed to be the killer. The world of the slasher has grown unstable in *High Tension* and, in fact, it is the character who is victimized through the film, Alex, who emerges as the Final Girl and fights back against her attacker. Aja's inversion of the trope works on an emotional and intellectual level. For horror fans, it is a fun payoff, but, unfortunately, a frustrating one for anyone concerned with actual plot and narrative elements. In his review of the film, Roger Ebert noted the plot discrepancies thusly:

> The rest of the movie you will have to see for yourself—or, not, which would be my recommendation. I am tempted at this point to issue a Spoiler Warning and engage in discussion of several crucial events in the movie that would seem to be physically, logically and dramatically impossible, but clever viewers will be able to see for themselves that the movie's plot has a hole that is not only large enough to drive a truck through, but in fact does have a truck driven right through it.[3]

Several story elements which are key to moving the film forward derive from the Le Tueur, such as his truck that transports the girls through the French countryside, are never explained when it is revealed that Le Tueur and Marie are the same person. In an interview with chud.com, Aja explains his original intent with the ending:

> It's kind of funny because the first draft of the script, the script we wanted to do, had the same twist but just in the final minutes. You started the movie in the hospital room and she's telling the story and then you come back to the hospital room in the end, so you have the feeling that the killer was the killer, but then the doctor brought a VCR into the room, watching the security video from the gas station and you realize she axes the guy. That was the final twist, and the twist was only saying, OK what you saw was her vision of the story and the truth is another movie. The producer, unfortunately, asked us to give up the last scene in the last reel, and I think that's where everything became more fragile. I understand the question of the viewers with the twist coming that way, which is not like the perfect way to bring it. I regret that we didn't have the time or the budget to shoot the two different endings and be able to, at least on the DVD, have the two different endings.[4]

To the majority of viewers, the plot holes are detrimental to the overall film, so much so that many genre buffs dismiss it outright. The twist is confusing if you take it literally, but taking under consideration the "gaze" of the film, it is primarily coming from the diseased mind of Marie. *High Tension* does suffer from the need for a final sting when Marie's true self is revealed. However, the film is ultimately about the terror of being trapped in an unreliable mind. What Aja and his producers utilized for the twist is actually the core of the film. By having the final moments effectively reset what the audience knew to be true, *High Tension* loses its power on subsequent viewings, but upon consideration, the emotional deception and subversion of popular horror tropes reveals and crystalizes its meaning. *High Tension* revels in what theorist Robin Wood identified as the "return of the repressed" in his book *Hollywood from Vietnam to Reagan...and Beyond.*

> It is necessary to offer a simple and obvious basic formula for the horror film: normality is threatened by the Monster. I use "normality" here in a strictly nonevaluative sense to mean simply "conformity to the dominant social norms": one must firmly resist the common tendency to treat the word as if it were more or less synonymous with "health."[5]

High Tension offers Marie's (perhaps) burgeoning sexuality as a threat to patriarchal heteronormative family. Several writers have defamed the film as homophobic, that Marie's love for Alex breeds destruction. Horror journalist Stacie Ponder wrote in her column "Taking Back the Knife" about the ending of *High Tension* and offered a more accepting view of the film, one that takes into consideration the mental battle of a character who is suggested to be, above anything else, schizophrenic.

> In a sense, however, this true ending—which finds Marie vanquishing the horrible man and admitting her love for Alex—is undeniably pro-gay: the lesbian is the hero of the story. On *High Tension*'s most basic level, we're rooting for Marie the entire time as she displays remarkable bravery and resilience in her quest to save her friend. Thematically, she's still the hero of the story even at the end: once Marie basically came out of the closet and admitted everything, the man was gone; it was the lying, the hiding and repression of her true nature and her true feelings that brought about all the violence and destruction. Simply put, coming out freed her from her mental anguish. That ain't homophobia.[6]

As Ponder points out, in Marie's gaze (which we, as viewers, break from when she is revealed to be the killer as well) fights her repression. In Marie's mind she has admitted her (albeit obsessive) love for Alex and that, perhaps, they can finally be together. Within the context of the film, Marie's repression of herself creates a monster. *High Tension* offers a problematic view of homosexuality which, depending on the audience's viewpoint, can be somewhat progressive or further stigmatized. For Carol Clover, who clearly identified and analyzed the tropes of the slasher film, the final moments of the prototypical slasher are all important to the societal and cultural conclusions of the film: "The last moment of the Final Girl sequence is finally a footnote to what went before, to the quality of the Final Girl's fight, and more generally to the qualities of character that enable her, of all the characters, to survive what has come to seem unsurvivable."[7]

Marie and Alex's worlds have both been irrecoverably altered: Alex, because she has lost her family; and Marie, because she has completely broken with reality. In previous incarnations of the slasher, Marie would have subdued Le Tueur, possibly saved Alex, and been able to revert to her previous feminine state. This lack of cohesion to previously understood tropes of the genre makes *High Tension* harder to read as it defies horror film coding. The chaotic nature of the film, mixed with the seemingly illogical ending, renders it understandable only through complete subjectivity. In order to make sense of the film, the audience must try to understand a schizophrenic mind because, logically, the events of the film could not have occurred in the way the audience has seen them. But through the transference of the Final Girl role to Alex, the audience lacks resolve for Marie's character, who manages to survive, but has not forgotten Alex. The audience understands that the nightmare of the film has not ended. While the monster may continue on in other iterations of the slasher film, it is a rare entry indeed that shows the audience that monster as their guide through the film, cloaked in their understanding of the genre.

The major concern in examining this film, especially within the context of New French Extremity, has to be the impact of the individual on society. Presently, the individual and one's identity have become transformative. The notion of self is at an all-time threat of being disabled. What *High Tension* illustrates is an internal trauma—or disorder—inflicting itself on the outside world. Marie's internal drama supersedes all the events and individuals around her. It is commonplace, when analyzing horror films, to identify the monster, or antagonist, as a repressed entity that has metaphorically evolved, to dominated the landscape. It also provides an easy scapegoat for the understanding of good and evil, us and them. These tropes commonly play out between the arrival of youngsters and the bizarre people who surround unknown territories, as in *The Texas Chain Saw Massacre* (1974), *Wrong Turn* (2003), and *Hostel* (2005). *High Tension* relies on the audience's belief and reliance on slasher tropes to provide an unpredictable outcome. In actuality,

High Tension plays out almost entirely in the mind of Marie. The truck, the chase—almost every scene that happens in the final two-thirds of the film are part of Marie's mind, not the actual events of the film. The audience is the victim of Marie's mind and her fevered imagination.

While Aja is successful in defining a new breed of horror film by absorbing the American structure of a slasher film, he is able to flip it on its head. The audience is fooled by its own preconceptions of horror. Because of this they are absorbed in Marie's reality, which becomes their own until the film's final moments. The horror of *High Tension* is not necessarily based in its depictions of violence, but in the knowledge that a psyche can be subsumed and overtaken by another.

10

Bon Voyage

Calvaire (2004), *Sheitan* (2006) and *Frontier(s)* (2007)

> But you have to remember ... that you can't run from unhappiness. You just take it with you.—*Karen Wheeler, Tout Sweet: Hanging Up My High Heels for a New Life in France*

Travel within French borders is easy, accessible, and a must for any resident or world traveler. Whether sightseeing in Paris or lying on the beaches of Nice or taking in the history of towns like Lille, France's economy receives a steady stream of income as locals and visitors continue to explore all that France has to offer. The films discussed in this chapter examine the forgotten space between departures and destinations, where the travelers are in limbo. Their focus is on the excruciating journey between expectation and reality, the real and imagined. The travelers in these films are searching for something new and are met by the deteriorating minds of the forgotten towns, cultures, and politics. The unrelenting terror that awaits them is only part of the terror.

Sharing a rather significant part of their borders, France and Belgium have developed a close and supportive relationship. From wartime to economic hardships, France and Belgium have remained close allies for centuries. When talking about Fabrice Du Welz's *Calvaire* in the context of New French Extremity it is important to note that it is a Belgian film, made by a Belgian filmmaker and starring two French actors (Jackie Berroyer and Laurent Lucas), and is a co-production between Belgium, France, and Luxembourg. *Calvaire* derives its New French Extremity label mainly from the fact that it is extreme, the script is in

French, and it deals with a particular space where violence from the past has reemerged in a rural landscape.

The 1980s and '90s in Belgium saw the rise of four notorious serial killers, the most notorious being Marc Dutroux a convicted murderer and child molester who kidnapped and assaulted six girls. Captured in 1996, his trial was held in 2004, which exposed the faulty and corrupt Belgium police force and led to an entire reorganization of the law enforcement. Michelle Martin, Dutroux's wife, who aided him in his crimes, was also sentenced to jail time but was released in 2012 to a convent where she promised to spend the rest of her sentence "in prayer." Michel Fourniret, also known as the Ogre of the Ardennes, was also put on trial in 2004 for the kidnapping, assault, and murder of multiple young women from 1987 to 2001, in both Belgium and France. The severity and implications of these murders shook the nation. As the salacious details emerged, they were splashed across the front of tabloid newspapers. It was yet another chink in the amour of social niceties and class that Western Europe propagated. While panic and fear spread that these kinds of crimes could happen in a civilized society, the authorities spun the story to ease the public's fear, assuring them that these crimes were committed by sick individuals who had removed themselves from society and were no threat if you stayed away from them.

The theme of the backwater, psycho-hillbilly has long been popular in the American horror genre, with films like *Deliverance* (1972) and *I Spit on Your Grave* (1978). For larger countries such as America, serial killings are a hazard of a large population, but they could happen anywhere. In the case of the Belgium serial killers, they had a great impact on the Belgium consciousness because their population is small by comparison. As Du Welz remarks on the crime history in Belgium and genre film's influence on his film:

> *Calvaire* has a connection with what happened in my country in the last decade. A lot of horror films that I admire so much are a witness of their country's dark times and murderers—*Texas Chain Saw Massacre, Zombie, Henry [Portrait of a Serial Killer]*, etc. But first with *Calvaire*, I tried to explore the genre. I wanted to experiment with the cliché of horrors; no pay-off, no twist at the end, no sympathy for the main character, sympathy for the psychopath ... that's also the limit of the film and that's also why *Calvaire* divided the critics so much.[1]

The notion that mental illness and solitude are bred by a removal from the industrialized city has been prevalent for decades. With all the amenities that the city can offer, why would anyone choose to remove themselves from it? As Kristin Ross writes in *Fast Cars, Clean Bodies*:

> France's own rural backwardness … constitutes the unmodern … economically, ideologically, and culturally, peasants inhabit an older time; they remain … a "distorted element" of an older economic consciousness in the midst of the flexible capitalist century, in possession of their own means of production, and tied to a seasonal, cyclical temporality. Peasants, like any other historical residue, enter the perceptive sphere of the already modernized as but one of two things: bothersome or picturesque.[2]

While Du Welz utilizes the common horror backdrop of urbanoia to situate his film, he delves much deeper into the concepts of isolation, obsessive love, and autonomy.

> We wanted to make a horror film without any women with big breasts, just like a lot of the cliché horror films. Also, I really didn't want to make a movie with music, because it's too easy, you know. So I had so many constraints, and I tried to experiment with all the clichés. I grew up watching horror films, and for me there are two horror films, *Psycho* and *Texas Chainsaw Massacre* that are "key films" for *Calvaire*. Between those two influences, I tried to find my own way, my own creativity, my own experiment, but, also, to reject all the pay-off, twists, you know, the fucking Hollywood conditioning. And yeah, of course, the pace is very slow, and the last 20 minutes is very, very brutal, but that's really how I wanted to construct the film and put the audience in a very strange atmosphere—a very strange fairy tale.[3]

Calvaire (French for *Calvary*; the English title is *The Ordeal*) begins a few days before Christmas, with entertainer Marc Stevens (Laurent Lucas) performing some songs at a nursing home. While his act is categorically cheesy, the audience—particularly the ladies—are clearly attracted to Marc; they reach out to touch him, to be near him. As he travels to his next gig, driving through the swampy Hautes Fagnes region of Liège, his van breaks down. He seeks shelter at a nearby inn, run by a man named Bartel (Jackie Berroyer). Marc explains his situation and mentions that he is a singer. Bartel immediately relates to the young man, saying that he, too, was an entertainer, a comedian in fact; he adds that his estranged wife, Gloria, was also a singer. He then promises to fix Marc's van, although he adds that this may take a while. Frustrated, Marc has little choice but to wait for Bartel to do the work as promised.

Early in his stay, Marc ventures out for a walk in the woods, with his host warning him not to go to the village. Marc heeds the warning but wanders by a nearby farm, where he hears strange noises. Venturing towards the sounds, Marc witnesses a teenage boy having sexual relations with a pig. Meanwhile, instead of fixing the van, Bartel is rummaging through his guest's belongings, which include some amateur pornographic photographs that had been presented to Marc by a female fan. When Marc returns to the inn, he discovers that the homemade porn has been rifled through and he angrily confronts his host. Bartel defiantly knocks Marc unconscious and proceeds to set fire to the van. The following morning, Marc awakens, bound to a chair and wearing a sundress. Bartel, it seems, is intent on turning Marc into his estranged wife, Gloria. He even shaves half of Marc's head to "protect" him from the villagers, all of whom, evidently, are male. When Bartel goes to inform these men that his wife has returned, they greet the news as fact. The townspeople gather at Bartel's inn for Christmas dinner and, upon seeing Marc in drag, there is a collective agreement that Gloria has indeed returned. In an intensely violent climactic scene (shot, incidentally, by Benoît Debie, who was also the cinematographer on Gaspar Noé's *Irréversible*), Bartel is shot to death, and another man briefly rapes Marc on the dining room table. Marc manages to escape and makes a run for it. Hot on his trail is a villager named Robert (Philippe Nahon), who falls into a marsh. Before being swallowed up in the mire, Robert proclaims his love to "Gloria." Marc, although he does not rescue the man, acknowledges the man's feelings and claims that "she" loves him as well. Robert dies, and Marc finds himself alone in the wilderness. It is at this moment that he has a major epiphany: his role on this earth is to be an object of desire. In a Christlike gesture, he absolves those who have wronged him.

Du Welz cleverly inverts the audience's expectations of the film by imbuing it with a pitch-black sense of humor and challenging the audience's sympathies. While the victim of abuse and torture is nearly always the protagonist, Du Welz and actor Laurent Lucas do everything in their power to set Marc up as the unlikeable hero. Bartel's quaint charm is infused through the film, and the character comes across as a lonely man who is simply looking for companionship, though his tactics to get it may be a bit extreme. Du Welz also negates the villagers' voices in the film. While they appear in several scenes, they seemingly act as one organism. In one of the most eerie and disturbing scenes in the film, the villagers begin to dance to discordant polka music. At first it is impromptu and then becomes almost ritualistic, as though they are preparing for battle. As Du Welz says of the scene:

[I]t wasn't in the script. At that point I tried to portray the villagers like an entity, a community. I didn't want them to speak, so one day, watching films at home, I saw André Delvaux's *Un soir, un train* [*One Night, One Train*, 1968]. It's an old film, a Belgian film. At one moment, a beautiful woman who probably represents Death invites Yves Montand to dance in a very Flemish pub. He resists, but finally he dances with the beautiful lady, and everybody else starts dancing too. When I saw that I thought, "Oh my God, that's the way I have to shoot that scene!" It's a dance scene. If you accept the dance scene, everything is complete and it's the key to open the film and accept the rest of the madness.[4]

The scene is filmed with a strange greenish hue, and the villagers' expressions seem somewhere between joy and madness. Their bodies sway back and forth as if in a trance. They collectively agree that something should be done about the return of "Gloria," adding another strand to the film's commentary on autonomy. No matter what Marc does, he cannot convince Bartel that he is *not* Gloria. The villagers, also believing (or wanting to believe) that Marc is Gloria, murder Bartel to get to Marc. Throughout the film Marc attempts to escape, make deals and flees the inn as fast as possible, only to be caught at every turn. It is not until Marc accepts his role in the final chase that the possibility of escape seems possible. The community perishes under the weight of the return of "Gloria." Essentially, Marc must fully embrace his role as performer and what it means to his fans, whoever they might be, and finally commit to a role.

When describing the elements that inspired him to make *Sheitan* (2006), director Kim Chapiron replied, "LSD and comics."[5] When asked about any regrets he had regarding the production, he answered, "Too much drugs on set. Staff overdosing.... Nightmare."[6] And with those answers, Chapiron sets himself up to be the next *enfant terrible* in French cinema. *Sheitan*, also Chapiron's first feature film, stars Vincent Cassel as an insane housekeeper named Joseph whose path crosses with a group of young Parisians. The film follows a more traditional horror movie format, with shadows of comedy infused throughout, mimicking the absurdist qualities of the Grand Guignol theater.

Sheitan, taken from the Arabic word for *Satan*, deals with the destruction of a society that is barely clinging to its civility. When a group of friends parties at a Paris nightclub called the Styxx Club, they meet Eve (Roxane Mesquida), who invites them to her family's country home. Both Bart (Olivier Barthelemy) and Thaï (Nicolas Le Phat Tan) are sure that at least one of them will get the seductive Eve into bed.

While staying at the house they encounter Joseph (Vincent Cassel), who monitors their every move with a gregarious nature. His oddity is assumed to be part of his rural character, but it hides something much darker. As the group is picked off one by one, and as Joseph's sister (also played by Cassel) is about to give birth on Christmas Eve, the siblings require more from Bart in particular.

Unlike its predecessors in New French Extremity, *Sheitan* offers an explicit look at youth culture in contemporary France. The Styxx Club is boisterous and energetic, and the men are constantly looking to seduce every attractive woman they meet. The first third of the film is spent in this world, with the characters looking to satiate their carnal desires; they readily resort to robbery, an act which seems commonplace rather than an abnormality. Portraying the realities of Paris's youth culture was important to Chapiron and, as he says, developed out of his rehearsal process:

> For me the best thing to show in a movie is the character: I love working with actors.... With *Sheitan* we had six months' rehearsal we were together doing improvisations around the basic idea. For me it's the most interesting way of working: I can catch something accidental, it might start off as a mistake. I love that feeling; it makes for a very natural feeling movie.[7]

Once the group arrives in the country, Joseph takes over, making suggestions, organizing activities, and generally becoming a nuisance, particularly to Bart, whose objective is to get to know Eve. Shortly after their arrival, Joseph convinces the group to pay a visit to the nearby hot springs. On their way, they encounter some of the young people of the town: the men who seem to be handicapped in various ways, and a particularly amorous young woman whom Joseph passes on to Bart. Once at the hot spring, the group takes off a few clothing items before getting into the water; the locals, however, prefer going naked. The young woman who seems intent on getting Bart's attention attempts to seduce him while also pleasuring a dog. Once in the water, she feigns being attacked by the men of the village, while the others look on concerned. The woman begins laughing, indicating that they were all playing; the majority of the group looks on, horrified. They then attempt to play-fight, during which the young woman rips out a hunk of Bart's hair; he lashes out, and the group has suddenly become suspicious of their surroundings. The hot springs scene makes clear the differences between the newcomers and the locals. The locals are portrayed to be primitive, animalistic in their sexuality, and mocking of the social norms of Paris. When the local woman pretends to be frightened of the male villagers, she is mocking not only mocking the urban fears which the newcomers know all too well, but also the audience by subverting its expectations of the subgenre. As Chapiron says:

> You see, *Sheitan* is a comedy first of all. A comedy but also scary and sexy. What I really want is reactions. When you see movies these days, you've often forgotten it immediately. With *Sheitan* my target is to achieve some kind of reaction.[8]

Chapiron utilizes standard horror genre film clichés, such as POV shots, lingering shadows, and characters who seem to have escaped from a North American film. Eve's house, too, is replete with disturbing puppets and dolls, an evocative trope of the more traditional contemporary horror film. But Chapiron is determined to outdo his American counterparts. The mentions of Joseph's sister grow more frequent as she is about to give birth. It is revealed that Joseph and his sister had engaged in an incestuous relationship, during which she was impregnated. He is now convinced that the Devil had tempted him to take part in this unholy alliance. The siblings decide to make a human sacrifice on the eve of the child's birth.

The stalk-and-kill formula is used throughout the climax of *Sheitan*, but the gravitas with which Cassel imbues the film, including its unflinching exploration of social taboos and violence, creates a worthy entry in the New French Extremity genre. Chapiron's protagonists are a diverse group whose members become increasingly terrified as they realize that the horrors of the city are nothing compared to those of the country. Chapiron also makes use of Christian iconography, with the events of the film set in the days leading up to Christmas. The arrival of a bastard child borne out of incest (believed to have been inspired by Satan) also heralds the arrival of the antichrist. While most human sacrifices are meant to be pure in spirit, the siblings decide early on to sacrifice Bart, the most violent and least socially apt of the group. The choice lends itself to a rejection of purity and an acceptance of chaos.

Sheitan fared well in French cinemas, with 500,000 tickets sold and distribution deals with thirty-four countries.[9] The success of the film stems, in part, from its pushing against the socially constructed boundaries of French society. At the turn of the millennium, there was a pervasive sense of fear concerning the youth that had had grown up in the outskirts of society, mainly within the Paris suburbs; their dependence on crime and violence as a way of life, it was reasoned, could lead to the destruction of culture. Chapiron, it seems, prefers to place the blame on the backward way of life still present in French culture: Christianity.

Xavier Gens's blood-soaked offering of 2007, *Frontier(s)* (French title: *Frontière(s)*), begins with what is arguably the film's most chilling scenes: footage of the real Paris riots that gripped the capitol beginning in 2005. These events stemmed from the social policies of Nicholas Sarkozy, a far-right-leaning interior minister (he would be elected president in 2007), and his efforts to police the suburbs of Paris, which are largely made up of immigrant families. After the accidental death of an eleven-year-old boy in La Courneuve in June 2005, Sarkozy stated that he would cleanse the area with "Kärcher" a German pressure-cleaning system, which drew parallels to Nazism. Sarkozy would echo this sentiment as the police were sent to quell the riots, causing increased tensions between the community members and the heavily armed law-enforcement officials. The riots at the turn of the millennium evoked the uprisings that had occurred in France since the Revolution, most notably those in May 1968. During the 2005 riots, Sarkozy advocated for increased police presence and a zero-tolerance policy to anyone thought to be a threat to public safety. The large Arab community in the suburbs felt particularly targeted and, with tensions rising, the demonstrations and riots became increasingly brutal. The antagonism in Paris swelled as those who felt targeted by the police took to the streets to demand fair treatment and an extension of civil liberties. Distrust of the French police dates back to World War II, when officers were appointed to protect the Vichy regime.

While Sarkozy did nothing to quell the fears of the communities who were being targeted at this time, France had come even closer to having an extreme ring-wing president in 2002. Former leader of the National Front Jean-Marie Le Pen, known to the liberal side of France as the "Devil of the Republic" (for his long-standing opposition to legalized abortion, same-sex marriages, and euthanasia, as well as his then-current advocating of the death penalty and immigration restrictions), progressed to the second round of voting for the presidency. Le Pen's startling success in the 2002 election caused a massive backlash among the liberals in France, leading to some of the biggest voter turnouts France had ever seen. Though Le Pen was swiftly eradicated from the race, it has not stopped right-wing support for increased social policing through political parties such as the National Front, members of whom were actively demonstrating against immigration, pointing at the influx of Syrian refugees in the autumn of 2015.

As Gens says of the inspiration for his film:

> *Frontier(s)* is about the evolution of the extreme right in France. In 2002, during the presidential elections, Jean-Marie Le Pen made it to the second round of voting for president, and that was the most fear I ever felt in my life. I wanted to translate that fear into *Frontier(s)*.... The French know the danger [Le Pen] represents, and everybody voted against him because when you see representatives on the extreme right making it to the second round of the presidential election, that's really frightening for everybody. You cannot accept that as truth.[10]

While using the chaos of the riots as a cover, a group of friends—Yasmine (Karina Testa), her brother Sami (Adel Bencherif), Alex (Aurélien Wiik), Tom (David Saracino) and Farid (Chems Dahmani)—a robbery, which results in Sami getting shot by the police. The group parts ways, with Alex and the pregnant Yasmine taking their friend to the hospital. In his final moments, Sami pleads with Yasmine not to have an abortion, which she has threatened. She consents to his dying wish. Meanwhile, Tom and Farid take the money and head to the border. Passing a countryside inn, they decide to stop there for the night, texting Yasmine and Alex their location so they can meet up later. But Tom and Farid are soon murdered by the strange family who manage the inn. When Yasmine and Alex finally arrive, they are, of course, completely unaware of their friends' fates and are soon held captive. The murderous family is revealed to be the Geislers, neo–Nazis who want to make Yasmine their eldest son's wife and raise her child as their own (their own inbred children rarely survive or, if they do, they are hideously deformed). Alex is killed, and Yasmine is adorned with a white dress and welcomed into their family. She resists, engaging in a bloody battle, during which the family members are killed. Escaping the scene in a car, Yasmine is eventually stopped by a police blockade. She pulls the car to a stop and exits the vehicle, with her arms raised.

Gens utilizes several elements from Tobe Hooper's *The Texas Chainsaw Massacre* (1974) and Jean-Luc Godard's *Weekend* (1967). Both films examine the fears surrounding the unknown elements and characters that exist outside of the urban landscape. While Godard's film was released a year before the riots of 1968, it captured the mood in France, where uncertainty and destabilization was growing due to the increasing distance between classes. Hooper's film captures the civil unrest in

America at the beginning of the 1970s and is viewed as an anti–Vietnam war film. Gens, however, inverts the structure of *Frontier(s)*. In *Weekend* and *The Texas Chainsaw Massacre*, the "othered" lower-classes are cannibalistic antagonists who brutalize the seemingly normal and relatable protagonists. The lower class seeks to devour the mobile class in order to survive. In Gens's film, the classically mobile classes (law enforcement, white rural–Nazis) prey on the "undesirables" represented by Yasmine and her friends, who are young and Muslim. The Gieslers capture Tom, Alex, and Farid in order to consume them, thereby carrying out the will of the Third Reich. Yasmine is going to be consumed by the family, but she appears to them passably Caucasian and the idea of a healthy baby proves too tempting to resist. Gens casts a critical eye on politicians like Le Pen and Sarkozy, who have more in common with the Geislers than the protagonists.

The bloody events at the inn act as a reaction to Kristin Ross's theories of cleanliness in *Fast Cars, Clean Bodies*. Though modernism was adapted by the French in the hopes of wiping clean their past, the past returns, and, in fact, exists around them despite their refusal to acknowledge its existence. While Gens's film is a work of fiction, the elements that inspired it are not. They are the cold, terrifying truths of a country which cannot accept its own past actions, allowing them to fester on the outskirts of society.

As the film progresses, the importance of Yasmine's child grows. In her opening narrative she mentions that she is three months pregnant and that every child is born equal according to the law. She then says she knows this is not really the case, and that she will do whatever it takes to protect her child from evil. Though Yasmine, who sees the world around her literally burning, seems unsure of whether she'll carry the baby to term, it is her brother Sami's dying wish that she keep it so as to continue the legacy of their Muslim family. Yasmine's child becomes a focal point once the Geisler family views the unborn child as a way to continue their own lineage. The patriarchal Karl von Geisler says to his son, whom Yasmine is to marry, that he is concerned about future daughter-in-law's dark hair and eyes but that he knows of no other option if the family is to continue. One of the daughter's cuts off Yasmine's hair until she resembles Maria Falconetti as the eponymously named saint in Carl Theodor Dreyer's silent film *The Passion of Joan of Arc* (1928). In a terrifying scene, one that mirrors a similar family meal

133

in *The Texas Chainsaw Massacre*, Yasmine is subjected to a dinner at which the Gielsers welcome her into their family. In an effort to escape and to save her unborn child, Yasmine attacks and fights her way out, while pitting one family member against another. Yasmine's child has transcended, from an object in her body, to a symbolic possession desired by both the biological mother and the Gielsers, each individual longing to raise the child in their own image and according to their own values. Yasmine's promise at the beginning of the film that she will protect her child from evil first seems to suggest an abortion to protect it from the world, but then it becomes a battle against neo–Nazis in an attempt to make the world a safer place. Yasmine's most progressive and defiant option becomes to have the baby and raise it as her own.

Gens frames his film as a criticism of authority in France by implicating the actions of law enforcement and the government as the catalyst for the events of *Frontier(s)*. The police use violent tactics to quell protests when an extreme-right-wing president is elected; Karl von Geisler, the patriarchal figure, is revealed to be a still-practicing Nazi who was also an army officer. In the film's closing moments, when Yasmine, covered in blood, surrenders to the police, Gens does not reveal whether the world is indeed a safe place for the young Muslim woman and her unborn child.

Froniter(s) offers a critique of France's present, as well as its past, by subverting established tropes of other horror films and functioning on a seemingly absurd presence, a neo–Nazi family residing in the French countryside. Gens, however, gleans this absurdity from his country's own history as a means of questioning what France's role was during the Second World War, and what, if any, residuals still remain.

These three films—*Calvaire*, *Sheitan* and *Frontier(s)*—are an exploration of the untended elements of society, the sections which are allowed to remain in realities that no longer exist in urban settings. They are films that challenge the notions of the beatific French countryside where atrocities have been committed for centuries, often unnoticed and undocumented. The characters in these films journey outside of their respective homes, out of either necessity or desire, and encounter darkness they could never have foreseen.

11

Enfant Terrible

Them (2006) and *The Pack* (2009)

> The French magazine *Parents* says that if a baby is scared of strangers, his mother should warn him that a visitor will be coming over soon. Then, when the doorbell rings, "Tell him that the guest is here. Take a few seconds before opening the door ... if he doesn't cry when he sees the stranger, don't forget to congratulate him."—*Pamela Druckerman, Bringing Up Bébé*

American writer Pamela Druckerman ignited a mini-fad with the 2012 release of her book *Bringing Up Bébé: One American Mother Discovers the Wisdom of French Parenting.* Druckerman was living in France at the time and wrote about the seeming abnormalities of French parenting, mainly that they did not coddle their children yet enforced simple rules on them thus creating mini-adults who knew how to behave in public. This trend was the next step in the further praise of the French woman who have been celebrated for their style and grace, which culminated in the book *French Women Don't Get Fat* by Mireille Guiliano (2007), sold as a "non-diet" book. These books propagate the myth that French women are a rarefied creature who excel at nearly everything. There was, of course, a backlash, with many parents and residents of France decrying the book for its inaccuracies surrounding French culture. As Pascal-Emmanuel Gobry wrote in *The Atlantic:*

> The way French education works, and I don't know if I could put it in a more charitable way, is that it seeks to mercilessly beat any shred of nonconformity out of children (the beating is now done mostly psychologically) so that they may be slotted into a society that, itself, treats nonconformity the way the immune system treats foreign elements.[1]

Writer Liz Garrigan went even further with her denunciation of French parenting on her blog, *I Am Carla Bruni's Neighbor*, in her post "French Children Don't Throw Food (When People Are Watching)":

> There is no doubt that French children are more behaved when they are being judged by their behavior than their American counterparts. French children know their parents don't mind exercising very unpleasant means of punishment should they fail to mind their Ps and Qs. But here's what happens—and again, this is such a universally accepted truth among everyone I know that it's offensive to us to see this style of parenting held up as the ideal: French kids don't have fun at home, they don't have fun at school, so when they get to a neutral place like the playground, where their mothers or nannies talk on the phone or take smoke breaks, they are often prone to act like wild animals…. So, not to put too fine a point on it, but while French parents may be able to get their children to sit at the table for dinner without throwing food or other unpleasantries, it looks to me like many of them are raising angry little monsters who resent their parents' methods.[2]

Nearly every culture emphasizes their children; they are the future, they are what will come after their parents. It is no surprise that a book preaching the effectiveness of simple yet absolute upbringing would cause a mild sensation, particularly in the parenting world, yet in the context of New French Extremity it rings as untrue. Though these books were being published towards the end of New French Extremity's life cycle, they are at odds with the virtues and condemnations that these films are dealing out and also at odds with the political climate. These books cultivate the notion of the France that emerged from World War II, one that tried to cleanse itself of the scars that it had accumulated. David Moreau and Xavier Palud's *Them* (2006) and Franck Richard's *The Pack* (2009) seek to show the scars that the sins of the parents inflict on their children.

Much of the French identity is tied up in pride—pride in the culture they have inherited and spread throughout the world, whether by influence or their colonial past. For many, France has upheld its traditions while maintaining its modernity through industrialization and expansion. In David Moreau and Xavier Palud's 2006 film *Them*, a couple moves to Romania and attempts to replicate France in their own backyard while shutting out their surroundings. Moreau and Palud create horror by adapting their story to a home-invasion scenario. This horror subgenre has long utilized this trope to illuminate fears surrounding the homestead, for what is more frightening than a violent assault on your personal space and possessions? The world may be dangerous outside, but the home can be controlled. Home-invasion films explore what happens when locking the door no longer suffices.

Them begins with a suspenseful scene in which a Romanian mother and daughter drive along an abandoned highway, get into an accident, and are attacked by unseen assailants. The film then cuts to a Romanian middle school where Clémentine (Olivia Bonamy) teaches French. She finishes her lesson, gets help from a colleague with the curriculum, and heads home to her boyfriend, Lucas (Michaël Cohen). Clémentine and Lucas share a large country house which is in a state of semi-disrepair. Clémentine and Lucas settle in for the night but are soon disturbed by noises. This quickly escalates into assailants attacking the couple, forcing them to make a run for it. Clémentine and Lucas nearly manage to escape but are killed by their attackers, who are revealed to be children. The film's coda sees the children running to get on a bus in the morning; text on the screen reveals that the couple's bodies were found by police and the children were detained. When asked by the police why the children did it, one of them replied, "Because THEY wouldn't play with us."

Them begins with a title card informing the audience that the film is based on true events. Many films, especially genre films, have relied on this trope to instantaneously fill the audience with dread. Palud and Moreau have admitted that the story's veracity comes from an amalgam of random instances of violence.

> The truth is that we started shooting a commercial and the driver became our friend and told us a story. We liked the idea about two people in the house being assaulted by unseen people. We wanted the end to be very strong. Are they good or bad? We don't really know, they're just here.[3]

The film does take some influence from the politics of Romania. The idea that wandering, violent children dealing out death is a stretch, but the idea that the country is overpopulated is not. Nicolae Ceausescu, Romania's first and last communist leader, led his country through fear and brutality. Among his rulings was Decree 770, a ban on birth control in hopes of seeing Romania's population grow from 23 million in 1966 to 30 million by 2000.[4]

> It was one of the late dictator's cruelest commands. At first Romania's birthrate nearly doubled. But poor nutrition and inadequate prenatal care endangered many pregnant women. The country's infant-mortality rate soared to 83 deaths in every 1,000 births (against a Western European average of less than 10 per thousand). About one in 10 babies was born underweight; newborns weighing 1,500 grams (3 pounds, 5 ounces) were classified as miscarriages and denied treatment. Unwanted survivors often ended up in orphanages. "The law only forbade abortion," says Dr. Alexander Floran Anca of Bucharest. "It did nothing to promote life."[5]

Ceausescu had women rounded up, examined, and questioned if they failed to produce a child in the expected amount of time. Districts were taxed if they failed to meet the birthrate quota, and sexual education was practically non-existent. Eventually, Ceausescu was overthrown in the Romanian Revolution of 1989, but the country still grappled to ensure that proper birth control and abortions were available after decades of misinformation.

Clémentine and Lucas, however, have no children. While Clémentine teaches children, she and Lucas enjoy a *lassiez-faire* lifestyle. While Clémentine works, Lucas writes. He seems to be writing a book but shows little interest in his subject matter, readily leaving his manuscript to play computer games or flirt with Clémentine. Their home resembles a rambling chateau, far too large for two people, but quite decadent in that regard. Clémentine has managed a job which relies on her speaking her native language, and she remarks to Lucas that her students were hyper but she managed to calm them by making them do French dictation, in essence commanding the students through language. As the audience sees Clémentine leave the school, she struggles to speak Romanian to her colleague, who speaks French to her. In this regard, Clémentine and Lucas have created their own mini–France in the property they occupy. They speak French to each other and marvel at how backwards the country seems to be, citing their shoddy telephone service and crass television offerings. When Lucas first exits the house to investigate the noises, he asks in French, "Qui va là?" ("Who's there?") The fact that such a grand house has fallen into disrepair also speaks to Clémentine and Lucas's feeling that the whole country is in disrepair. It is through this lens that the final revelation from the children attacking Clémentine and Lucas that the French couple are "Them," the other, the intruder in their country. The declaration coming from a child adds a chilling note since the audience is asked to identify and sympathize with Clementine and Lucas. When they manage to kill some of the children, the audience feels vindicated as they root for the protagonists to survive. The final note that the titular "Them" is, in fact, the audience brings into question the very nature of national identity and assimilation.

While *Them* could be seen to offer a too-easy take on the subgenre, implying the decadence of moral and social fiber through the underclasses, attacking the bourgeoisie, it is merely a reflection of conflicts that have continued to occur throughout history, especially in France.

Them can be read as a critique of complacency, of assuming too much from foreign lands, a specter of France's colonial past. The story unfolds, demonstrating how the destruction of moral and social values impact Clémentine and Lucas, tearing away at their values until they react violently. As director Moreau says in an interview:

> When you just have one point of view it's very difficult to give reason to a scene because there's knocking on the door and you don't see what's behind. If you see the people behind you give more sense to the scene. But there's more tension when you only give one person's point of view. There is suspense when there are two people in the café and they don't see that under the table there's a bomb. But it was not a suspense movie because we never show the bomb so it was very difficult. But it was really interesting.[6]

In the wake of World War II, talks began which would eventually form the European Union. France was among the first to join, in 1957, in hopes of never allowing the trauma and tragedy of World War II to recur. More countries were added to the union, and it continued to grow, eventually adding all the countries on the continent. This led to growth and trade, but it also put tremendous financial stress on countries that were struggling, forcing the rest of the union to assist them in the form of loans. In 2002, the French gave up their currency, the Franc, and replaced it with the Euro, which was to become the one currency across the union. As is the case with any currency, it is only as strong as its weakest link. As the French government and people assumed their place in the European Union, the question continued to arise: What did it mean to be French if elements of their culture were continually subsumed. *Them*, therefore, functions as an allegory in which a typical French couple cannot assume or adapt to their position in a new country; they continually try to encase themselves outside of the native society and make their own life. Because they cannot adapt, they die.

Them establishes its specific look through contrasts. The school, highways, and brief shots of the city all appear modern if slightly too efficient, a symptom of the fallen Communist regime. Palud and Moreau waste no time establishing the size of the couple's house, along with its peeling paint and sparse furnishings. It is as if Clémentine and Lucas are still residing in the Palace of Versailles, which is slowly crumbling around them. As Clémentine tries to find a way out through the attic, she is attacked by one of the assailants. The two struggle as if in a pseudo version of hide-and-seek. The attic is encased in hanging plastic sheets, a symbol of disrepair and lingering renovations. When the couple finally escapes, Clémentine is captured and held by the children in an elaborate underground sewer system. Lucas comes to save her, but is killed. Clémentine sees a light and runs towards it, only to find the opening barred. She reaches out frantically, screaming as cars pass by, before she, too, disappears. The viewer last sees Clémentine, dirty and injured, screaming (in French) for anyone to help her. When she disappears, the cars continue to pass by. Their efficiency and the clean roads are no place for Clémentine or Lucas. Palud and Moreau also manage to make the large house claustrophobic, and the surrounding woods full of terror and menace.

The film's ending states that the children were picked up by law enforcement in the Sagnov region, a place the Romanian government is intent on making attractive to tourists. Plans were made for a Disney-inspired Dracula theme park in the area, since the remains of Vlad the Impaler (the supposed inspiration for the Dracula mythology) had been found. Romania has remained a source of inspiration for horror writers, not because of the political ideology that almost brought down the nation, but because it offers a sense of the undiscovered, with many folkloric tales emerging from throughout the country, with a prevailing sense of mysticism and the occult permeating the land.

Them is one of the few films of New French Extremity to receive an American remake. The year 2008 saw the release of Bryan Bertino's *The Strangers*, starring Liv Tyler and Scott Speedman. The film took the original's based-on-a-true-story device, as well as the home-invasion aspect, but changed the killers significantly: they are not children, but adults. The attackers wear masks which obscure their faces but also create an iconography for the film. American genre films are constantly on the search for the next Jason Vorhees or Freddy Kruger, and the addition of the masks helps elevate *The Strangers* to that aesthetic. The end of the film, however, offers no closure. The assailants escape, but not before protagonist Kristen (Liv Tyler) asks them why they did it. "Because you were home," one replies. Unlike *Them*, *The Strangers* maintains that the killers are the "Other." *The Strangers* reads as a film indebted to the post–9/11 era when attacks were violent and random, and the nice couple did nothing except inhabit their home. *Them* reads as a response to the loss of identity through France's entrance into the European Union, as well the mounting fears of violence and destabilization in the suburbs. Palud and Moreau never reveal the faces of their children, except in brief glimpses. The children remain anonymous, essentially a threat that could emerge anywhere.

The Pack (*La Meute*) was made and released towards the end of the New French Extremity movement as it existed in France. Made by first-time director Franck Richard, *The Pack* received most of its notoriety from a failed public screening at the Cannes film festival. Originally scheduled as part of the Cinema de la Plage series, which screens free films for the public, *The Pact* was pulled when it received a restrictive rating, causing organizers to worry about the level of gore that was about to be displayed to a potentially unsuspecting audience. Cannes rescheduled a screening in a cinema, where it was met with a tepid reception.

The Pack begins with Charlotte (Émilie Dequenne) driving along a rural French road. When she sees a police car potentially following her, she opts to pick up a hitchhiker, Max (Benjamin Biolay). After they make small talk they decide to stop at a nearby restaurant; during their meal—as they openly flirt with each other—they are attacked by a biker gang. The gang is thwarted when the restaurant owner, La Spack (Yolande Moreau), pulls a shotgun on them and orders them out. Max goes to use to washroom to pull himself together while Charlotte waits in the restaurant. After a long wait, Charlotte inspects the washroom to see what became of her companion and finds no trace of him. As she's leaving she encounters Chinaski (Philippe Nahon), a retired police officer who takes her name and number. He promises that he will look into Max's disappearance, and then adds, informally, that not many women as attractive as Charlotte come out this way. Charlotte drives off but later returns, still concerned for Max's welfare. La Spack knocks her out. When Charlotte awakens, she finds herself imprisoned alongside others who about to be fed to zombified mutant creatures.

More than an example of French New Extremity, the film is beginning to resemble an entry in the torture-porn subgenre which rose to popularity in American with films like *Saw* (James Wan, 2004) and *Hostel* (2005, Eli Roth). Charlotte is bound, beaten, force-fed, and drained of blood, all in the name of feeding the grotesque creatures. The audience is provided with little to no context as to why this is happening to her. There are no outside forces or ideologies which spur these punishments, at least not at this point in the film. The camera lingers on the scenes of abuse, challenging the viewer to keep watching. *The Pack* only moves into the realm of New French Extremity when the characters' motivations and backgrounds tie them—and the horror they inflict—to the French landscape.

Having survived her first night, during which the creatures appear to tear apart another captive but only nibble on Charlotte, Chinaski makes good on his promise and returns to the restaurant to figure out the mystery. He tricks La Spack, knocking her out with the poison that she meant to use on him. He then frees Charlotte, who attempts, unsuccessfully, to escape. Meanwhile, Max has finally reappeared. He reveals to the terrified Charlotte that he and the mutant creatures are all La Spack's sons; his brothers, it seems, had been working in a mine when it collapsed. The officials decided it was better to let a few men die rather than risk a large explosion. The miners were reborn: they now emerge from the earth at night to drink blood and consume flesh. It is time, Max tells Charlotte, for these unfortunate creatures to be finished off, once and for all.

The use of a mine explosion, resulting in the demented monsters, seems to stem from the Courrières mine disaster of 1906. The mine, located between several small towns and north of Paris, exploded, killing an estimated 1,099 people (including many children), making it Europe's worst mining disaster. The explosion was caused by coal dust and may have been triggered by a mishandling of explosives or an open flame. Rescue attempts began almost immediately, but were hampered by the lack of training for such an incident, creating tension among the distraught families and the mine's owners. Approximately six hundred miners were able to reach the surface in the hours following the explosion; these individuals suffered the effects of mine gases or were severely burned. A group of survivors were found twenty days after the initial explosion, having subsisted on, among other things, a horse used in mining operations. The Courrières mine disaster would serve as a rallying point in the French media for proper training and insurance for all laborers. The mining industry in France was a high point of the country's attempt to industrialize and modernize their country in the 20th century.

In recent years, the French government has sought to revive the industry so as to produce its own resources. As recently as 2014, market analysts reported:

> The founding of CMF, France's first state industrial startup [in] 20 years, marks a throwback to the country's previous historical successes 200 years ago in mining coal

and iron ore.... French Industry Minister Arnaud Montebourg says the government considered the state as an intelligent economic actor serving the interests of the nation. "Francophone African countries, notably, would like to work with us rather than do business with foreign multinationalism.... Colbertism is coming back and that is good," he proclaimed last week, referring to Jean-Baptiste Colbert, 17th-century finance minister under Louis XIV and the pioneer of French dirigisme.[7]

Many have viewed mining as a throwback to a developing nation, with several companies attempting to mine for oil in hostile countries. The mining industry served to employ millions at its height, but is now controlled by multi-national corporations who prefer to do business overseas.

Today the global landscape of mining is dominated by multinational firms, some of which are among the largest companies in the world, who operate in exotic, remote, and sometime hostile locations. The challenges in constructing and operating their high-technology sites and delivering the precious materials into a global supply chain are known only too well to managers and investors in this sector. Junior miners who are often responsible for much of the exploration and development face even greater challenges due to the enormity of the financial risk relative to their balance sheet. Overarching the operational and financial risk dimensions to mining, significant pressure has been applied to the sector due to the introduction of environmental, regulatory, and taxation reforms which have further complicated the investment cycle and provided new business challenges for investors and managers in this critical industry.[8]

La Spack's restaurant is run down and occupied only by the occasional local drunk. Any remnants of a population that existed because of the mining community in the small town have long since vanished, creating a ghost town. La Spack's scheme relies on the kindness of strangers to pick up Max and grow concerned for him after he seemingly disappears into the restaurant. Implied throughout the film is that Max and La Spack have run this arrangement time and again. La Spack insists that the earth demands blood; and blood and flesh is what seems to sustain the creatures, as if they have been consumed by the earth after a long and painful period during which they were left to die in a mine shaft.

Upon its release, *The Pack* was met with less-than-enthusiastic reviews, with many writers proclaiming it the end of the surge of originality that had accompanied French horror films in the previous decade. As James Dennis, at Twitch Film, wrote:

The Pack does have some memorable, striking shots (beware the moon...) and suitably gory moments. So too it continues a tradition of extreme cinema following through with its singularly grim trajectory to the bitter end. Overall though, Richards flirts with far too many subgenres whilst never truly satisfying any of them. It's a prick tease of a movie.[9]

The Pack was written off as having too many influences: Night of the Living Dead (George Romero, 1968), The Texas Chainsaw Massacre (Tobe Hooper, 1974), and My Bloody Valentine (George Mihalka, 1981), among others. What reviewers often failed to mention is that the wide variety of genre films that influenced Richards, coding The Pack as a throwback film encompassing North American genre tropes as well creating a tone and style all its own. "I have liked genre films ever since I was a child," said Richards at the time of the film's premiere at Cannes. "Back when this term that is so overused today was not just used for horror films but also for a whole complex of genres ranging from action films to detective films to adventure films."[10] The Pack offers a thrilling blend of multiple genres, making for an entirely new film which, while at the end of the New French Extremity movement, serves to show that the horror genre in France has been established in the short time since the release of Aja's High Tension.

The Pack owes a debt to Tobe Hooper's The Texas Chainsaw Massacre, which, in effect, is a kind of godparent to New French Extremity. As America teetered on social and cultural collapse in the early 1970s, The Texas Chainsaw Massacre offered an unflinching and terrifying look at a world gone berserk. In the words of film writer John Kenneth Muir:

> Over and over again, disorder reigns in The Texas Chainsaw Massacre. A spider web flourishes inside a house, a human dwelling. There's talk of a watering hole … but it's just dry earth. The kids visit a gas station, but there's no gas. Again and again the audience's expectation of order is confounded. Insanity has supplanted sanity in the film, right down to its core, taboo-breaking genetic structure.[11]

Richards's film continues that tradition by merging and marring the audience's expectations of what is about to happen. While The Pack is imperfect, it offers a view of the genre that happens to be as much, if not more, challenging than its American counterparts of the new millennium. Much of the horror of The Pack stems from its location. It exudes the sense of a place that time and history has forgotten. Something is truly rotten in the ground, and it has begun to fester.

Many reviewers felt that The Pack's promising first half was let down by a disappointing and confusing conclusion. While the conclusion of the film offers few complete answers, it does offer an exhilarating rebirth of the Final Girl trope. In the film's concluding moments, Charlotte runs from the house where she, Max, and the bikers from earlier in the film, have holed up in an attempt to finally kill the creatures. The plan goes awry, with Charlotte running out of the house as it's consumed by flames. She is hunted by the creatures, who stalk her through the deserted countryside. She falls, ensnared by a trap as the creatures begin to eat her flesh. The film then cuts to months later, with Max leading yet another attractive young woman into the restaurant. The camera pans to reveal Charlotte behind the counter, heavily pregnant, and watching Max's interactions with this new young woman. The film then reveals that Charlotte was not eaten by the creatures but rather hung up by them after the events of the standoff. Charlotte has been consumed by the family and has, ultimately, joined them.

Throughout the film, Charlotte takes on the characteristics of what theorist Carol Clover dubbed the "Final Girl," the female protagonist of a horror film who survives to the end:

> She is the one who encounters the mutilated bodies of her friends and perceives the full extent of the preceding horror and of her own peril; who is chased, cornered, wounded; whom we see scream, stagger, fall, rise and scream again. She is abject terror personified. If her friends knew they were about to die only seconds before the event, the Final Girl lives with the knowledge for long minutes or hours. She alone looks death in the face, but she alone also finds the strength to either stay the killer long enough to be rescued (ending A) or kill him herself (ending B).[12]

In *The Pack*, Charlotte lives long enough to be rescued by Chinaski, but is determined to end the creatures rather than run from them. Despite her heroic and strategic attempts to destroy any remains of the creatures, they continue to come for her. Richards offers a particularly nihilistic view of the Final Girl, one rarely seen before, where she herself turns into the killer of Final Girls. Charlotte watches Max flirt with the potential new Final Girl at the end of the film; they share a knowing look as he enters the washroom and she rubs her pregnant stomach. Charlotte's grab for power was to become the matriarch of the diseased family who control this forgotten region of France. Charlotte replaces La Spack, and her blood which fed the creatures when she was first captured will fuel a new generation of terror.

Both *Them* and *The Pack* offer a view of the effects of the sins of the parent or community has on the society around them. In *Them*, the children are a force to be reckoned with, not negotiated with. They control the present and the future, rendering the adults they encounter as null and void. It is a film that is hard to stomach because it confronts the audience with the premise that they are no longer in control—the next generation is. *The Pack*, on the other hand, is about the lengths to which a mother's love extends. Charlotte seems to take up the mantle of La Spack, the matriarchal figure of a demented family content with murdering others to ensure their survival. The town they inhabit has been all but abandoned, but the family continues to feed the land with those few, unsuspecting passersby. In both films, families try to create their own homes: in *Them*, Clémentine and Lucas attempt to build walls around themselves to protect their French-ness; in *The Pack*, La Spack and Max (and later, Charlotte) trap those who have moved on and forgotten about their world. Both films prove that no family is an island.

12

It's So Easy to Create a Victim
Martyrs (2008)

Kill a man, one is a murderer; kill a million,
a conqueror; kill them all, a God.—*Jean Rostand*

For all of the blood, guts, and taboo subjects that New French Extremity has waded through, two films have risen to the top of most upsetting, terrifying, and morally corrupt—Gaspar Noé's *Irréversible* (2002) and *Martyrs* (2008). Pascal Laugier's 2008 film has been called the most extreme of the New French Extremity movement; it is also the film most frequently labeled as torture porn. While the film does use elements of torture porn, it does not revel in the audience's squeamishness. *Martyrs* depicts the aftermath of agony and suffering. *Irréversible* deals with the trauma and depravity of the cityscape, making the familiar unfamiliar and terrifying. *Martyrs* employs a far more familiar horror film structure, but, as its predecessors in this movement have shown, the films of New French Extremity rarely do anything by the book.

Pascal Laugier's *Martyrs* is possibly the most nightmarish film in contemporary horror cinema; it is also lauded as one of the best contemporary horror films. It attacks its viewers on almost every front. It is a horrifically fascinating look at religious extremism, social bonds, and the right to knowledge. The film begins with a young girl named Lucie (Jessie Pham) escaping from a warehouse where she is being tortured. She is then put in an orphanage where she is befriended by another young girl named Anna (Erika Scott). As Anna helps put Lucie at ease she discovers that Lucie is tormented by a disfigured woman only she can see. The film picks up fifteen years later: a grownup Lucie (Mylène Jampanoï) bursts into a seemingly normal family's home, killing them all. Anna (Morjana Alaoui) arrives on the scene, but is too late; the two try to clean up and escape. Lucie, however, is still being viciously attacked by the disfigured woman (who is revealed to be a product of Lucie's tortured psyche). Realizing she will not escape her tormentors, Lucie kills herself. While mourning her friend, Anna discovers a secret lair in the house used for torture, proving that Lucie's stories of abuse were indeed true. A secret society arrives and informs Anna that they are trying to learn the secrets of the afterlife by attempting to create martyrs, and that Lucie was a failed experiment. They reveal that they have never successfully created a martyr, only victims. Anna is then taken by them and tortured. Lucie appears to her in a dream and tells Anna to "let go." Anna does, and in doing so, goes further than any other torture victim. She is then flayed alive and achieves transcendence. When the head of this secret society, the Mademoiselle (Catherine Bégin), arrives to find out what she has learned, Anna whispers something inaudible in her ear. When one of the followers asks what she said, Mademoiselle says, "Keep doubting," before killing herself.

Violence infiltrates almost every scene in *Martyrs*. If the audience, like a martyr, is not witnessing a horrific act, then they are watching the aftereffects of the psychological trauma of a victim of violence. *Martyrs* mirrors the reverse fashion of *Irréversible*. While *Martyrs* does follow a linear timeline, the audience sees the effects of violence in reverse. The beginning moments, with Lucie killing this seemingly random family, is over a decade after her initial experience with torture and she hopes the murder of this family will clear her scars and traumas. Even after this massacre, she is not at peace and takes her life as a result. The middle portion of the film, when Anna finds the torture victim held captive within the house and tries to help her until she no longer can, speaks to the present effects of torture on her mind and body. The final third of the film deals with the initial capture and torture of Anna, in essence the indoctrination and resignation to torture. The audience experiences what these women have, in reverse. The beginning of the film deals with the aftermath of trauma, the midsection of deals directly with the trauma, and the final third deals with the initial capture and torture. The weight of Anna's capture is all the more terrifying because the audience has witnessed the extent of suffering experienced by Lucie and the captured woman.

Religion and horror may seem like strange bedfellows, but since William Friedkin's *The Exorcist* (1973) became a cultural touchstone, the two seemingly disparate ideas have supported each other. *The Exorcist*, *The Omen* (Richard Donner, 1976), *Rosemary's Baby* (Roman Polanski, 1968), and *Rec 2* (Jaume Balagueró and Paco Plaza, 2009) all set out to prove that the Devil is not only very real, but that the way to defeat him is through a strong Christian belief. While some claimed the release of these films were affronts to religion, in many ways the films actually reaffirm and reify the importance of Christianity as a tool to defeat evil and restore order. In these kinds of films in particular, religion serves to stabilize humanity, whereas the Devil and his minions are a constant threat to civilization.

> The act of religion is the act of constructing and maintaining a set of beliefs and material practices which provide meaning to one's life amidst the universe of known experience. This set of beliefs offers more than a way of answering the question, "Why am I here?" It provides a framework by which one sets oneself among others, identifies a purpose in life, hope for the future and a pathway for the rest of one's life.[1]

In many ways these religious-themed horror films serve to reinforce the patriarchal world order by suggesting that chaos and temptation will lead to humans' eventual downfall. *Martyrs*, however, is a condemnation of religion. The audience sees the before, after, and current effects of the lengths to which this secret society will go to achieve their goal. To Laugier, nothing is sacred. Laugier sets his potentially nihilistic film against the clean stainless-steel backdrop of the upper-middle-class bourgeois family, who also happen to be part of a network that destroys young women as a perverted means of affirming the existence of an afterlife. The antagonists are the clean, well-dressed, educated elite who brutally torture innocent subjects with the same clinical organization they utilize to maintain their immaculate homes.

When the head of the organization, the Mademoiselle, reveals their objective, she also reveals that their methods have resulted in many victims, but no martyrs. The Mademoiselle tells Anna that part of the torture process is that the subjects begin to hallucinate. Lucie, for instance, saw the woman she could not save; the Captured Woman saw bugs on her skin; but Anna is able to hear comforting words and feel a comforting presence through her hallucination, which is what sets her apart.

Interestingly, Carol Clover identified the victims in slashers as being punished for their sexual transgressions: "Boys die, in short, not because they are boys but because they make mistakes. Some girls die for the same mistakes. Others, however, and always the main one [victim]—plot after plot develops the motive—because they are female."[2] The Mademoiselle tells Anna that they perform their experiments on young women because they are more sensitive and susceptible. *Martyrs* focuses on the punishments inflicted on the female body. Even the victims who do not survive the torture manage to live through horrific procedures that render them unrecognizable as humans.

Laugier ends his film with a definition of the word *martyr*: to bear witness. However, the Merriam-Webster dictionary defines "martyr" as:

a person who is killed or who suffers greatly for a religion, cause, etc.

a person who pretends to suffer or who exaggerates suffering in order to get praise or sympathy.

a person who suffers greatly from something (such as an illness).[3]

Indeed, the most common definition of martyr depends on the implication of a religious aspect or principle. In the final moments of the film, Laugier strips the word of the audience's expected meaning and returns it to its more inclusive, understanding state. The audience knows that Anna is the true martyr, the end game this secret society had been looking for because she bore witness to her own pain, suffering, and humanity. The audience, in turn, has borne witness to her plight. The audience identifies with the suffering because Laugier has situated the final half of the film within Anna's perspective. For Laugier, a martyr takes power from their powerlessness, understanding that they can rise above the trappings and meaningless gains afforded to those with privilege. As Laugier says:

For me, the martyr represents the one who, having no other choice but to suffer, manages to do something with this pain. Of course it's an extreme projection, entirely disenchanted, of what I was telling you about today's world. Since we don't believe in anything, since the world is increasingly divided between winners and losers, what is left to the losers but to do something with their pain? Deep down, it's what the film is about.[4]

While doing press for *Martyrs*, Laugier was upfront about his own upbringing in the Catholic church and the effects it had on him. France's relationship with religion has been a tumultuous one. The Catholic church of France is often referred to as "the eldest daughter of the church" because of France's almost uninterrupted relationship with Catholicism since the second century AD. While the political and social revolutions of France began to disrupt this holy union, it was not until 1905 that France began the practice of separating Church and State; despite this, France's history with the Catholic church led to much friction through the 20th century and up to the present day, with France's xenophobia toward the Jewish and Muslim religions in particular. While many in France have moved away from the Catholic church, with many practicing Catholics only casually attending Mass, if at all, there is an undercurrent of the traditional French identity in the face of the mass immigration experienced by France. With *Martyrs*, Laugier examines the anti-humanistic side of religion. The killing and desecration that is done in the name of a religious sect is shown to be monstrous, as we encounter Lucie's trauma from the events of her childhood to Anna's present imprisonment. *Martyrs* deals with the trauma, sacrifice, and redemption that was once the basis for religion rather than the inclusive clique it has become for many. As Laugier said in an interview:

> I really wanted to give answers to the audience for the amount of violence I was putting them through. I'm not the kind of guy who can show very brutal sequences without a reason behind it. It wasn't a matter of self-justification—because I hate that—it was more a way of helping to relieve the audience, to give the audience a reason to stay in the theatre. Believe it or not, I didn't make the film to shock or create any sort of scandal. I wrote the film in a very sincere state of mind. I was feeling pain and I wanted the audience to share the pain as part of a very honest process. I wasn't aware at the time that I wrote it that I was crossing any lines. I was thinking I am going to make the audience feel the real pain. I'm going to make the audience share the real experience of pain and violence as a way of communion. It was a very Catholic process. I have a very Catholic mind. Let's share together what's worst in life—the very worst of the human condition—and maybe we can reach another state after the screening. That was much more my intention. Also, my feelings are very compassionate with my characters.[5]

Laugier has been vocal in his belief that he and *Martyrs* do not belong to the New French Extremity movement. However, it is hard to separate the two. *Martyrs* shares a similar aesthetic to that featured in other films in the movement and creates some of the most brutal imagery in contemporary cinema. While the film was a co-production between France and Canada, the ties to the landscape of France cannot be ignored. The bourgeoisie lifestyle façade feels deeply French, especially in comparison with other films in the movement. *Martyrs* may be the epicenter of New French Extremity, and it is where it was destined to go. In *Martyrs* there is beauty in degradation, hope in loss, and triumph in darkness. *Martyrs*, more than the rest of the films in New French Extremity, brings these themes to light while challenging its audience to keep watching. As Laugier says:

> It's the matter of what horror is, if you want my opinion. As a fan of the genre, I was very tired of horror films that said nothing to no one. That's one of the traps of the genre. The genre can be made from fans, for the fans and it's in a kind of ghetto. It's totally powerless. I wanted to make the genre offensive and disturbing again. Once again, the genre first existed for that kind of purpose. Trying to offend the dominant thoughts, the dominant people and trying to express something else. Trying to express something more real, the kind of reality that society doesn't want to reveal.[6]

Horror films have often offered a subversive alternative to the status quo of popular entertainment. While many horror films provide glimpses of this, they often return to a patriarchal normality in the end. Carol Clover readily identifies this in her analysis of the structure of a slasher film. The Final Girl may fight back and subdue the monster but, in the end, she drops her weapon, returning to a feminine state and is often rescued by a male figure of authority (i.e., doctor, police officer, etc.). Some view *Martyrs* as a completely nihilistic film, as what Anna sees through her martyrdom causes the Mademoiselle to commit suicide, an act that could effectively bring about the end of this secret society. Anna has risen above her torturers, attaining a status they never could. Anna may not survive her ordeal but what she leaves behind is a brave new world where the power structure is in flux, one that may be open for something new to emerge. The former order of this world is in question and not likely to survive. Laugier elaborates:

> It's not really a fascination, but a questioning. The film is a personal reaction to the darkness of our world. And I like the paradox within horror film: take the worst of the human condition and transform it into art, into beauty. It's the only genre that offers this kind of dialectic and I have always found this idea very moving—to create emotion with the saddest, most depressing things in existence. I've always felt that horror was a melancholy genre.[7]

Martyrs is a film very much about life: living it and being able to live your own. In a first-world culture which is wealthy enough to worry about the afterlife, a secret society has come together to murder woman after woman in the hopes of validating the society's existence. They kill in order to give themselves a reason to live on; their luxury, based in wealth, causes the pain and suffering of those who fall beneath them.

While the film opens with Lucie as a young girl in the flashback, and as a young woman when she enters the family's house, she crumbles beneath the weight of what she has had to bear and takes her own life. The film is *her* journey, one that she starts but is unable to finish. In this case, the monsters are the members of the secret society, and they have managed to create another victim. Anna is a motherly figure from the outset, taking care of Lucie and encouraging her both in childhood and as adults. Her inability to leave her friend is ultimately what lets her fall into the hands of the secret society, but also, what allows her to free herself from the torture they inflict on her.

While the final moments of the film show the leader of this secret society killing herself, the audience is left with a feeling of uncertainty. However, the ultimate victim and sufferer, Anna, is no longer disempowered. She is, spiritually, the most powerful character in the film and causes the seeming downfall of the organization through her suffering and ultimate transcendence. Suffering, transcendence, love, acceptance— these are more powerful than some elitist society which is more than happy to sacrifice Anna's life for their experiments. As Laugier says of Anna's character:

> That was a crucial element for me. I didn't enjoy making this film very much. Everything, from writing the script to editing, was, for different reasons, very difficult. What gave me the strength to tell this story, to spend two years of my life in such a dark world, was the love story between Anna and Lucie. It was what connected me viscerally to the film. It's a love that is not shared. Anna loves Lucie unconditionally and this love will kill her. That's something very real that we all experience: to fall in love with the wrong person, the one who, without consciously wanting to, will destroy you. Just because they are what they are. Anna loves in an absolute manner, and in that sense, she is a sort of modern saint. She gives all of herself and she will pay for it very dearly. The world and its trivial reality are fatal to people like her.[8]

Lucie could not survive because her torture stripped her of those traits, but because of Anna's social and innate adherence to them, she survives, in a sense at least.

Martyrs challenges the boundaries of good taste but ultimately rewards its audience with a nihilistic yet strangely uplifting ending. Anna has transcended something no other character in the film has been able to achieve because she loves unconditionally. By doing so, Anna destroys her captors. Even the film gives her the power of knowledge by allowing her to keep the secret of what she sees on the other side. Many articles and blogs have theorized about what Anna said that could make the Mademoiselle kill herself, but as Laugier insinuates, that's for Anna to know and everyone else to find out on their own.

13

Living Womb
Inside (2007)

A mother's arms are made of tenderness and
children sleep soundly in them.—*Victor Hugo*

Impending motherhood is generally a time when the expectant
woman is surrounded by those she loves. The old adage, "It takes a village to raise a child," represents the notion that a child is not just the sole
property of its mother and father, but also of its community. It is the
next generation that will keep society's values and interests intact. But
what is it to be an isolated mother? One cut off from everything else,
seemingly stunted because of a painful memory. This is one of the questions that Alexandre Bustillo and Julien Maury's *Inside* (*À l'intérieur*)
asks during its blood-soaked eighty-two-minute running time.

The film begins with a gestating baby in its mother's womb. The
audience sees the baby disturbed by an outside occurrence, during which
the camera pulls out to reveal a car accident involving expectant mother
Sarah (Alysson Paradis). Sarah has received a heavy gash to her face and
looks over at the passenger—later revealed to be her husband—who is
unresponsive. The film cuts to four months later, on Christmas Eve.
Sarah is now heavily pregnant, and the doctors advise her that she will
be admitted the next day to give birth. Sarah refuses the attentions of
her mother and asks her employer (and possible love interest) Jean-
Pierre (François-Régis Marchasson) to pick her up the following morning to take her to the hospital.

Sarah's night is spent alone at her own behest. She watches television and, at one point, dozes off and dreams that she is vomiting milk
and the baby comes out of her mouth. At that moment she is awoken

by the doorbell. The person on the other side of the door asks to use her phone. When Sarah refuses, The Woman (Béatrice Dalle) reveals that she knows not only Sarah's name but also that her husband is dead. Scared, Sarah calls the police, who arrive despite the encroaching riots in the Paris suburbs. The police check the grounds, find nothing, but promise to have a squad car stop by later in the night. Sarah then settles in for the night, not seeing the eerie figure of The Woman hovering by the house windows, watching her. Once Sarah is asleep The Woman enters the house and begins to attack the expectant mother in an attempt to retrieve the baby by cutting it out of her womb with a pair of scissors. Hapless passersby stop to check on Sarah, including Jean-Pierre and Sarah's mother, all of whom meet a grizzly fate. The police return later on in the night as promised and are dispatched by The Woman in equally gruesome ways. In the final twist of the film, it is revealed that the embryo the audience first saw was not Sarah's but The Woman's. The Woman was in the other car in the accident and the crash killed her unborn baby; she now views her actions as justified, rightfully reclaiming what should be hers. In the climax of the film, Sarah goes into labor, but the baby is stuck in her uterus. The Woman performs a cesarean, which kills Sarah but allows the baby to live. The final image is of The Woman scarred and badly burned from the night's happenings, gently cradling the newborn who gurgles softly in her arms.

Bustillo describes the inspiration for the film as:

> A friend of mine was pregnant and I asked myself what a pregnant woman alone at home at night would feel. It certainly must be a weird feeling. My first idea was to have a struggle between the pregnant woman and a serial killer who hunted her to eat her placenta. But it was too basic; like every slasher movie with a fucking bad guy on one side and a poor innocent girl on the other. Changing the sex of the boogeyman was more interesting, more original, a real struggle for life.[1]

Bustillo and Maury certainly do not make Sarah an innocent character, nor do they seem concerned with making her likable. Sarah continually refuses help before The Woman enters her life, preferring to isolate herself and deal with the trauma of her husband's death on her own. She rejects any help that is offered to her and even seems irritated at her own unborn child. Any discussion of going to the hospital to give birth comes across as Sarah getting a wart removed by the doctor. As the audience learns through the film, Sarah has not come to terms with her husband's death, and the birth of their child seems like the final chapter in their story. A child, which should be the solidification of a nuclear family, will only serve to remind Sarah of the past she so desperately wants to forget. From the outset, however, The Woman clearly desires Sarah's baby. In *Inside*, two seemingly disparate themes emerge: obsession and sacrifice. When Sarah is cornered by The Woman, she threatens to harm the baby, pointing an implement directly at her stomach. This catches The Woman off guard as she cannot harm Sarah at this moment without risking the baby's life. The Woman seems only to realize in this moment that her obsession, the baby, and her enemy, Sarah, are linked. Sarah is not merely an incubator for the unborn child, but its only chance at survival.

Throughout the film, Sarah loses all her safeguards. Her mother, her employer/lover, and even the proactive law enforcement are of no help to her. Her mother, in particular, whom she dismisses in the hospital parking lot at the beginning of the film, is an important character in the story. But her concern for her daughter and her unborn grandchild merely grates on Sarah. When the mother arrives at the house, The Woman is holding court with Jean-Pierre, having convinced him that she is Sarah's mother. Sarah's mother, upon seeing this, bounds up the stairs to look for her daughter, who has locked herself in the bathroom. Hearing footsteps coming towards the door, Sarah arms herself and attacks, unintentionally killing her mother, whose blood splatters across the walls. Sarah meekly cries, "Mommy!" as her mother dies in front of her. Sarah's accidental killing of her mother removes any safety net—either present or future—from her life. No other family members seem to be present. This moment leads to Sarah's transformation from reluctant child into a fiercely determined adult.

Sarah's physicality epitomizes the desired mother. She is financially stable, attractive, and gainfully employed (as a newspaper photographer). She is exactly the type society desires to be a mother, even though she herself seems uninterested in the job. Scholar Ashley Nunes describes the potential coded understanding of Sarah and her transformation thusly:

> [S]he wears a white nightgown. The white signifies her cleanliness, her purity, which, in relation to the child's development signifies Sarah's ability to properly convey maternal authority.... Furthermore, *Inside* presents Sarah as a modern day Virgin Mary, who is the ultimate representation of the perfect mother. In the film, she is scheduled to deliver on Christmas Day, thus linking the birth of Sarah's baby to that of Jesus. Moreover, unlike the Woman's situation, where there is no father, Sarah's

husband is dead. Like God, the father of Sarah's baby is not present because he is in "heaven," which further links Sarah to the Virgin Mary.[2]

Sarah's transformation begins with the death of her mother, then of her implied lover, and, finally, when the social safeguards provided by the police are thwarted. Her final step towards true adulthood and motherhood comes when she turns to The Woman for help when her baby is stuck. In that moment she allows The Woman to cut into her, knowing that she must sacrifice herself to give her child a chance in the world, whatever that world may be.

The Woman's obsession with Sarah stems from what Sarah has inadvertently taken from her, her child. The opening of the film which features a CGI baby in utero is shaken by the car accident which Sarah either caused or was at least involved. In an effort to right the perceived wrongs, The Woman decides to reenact the crime on Sarah's house and body. As writer Donato Totaro elaborates on the breach:

> [Home invasion] is a type of crime that seems to be on the rise in North America, or at least there is a rash in the reporting of home invasions, which is one of the most frightening crimes imaginable for a society living in an otherwise safe, "civilized," well-to-do nation. It is one thing to feel fear or to be on your guard when out in urban city streets, especially late at night, but quite another to fear for your own safety in your own home, where we feel the most vulnerable because we feel the most safe.[3]

For The Woman, Sarah began the fight when she disrupted her child's safety within her womb. Throughout the film, Sarah's bland, urban home seemingly transforms into a living womb, with blood covering the wall and the lights dimmed or knocked out. Even The Woman's entrance into the house, though a mystery, is suggested to be violent. During their first encounter (before Sarah calls the police), The Woman stares defiantly at Sarah through a glass patio door. Sarah begins to take photos of The Woman as a means of intimidation, but also to capture her image. The Woman aggressively punches the glass, creating a crack like the first contraction in labor. When Sarah first locks herself in the bathroom, The Woman bangs on the door, to no avail. Eventually she takes the scissors, which have been her primary tool of attack, stabs the door until she creates a vaginal-like hole, allowing her to grab at Sarah. The Woman refuses to let Sarah hide from her or from herself. The Woman continually confronts Sarah with her own life and when Sarah seems to have the upper hand, The Woman tells her that she has already killed her when she killed her baby. Sarah is forced to look beyond her own suffering

157

and accept the traumatic effects that the initial act of violence (the car crash) had on others. The Woman's obsession with Sarah and her unborn child forces Sarah to look inward and abandon all that she had known and attempt to recreate herself.

Bustillo and Maury are careful to ensure that the band on The Woman's ring finger is shown throughout the film, hinting that there is—or was—a husband in her life and was, presumably, the father of her unborn child. As Sarah finally and aggressively fights back against The Woman, she screams, "Who would ever want to fuck *you*?" implying that no man would touch a woman as crazy as The Woman appears to be. But who, if not the Virgin Mary, bore a child without the help of a physical man? The appearance of The Woman's wedding band and lack of mention of any husband (The Woman's POV shots of the accident reveal no one else in the car) offers the suggestion that there once was someone with whom she shared an attachment. The Woman's child can be seen as a building block in her family—an attempt to normalize or solidify what she already had. The creation of a child through marriage can be seen as the completive step in maturity, forcing the parent or parents to care for something more than they do themselves. A child is also the product of idealism, an attempt for the parents to teach and pass down their values and, in many ways, allow the child to live on beyond their own life spans. The Woman's final and brutal victory hints that the child will forever be tainted with the events of that night.

Inside depicts a contemporary Paris household, one of clean blandness and excess, with hints of riots raging not far from its doorstep. Sarah begins her final evening resplendent in a clean white nightgown, which soon becomes caked with her own blood and that of others. As the bodies pile up—there is a total of nine deaths in the film—over what appears to be a two-story, two bedroom house, the walls also become encrusted with blood and flesh, creating, as mentioned before, a kind of makeshift womb and a house marked by violence. Director Maury describes the evolution of the aesthetic of the film:

> Since the beginning, we decided to do a good-looking movie. We always wanted to show the worst thing you can imagine, but in the best way possible. So we didn't want to use shaky cam and we always wanted a structured way to direct. The use of light was really important to us and the work with the director of photography began really early in the film process. We had long discussions with Laurent Barès, our director of photography. He had just finished *Frontière(s)*. We wanted to begin the movie in a really realistic way and have an image that looks like a cold, rainy day in winter. We

wanted to reflect the mind of Sarah. She's depressed [but] she doesn't have the strength to cry, she's totally destroyed on the inside. So we wanted to begin in a very realistic way and then, step by step, go to fantastic imagery, and by the end, we wanted the movie to look like a dark fairy tale.[4]

When the second squad car arrives to check on Sarah after The Woman has begun her attack, the police have in their custody a young man they arrested during the riots. Of Muslim descent, he immediately becomes a suspect whose ethnicity and religion are mocked by the officers; in fact, the young man appears to be the most innocent and articulate character in the film. He maintains that he has done nothing wrong, reasoning that if he was taking part in the riots, why would he be carrying his identification with him? Though it is suggested by his calm, cooperative demeanor that he is indeed innocent, he is not spared from the violence within the house when he is forced by the officers to enter the dwelling.

As Bustillo says of the inclusion of the riots as a backdrop to *Inside*:

The real-life shots of the riots were very important to us because they're the only real violent images in the movie. We hate Sarkozy and his politics. I live in a suburb, one of the biggest in Europe, and when I hear the president insult people who live here, I shake with anger. But that's not the theme of *Inside*. Neo-conservative politics have been here for more than fifteen years now. Sarkozy is not a newbie. Chirac was here before him.[5]

Indeed, politics are embedded in the world of the film: from the silence on the streets—suggesting that everyone in that area has barricaded themselves in for the night—to the police officers' seemingly nonchalant attitude toward the riots. The constant influx of violence has desensitized the French population, causing some citizens to retreat further into their homes and not engage with their community. At one point, early in the story, Sarah's boss relays the paper's demand that the riots receive front-page coverage the following day; he then laments that Sarah is unable to photograph the events as they unfold. The society in which Sarah and Jean-Pierre live is more than willing to document the very real struggles against conservative politics and splash violent images across their front pages, but is unable to deal with violence when it literally knocks at their door. As Maury says:

In France, you have heavy, strong images in cinema. Here, cinema is considered really as an art and not entertainment. That's the vision we all have, the directors of horror movies. We don't want to do popcorn movies. Maybe it's because we've been raised in a culture that tells you to go further with the exploration of your subject. But here the cinema is always clever and if you do an entertaining movie, the critics are merciless. For Alex and me, we have a dark vision of life. We prefer living at night. We are night birds. We don't trust the future. What we see in life despairs us, so we don't want to tell happy stories with happy endings because that's not how we see life.[6]

The end of the film offers a truly chilling image and makes good on Bustillo and Maury's vision of a realistic film that descends into the aesthetic of a dark fairy tale. The Woman has been badly burned and sits in the rocking chair that was formerly occupied by the pregnant Sarah. The camera pans over Sarah's lifeless body which now bears the scars, not only of the night's violence, but of the improvised caesarian section which The Woman had to perform. In Western culture, pregnancy is still widely revered, although the markings of pregnancy are to be covered up and hidden as quickly as possible. Bustillo and Maury show the unhealed wounds and the uterus that has been cut open and overflows on the stairs of a family home. The Woman sits, rocking the child, lit only by an overhead red light. Her face is disfigured but her expression, serene: she has her child.

> [The] two women are strongly linked through a common deep grief: The Dalle character [The Woman] from the loss of her baby, and Sarah from the loss of her husband, who died in the same car crash. The tragedy caused by the opening car crash acts as a symbolic umbilical cord tying the two women together until the very bloody end.[7]

In the final moments of the film, the audience sees the severed umbilical cord hanging out of Sarah's body, her attachment to the remorse of grief surrounding the accident and the death of her husband has been extinguished as a final act on her body. The Woman has taken the child she believed to be hers. The wrongs of the crash have been righted, the tragedy ended.

14

American Remakes in New French Extremity

The Hills Have Eyes (2006),
Mirrors (2008), *The Eye* (2008)
and *Maniac* (2012)

Beware of false prophets who come to you in sheep's
clothing, and inwardly are ravening wolves.—*French proverb*

To remake a classic (or not so classic) horror film is tantamount
to sacrilege. With few exceptions, horror remakes are almost instantaneously dismissed by fans and critics alike as they leverage the watered-
down nature of a reproduction of a beloved original. While certain
aspects, such as budget and star-power, may aid the remake in reaching
a new audience, for fans of the classics, they offer a milquetoast mirror
image of what was once new and daring. Film studios produce these
remakes (particularly after the 2003 remake of *The Texas Chainsaw Massacre*) because they have a certain amount of cultural cache and name
recognition, making them more likely to turn a profit. They also offer
an opportunity for emerging directors to stake a claim on reinterpreting
a story with their own aesthetic. While none of the films of New French
Extremity made a significant impact in terms of box office in North
America, they did amass a cult following. More intelligent than torture
porn and more brutal than the J-Horror trend, New French Extremity
began to find its home with international horror audiences, which can
be seen with the multiple horror magazine covers featuring them (e.g.,
Rue Morgue #37 *High Tension*, *Rue Morgue* #78 *Inside*, and *Rue Morgue*

#87 *Martyrs*). Studios were eager to capitalize on the underground success of these films and continue the remake trend, producing strong box-office returns.

Greek philosopher Aristotle wrote the first treatise on dramatic theory and addressed the need to mimic or replay events from past creative or historical works as the human need to control and gain mastery over these events. By distilling and retelling stories, Aristotle believed, the audience gains a deeper understanding of the events, pulling them into focus.[1] In the introduction for their book *Fear, Cultural Anxiety, and Cultural Transformation: Horror, Science Fiction and Fantasy Films Remade*, editors Scott A. Lukas and John Marmysz explain an audience's need for repetition of that which terrifies them:

> [T]he remaking of horror ... films involves an attempt dialectically to work through and linger with our collective experiences of fear, anxiety and transformation. Fear and anxiety are essential elements in horror films, and it has often been noted that there is something mysterious about the fact that the audience, first of all, derive enjoyment from exposure to fearful and anxiety-inducing performances and, second of all, that they desire reexposure to these stimuli again and again.... The desire repeatedly to engage in encounters with fanciful and dreadful characters within the illusory realm of the cinema attests to our need to experiment safely with our own reactions to fear and anxiety.... [T]hough we may never learn everything, we can in the meantime at least learn something about ourselves and our feelings about the world. Such is the positive potential of the remake.[2]

The remakes that have emerged from some of the most prominent members of the horror section of New French Extremity have sought to explore the horror films of the 1970s, furthering the movement's attachment to the New Hollywood that emerged in that time period. The other trend that was tasked to these directors was the J-Horror (or Asian Horror) movement which began with Gore Verbinski's *The Ring* in 2002. While the films that originated in the 1970s encapsulate goriness mixed with a cultural message, an intrinsic part of New French Extremity, the J-Horror films offer an air of austerity. The remakes discussed in this chapter explore what happens when French directors are tasked with a reinterpretation of Americana, even though they are already outsiders. According to director Wes Craven, this is not necessarily a deterrent to making a successful film:

> To be fresh, a horror movie has to get under people's skin in unexpected ways, with things that make them profoundly uneasy. Horror movies have to show us something that hasn't been shown before so that the audience is completely taken aback. You see, it's not just that people want to be scared; people *are* scared.[3]

162

Director Alexandre Aja (and his creative team—collaborator Grégory Levasseur, cinematographer Maxime Alexandre, and editor Baxter) followed up their international genre sensation, *High Tension*, with a remake of the 1977 Wes Craven cult classic *The Hills Have Eyes*. The production was decidedly "Hollywood," with the film distributed by Fox Searchlight Pictures and the use of the famous KNB Effects (*Men in Black*, *Kill Bill I & II*, *The Walking Dead*) for makeup and prosthetics on the shoots. The original Wes Craven film was essentially an examination of one family versus another. The Carter family takes a shortcut while on a road trip to Los Angeles, and gets lost in the desert. They get in a car accident while driving through the surrounding hills and, as they attempt to figure out what to do, they are attacked by cannibalistic mountain people.

Aja's version sees the addition of a back story which indicates that the cannibalistic mountain people, the Jupiter family, are the result of the inhabitants of a mining town refusing to leave their homes during nuclear testing in the area, turning them into mutants. The opening of the film shows what is essentially, especially in the eyes of this film, American propaganda. As the government turned to nuclear weapons as an option in the midst of the Cold War, the weapons needed to be tested; members of the military then sought to find deserted areas in the States in which to perform these tests. The utilization of American nuclear technology went hand in hand with the idealized American dream of the 1950s. Kathleen A. Tobin expands on the effect that the nuclear arms race had on the country's reorganization:

> It is wrong to believe that postwar American suburbanization prevailed because the public chose it…. Suburbanization prevailed because of the decisions of large operators and powerful economic institutions supported by federal government programs … ordinary consumers had little real choice in the basic pattern that resulted…. Essentially city planners saw the atomic threat as a means to accelerate the trend of suburbanization. Plans to circle American cities with open spaces, highways and circumferential life belts was long overdue…. The federal government played a more effective role in reducing urban vulnerability [to atomic attack] in future residential development by working through the Federal Housing Administration [FHA], The Housing and Home Finance Agency and the Federal National Mortgage Association [FNMA]. As the FHA and the FNMA annually guaranteed federal liability for hundreds of thousands of dwelling units, the federal government could mandate that in the future they all be subject to urban defense standards.[4]

The notion of the American Dream as a large house in the quiet suburbs was a result of American military planning in hopes of ensuring the survival of at least a portion of the population outside urban targets. Aja builds on Craven's sense of threat of what exists in the uncivilized portions of America and made it even more sinister by implicating the American government in the creation of the mutants. A title card appears on the screen stating, "Between 1945 and 1962 the United States conducted 331 atmospheric nuclear tests. Today the government still denies the genetic effects caused by the radioactive fallout." After a sequence where two men in hazmat suits are attacked and killed by unseen assailants, the title sequence begins with Webb Pierce's song "More and More," providing the background with images of an idealized 1950s America. These idyllic scenes are soon interspersed with photos of newborn babies with birth defects and deformed body parts, the tragic result of nuclear testing on home soil. For Aja, the American Dream came at the price of the American body.

The conservative Carter family, led by patriarch Big Bob (Ted Levine, best known as Buffalo Bill in Jonathan Demme's *Silence of the Lambs*, 1991), are traveling in their car when one of the tires are blown out by a trap in the road. Big Bob is directed to a shortcut by a gas station attendant (Tom Bower); the family soon becomes the prey of deformed mountain people. Aja oscillates between the Carters and the mountain family, the Jupiters, as in the original, but keeps the allegiances ambiguous. The Carters represent the political and ideological antithesis of the mountain people. Being conservative, Big Bob would undoubtedly be in favor of nuclear testing as a means of safe-guarding his family and their homeland. The Jupiters were miners who had protested the use of nuclear testing, hiding in the mines to keep their land but facing the fallout of the testing. The government's negligent lack of foresight caused the mutations in the mining family, then created a force that seeks to destroy what they initially meant to protect. "It was mainly finding out what's going to make the difference," said Aja of approaching his version of the cult-classic film.

First of all, to come up with the idea of the back story of the hill dwellers, something that justifies their presence and their rage, the way they act towards the travelers crossing their area. And so that's why we came up with the nuclear testing history.... You know, it's funny, five or six years ago, before September 11th, this would have been a different kind of film. In a strange way, American culture as I see it now—coming from another country, and too young to have lived in the '70s—reminds me of what I've heard about the '70s. I mean, the fact that some people, like the Carter family, are so conservative, so religious. We keep that subtext in my movie; I think we even increase that subtext. "Who's the bad guy? We're the good guys." Even if you are always on the side of the victims at one point you start wondering, "Who are the real victims in the story—the Carter family or the hill dwellers?"[5]

After the Carters are attacked and several of their family members dispatched, the oldest daughter's husband, Doug (Aaron Stanford), goes to the Jupiters' territory in order to retrieve his infant daughter, whom they have kidnapped. Doug finds what appears to be a model home village in the midst of the hills which still maintains an idyllic, if somewhat damaged, vision of 1950s Americana. Doug's journey to save his daughter is not unlike Marie's in *High Tension*: In order to rescue his loved one he must transform himself from clean urban dweller to a blood-soaked madman. (This is a marked difference indeed from the idealistic Democrat and cell-phone salesman who is mocked by his Republican father-in-law early in the film.) By the time Doug has finally been able to claim his daughter, he has murdered most of the Jupiter clan and is now caked in blood; he is barely recognizable as his former self and all but indistinguishable from those he has just killed.

The Hills Have Eyes includes another notable link to *High Tension*, that of the unreliable gaze. Several times in *The Hills Have Eyes*, what seems to be an establishing shot of the Carter family stranded in the desert pulls away and keeps pulling away until the frame becomes punctuated by binocular frames, indicating that the POV belongs to that of the Jupiter family. Aja uses this technique twice—the first time, midway through the story; the second time, at the conclusion. Throughout, particularly during Doug's journey into the Jupiter family's de facto town, the camera begins as an establishing shot and pulls away, suggesting that the gaze of the camera is not the objective one of the film, but the subjective viewpoint of a member of the Jupiter family.

Aja's remake ends with the remnants of the Carter family reuniting. All of the survivors have committed murder, linking their capacity for violence and destruction in the name of saving their family and retribution, not unlike the actions of the Jupiter family. *The Hills Have Eyes* also serves as a condemnation of the nuclear bomb by showing its destructive effects on one family and another family's reaction to its fallout. The extreme measures taken by the Jupiter family have not caused the Carters to react in kind but pushed them to it, suggesting that the capability of destruction is an element consistent across humanity, one that can emerge the farther away from the watchful eye of civilization one gets.

The new millennium seemed to dictate a new trend in Hollywood horror films. *Scream* (Wes Craven, 1996) had reignited the subgenre by galvanizing audiences and the box office, leading to a slew of similar slashers, such as I *Know What You Did Last Summer* (Jim Gillespie, 1997), *Urban Legend* (Jamie Blanks, 1998), and *Final Destination* (James Wong, 2000). By 2000 the slasher well was beginning to run dry. After the events of 9/11, American audiences became stoic, wary of what they would pay to see, which resulted in the financial decimation of several big-budget films like *Collateral Damage* (Andrew Davis, 2002). It would be Gore Verbinski's *The Ring*, released in 2002, which would generate an excitement for horror that had not been seen since *The Blair Witch Project* (1999), and result in a trend known as J-Horror (or Japanese Horror, though the films in this trend came from all over Asia) remakes. The films were brought to major studios by would-be producer Roy Lee, who helped broker deals between the American and Asian studios.[6] Following the success of *The Ring*, which wound up with an almost $250 million worldwide box office,[7] more remakes followed, including *The Grudge* (Takashi Shimizu, 2004) and *Dark Water* (Walter Salles, 2005). These new versions upheld the sinisterly austere aesthetic of the originals, creating a more "mature" take on horror films. It also brought in decent box-office returns for a few years.

New French Extremity would clash with the J-Horror remake boom in 2008 with the release of Alexandre Aja's *Mirrors*, David Moreau and Xavier Palud's *The Eye*, and Eric Vallette's *One Missed Call*. (The latter is widely regarded as one of the most reviled contemporary horror films, holding a 0-percent rating on the Rotten Tomatoes website.[8])

Mirrors, a remake of the South Korean film *Into the Mirror* (Sung-ho Kim, 2003), is sometimes overlooked in analyses and histories of the J-Horror boom in North America, not because its source is a South Korean film but because it simply does not evoke the coolly isolating atmosphere of that ilk. Aja retained control over the film by bringing back his creative team of Gregory Lavasseur, editor Baxter, and director of cinematography Maxime Alexandre. It was widely publicized at the time of the film's release that Aja took inspiration from the original film, with nods in several scenes, but, ultimately, *Mirrors* is Aja's interpretation of a supernatural possession/ghost story. The story concerns Ben Carson (Kiefer Sutherland), a former police officer who was let go from the force after a fatal shooting. Needing money, Ben takes a job as a night watchman of the dilapidated Mayflower department store in downtown Manhattan. He lives with his sister Angela (Amy Smart) while trying to repair his relationship with his estranged wife and children. The Mayflower store suffered a massive fire decades earlier and has been all but abandoned. As Ben settles into his job, he notices there is something wrong with the mirrors throughout the store. Soon, mirrors everywhere begin haunting Ben and his family, forcing him to uncover the mystery behind them.

Mirrors became notable on its release for bucking trends in previous J-Horror remakes by being extremely gory. The film is rife with jump scares and atmospheric elements, but it is Aja's use of disturbing effects that allowed *Mirrors* to stand out from other entries in the subgenre. Arguably the most shocking and disturbing scene—even for diehard horror fans—is the one in which Ben's sister Angela is attacked while taking a bath. "What would be the worst of the worst of the worst?" asked Aja when discussing the scene:

> I thought about a nice, pretty girl getting ready to take a hot bath. She's undressing and it's so pretty. Then at one point, *boom*! Her reflection stays [in the mirror] and you know something really, really bad is going to happen. I was thinking about what would scare me the most and I was thinking, okay, if the reflection doesn't feel pain because it's something supernatural that can do anything why not have it do the worst thing that can happen to a girl, being disfigured.[9]

Mirrors plays with several tropes Aja had already explored in his previous films, the obvious example being the use of mirrors as a reflection of self and a forgotten piece of American nostalgia. The character of Ben is at his weakest—indeed, the lowest point of his existence—at the beginning of the story. While trying to get his life back on track he is forced to stare at himself every night with the mirrors that cover the walls of the Mayflower—the ones that which were mysteriously undamaged in the fire decades earlier. As Ben seems once again on the verge of becoming unhinged, his family fears for his mental health; this forces him to come to terms with the damage he has done to his family and the role he has played in the disintegration of his life. Aja explored the mirror analogy in *High Tension*, but whereas Marie was unable to truly see herself or her actions, Ben is all too aware of his past. The use of the Mayflower as a symbol of an Americana spirit that has fallen into disrepair was also explored by Aja in *The Hills Have Eyes*, with the inclusion of the model town. The Mayflower, named after the puritan ship which brought European settlers to America, is now a burned-out shell of its former self, the department store offering an all too apt parallel for the economic downturn following the stock market crash on September 29, 2008. The first third of *Mirrors* is nearly a one-man show, with Aja's camera trained on Ben as he wanders through the department store every night as his visions and suspicion of the mirrors escalates. Despite being long out of business, the Mayflower still has mannequins, hangers, and assorted goods scattered throughout the store that no one had bothered to retrieve. America is still flush with capitalistic hunger, but, after the recession, the faded glory that still surrounds America remains for sale.

During the press tour for *Mirrors*, Kiefer Sutherland was asked by a journalist of the horror website Bloody Disgusting what his thoughts were on the emerging horror trend from France. He replied: "Once you start to parody it [the horror genre], you open up a whole other frontier where another group of people say, no—this is serious stuff here and we're going to reinvent it and start tooling with it. Once you start a parody of anything, it's died in that format."[10]

With *Mirrors*, Aja was able to merge his tastes with the framework of what was currently selling tickets. While *Mirrors* divided audiences with its gory effects and divergence from the source material, it remains a film that partnered the aesthetics of New French Extremity with the basis for a South Korean film and made it (somewhat) palatable for American audiences.

David Moreau and Xavier Palud's *The Eye*, also released in 2008, failed to stir any kind of response from critics or audiences. With an American box-office take of just over $30 million and a worldwide take of $56 million, the film barely recouped its costs and was savaged by critics. Jeanette Catsoulis, of the *New York Times*, wrote:

> The original "Eye," directed by the Thai filmmakers Danny and Oxide Pang, was an insinuating ghost story that cleverly exploited cinema's fascination with all things ocular. But what the Pangs accomplished with little more than a talent for framing and focus, this remake (directed by David Moreau and Xavier Palud) fails to achieve, despite an arsenal of strobe lighting and crashing chords.[11]

Many horror fans wondered what happened to the directors who had made the chillingly claustrophobic *Them* just two years earlier. Did they simply not have it in them to deliver the gut punch that *Them* elicited?

Or was it the forceful hand of a Hollywood studio that took the film away from them? An Australian reporter asked that very question of Moreau, who responded:

> Meeting Jessica [Alba, star of *The Eye*] was marvelous. But when you meet a Hollywood star you have 15 people telling you how you should behave and act [with them]. First never say, when you're shooting, if you think it's bad, never say it's bad; you have to say, "It's great, but it could be better." ... [Jessica Alba] was really happy to work with "European" directors who are supposed to be more crazy. We're not crazy; we're just having an accent. So that part of the shooting was marvelous, working with [Alba] was marvelous, but the editing is something different where basically you're not in control if they don't like what you did, which was the case. So the movie that you saw was absolutely not the movie we wanted to make.... They don't tell you [that they don't like what you've done], they let you understand. It's not, I'm not happy with this. For me, it was coming back to the editing room. You leave the editing room on Friday and the editor tells you, "Great job, it's going to be a marvelous movie." Then you come back on Monday and he says, "What are you doing here? You're not supposed to be here." "Um, I'm the director." "Well, you should call your agent." [The premiere] was probably the worst evening of my life. [But] you need to be there, just to close it from your memory.... Your dream is taken and smashed on the ground. But I survived.... In France we are in total control. If a producer says, "You do this." I say, "Yeah? *Non!* I'm the director. I have the power."[12]

The Eye is a forgettable film, transparently designed as a star vehicle for actress Jessica Alba after *The Ring* helped Naomi Watts achieve A-List status in Hollywood. Alba portrays Sydney, a blind violinist who receives a retina transplant. The operation allows her not only to see, but, to paraphrase another famous contemporary horror film, she sees dead people. *The Eye* is a resoundingly flat film with none of the terrifying sense of panic that permeates *Them*. *The Eye* is a bland, Hollywood cash-grab that resulted in both David Moreau and Xavier Palud returning to their home country to continue their careers. As horror critic John Kenneth Muir pointed out in his book *Horror Films FAQ*: "In these J-Horror remakes, the would-be victims do literally nothing to deserve their fates. They're merely accidental tourists, and so relatively passive acts, such as spectatorship, bring about their destruction."[13] While that sentiment resonated with American audiences of the new millennium who watched as their country went to war, nearly bankrupting them, the same could also be said for any audience members who paid to see *The Eye*.

In keeping with his formula for drawing on the basic plot of his source material, Aja's next project was a remake of Joe Dante's 1978 film *Piranha*, notable for being the first in a long string of *Jaws* (Steven Spielberg, 1975) retreads. The film even won the plaudits of Spielberg himself, who called *Piranha* "the best of the *Jaws* rip-offs."[14] Dante would go on to become a well-respected genre director, with such box-office hits as *The Howling* (1981) and *Gremlins* (1984). For Aja, however, he saw his version, entitled *Piranha 3D* and released in 2010, as his own film: With *Piranha*, the studio [Dimension Films] bought the title but it's not a remake—it's a completely different story, completely different characters, different script. It's more like a new movie than a remake of the Joe Dante's film. It's so different that the Writer's Guild decided that it's not a remake.[15]

Unlike Aja's *The Hills Have Eyes*, which included political and social elements by way of the military's testing of the atomic bomb, Aja eschewed Dante's take (which had the piranhas becoming aggressive due to military testing) and replaced it with an earthquake that releases a prehistoric version of the piranha; the species then wreaks havoc on local spring-break festivities. *Piranha 3D*, so named for use of 3D technology as well as the many ample bosoms on display, stacks its cast with recognizable names, such as Elizabeth Shue, Adam Scott, Ving Rhames, and Christopher Lloyd, with cameos by horror director and actor Eli Roth and *Jaws* alumnus Richard Dreyfuss. The plot of the film is relatively threadbare: the main characters get separated and attempt to find their way back as the piranhas begin to attack. The main set piece, though, is the piranha's attack on the large-scale spring-break party on a local beach. Utilizing KNB Effects, the piranha attack is a orgy of blood, guts, and disintegrating limbs. "We went so far, I think we beat *Kill Bill*," remarked Aja. "There was more blood used in this movie than in any other movie ever made. I think that gore is sometimes more acceptable than violence, like in *The Hills Have Eyes*, which was more visceral. You know, it's such a fine line—you don't want people to run away from the theater, puking. There has to be a fun component. That's why spring break really saved us because we needed it to be very violent, gory and suspenseful, but also very fun and light somehow."[16]

While *Piranha 3D* wears its blood proudly, it is significantly lighter, both emotionally and intellectually, than Aja's previous efforts. There is no condemnation of law enforcement or the town. The closest element that comes close to criticism is the portrayal of Derrick Jones (Jerry O'Connell), a sexually aggressive and disturbed soft-core porn impresario. The design of *Piranha 3D* is slick and glossy, owing to the budget Dimension secured for the production, but also from the sunny landscapes and attractive actors. If anything, *Piranha 3D* falls more in line with the torture porn trend—exemplified by *Cabin Fever* (2002), *Hostel*, parts I and II (2006, 2007), and the *Saw* series (2004–2010)—than anything resembling New French Extremity. While Aja has repeatedly called *Piranha 3D* his fun "popcorn" movie, it is also his most vacant. If anything, the true stars of the film are KNB Effects for their work on the attack and grisly aftermath of the piranhas. *Piranha 3D* relinquishes the fun and heart of *Jaws* and the original *Piranha* in favor of attractive actors being repeatedly savaged, rendering *Piranha 3D* a soulless contribution to Aja's oeuvre, but one that remains his nonetheless. "I've tried as much as I can to apply in the States the same way I make movies in France," said Aja in the lead-up to *Piranha 3D*'s release. "[Full] creative freedom and working the way I want and writing my own scripts. [Aja is not credited as a writer on *Piranha 3D*]. It's not easy every day and there are lots of fights, but mostly I've been lucky so far."[17]

For Aja's next project he stepped away from the camera to produce and write the remake of William Lustig's grimy 1980s slasher *Maniac*. Released in 2012, this version of *Maniac* was helmed by Franck Khalfoun, another of Aja's collaborators, who had appeared in *High Tension* (as Jimmy, the store clerk) and in *Piranha 3D* (as a deputy). Khalfoun's first directing credit was *P2* (2007), a violent survival horror, set in an underground parking garage on Christmas Eve. Though *P2* did not fare well at the box office, Khalfoun proved that he could master turning familiar spaces into menacing ones, making *P2* a sharp, engaging thriller. Aja, along with writing partner Gregory Levasseur, showed the script to Khalfoun, who agreed to direct. The result is a terrifying—and not easily forgotten—look at madness in the contemporary landscape of L.A. This became one of the last films to uphold the tenants of New French Extremity Violence, not for violence's sake, but because violence exists throughout society.

Lustig's original film is an emblem of a New York City that most would like to forget, dilapidated and crime ridden. Chronicling the downward spiral of Frank Zito (Joe Spinell) as he attacks women, killing them and taking their scalps which he places on mannequins in his apartment. Aja and Levasseur's script once again keeps the basic premise—including the implication that Frank's anger toward women stems from an absentee mother, and his unraveling being the result of falling for a beautiful photographer—but adds an iconic element. Khalfoun's

Maniac is shot almost entirely from Frank's (Elijah Wood) POV, save for flashbacks. As Khalfoun recalled on the press tour for *Maniac*:

When Aja and I were talking about the best way to handle the script he and Greg handed me ... we wracked our brains on how to create that [empathy], how to bring the audience close. And how to do it knowing [the audience] are not only genre fans but cinephiles who love movies. We knew in essence if we made a cool film that stood on its own, it would be respected. That's where the POV started coming from ... it reminded us of *Peeping Tom* and early horror movies. It fit, like coming back to where it started. Some of the scariest moments in horror films were the stalking from behind the bush scenes, and then we thought of today's audience—because of first person shooter [video games], and this found footage stuff and that we all have camera phones—are ready to accept a film shot entirely like this.... A lot of serial killers talk about these out-of-body experiences and a light bulb went off. That would be a perfect way to see our character as well.[18]

Some of the most famous example of POV shots used in horror films, such as the aforementioned *Peeping Tom* (Michael Powell, 1960), *Black Christmas* (Bob Clark, 1974), and *Halloween* (John Carpenter, 1978), serve as a tactic for suspense. The audience can see the killer's impending arrival, but the camera returns to its objective status following the victims. Film scholar Laura Mulvey looked closely at the phenomenon of cinema imbuing itself with a "male gaze," and in her book *Men, Women and Chainsaws*; scholar Carol Clover elaborated on the idea, writing, "[POV shots have] us looking at women in the way men do. The cinematic apparatus ... is characterized by the fixing of the female body as the quintessential and deeply problematic object of sight."[19] Much like Marie in *High Tension*, but in a far more obvious way, Frank is the unreliable narrator of *Maniac*. His twisted desires result in chaos. In Khalfoun's *Maniac*, Frank is around every corner, watching and waiting for his chosen victims. The violence is unrelenting because the camera rarely breaks from Frank's gaze. In effect, the remake of *Maniac* is the male gaze run amok, seeding from the terrifying fears that enter the minds of many women who live in urban settings. Frank, of course, sees nothing wrong with the killing and scalping of his victims as he staples their hair on the mannequins he works to restore. Metaphorically, a mannequin should be the perfect woman to Frank, silent and always present. Frank's mind, however, develops narratives for the mannequins as he treats them like girlfriends; he cannot stop his mind from corrupting the inanimate objects to the point where they fight among themselves and eventually turn against him.

The only person able to get close to Frank—and break his POV in the film's narrative—is Anna (Nora Arnezeder), a beautiful photographer. Frank and Anna share a similar relationship with the mannequins: both try to bring them to life, and both share a kind of love for them, a point on which Anna remarks when she first views Frank's collection of vintage mannequins. They develop a friendship, and Frank's affection for her grows. As Khalfoun mentioned a typical serial killer's out-of-body experiences, Frank's out-of-body (or out-of-gaze) experience happens when he and Anna sit by a pond in a park. The camera shifts from Frank's gaze to an objective viewpoint of the two of them sitting, side by side. Frank returns to this memory—and the film uses this specific shot several times—as he learns that Anna has a boyfriend, and as he is about to attack her. The film's one moment of objective clarity is when Frank seemingly falls in love with the kind-hearted Anna, and it is a shot that tortures him for the rest of the story. He cannot return to that out-of-body (or out-of-POV) moment, and no amount of murder or coercion will remedy that.

Anna's profession as a photographer is what brings them together initially, but it also presents an interesting parallel in the film. Anna asks to photograph Frank as he restores a mannequin, and her photos represent the few outside glimpses the viewer has of Frank that are not in a flashback. He is no longer anonymous with Anna as she casually snaps photos of him, documenting him and his existence. As Susan Sontag wrote about *Peeping Tom*: "To photograph people is to violate them ... to photograph someone is a sublimated murder."[20] Anna's ability to photograph allows her an outside perspective on Frank: she is in control of her gaze; she has not been solely subjugated to Frank's.

Maniac embraces 1980s and American nostalgia with a synthesizer-based score, written and performed by Robin Coudert and Chloe Alper, and a slickly neon aesthetic which hints at its L.A. setting in conflict with the violence realized on screen, functioning as an almost anti–*Piranha 3D* where the gore is dependent on the film's nihilistic, visceral quality. *Maniac*'s aesthetics work in opposition to the film's bleak outlook. Frank's inner monologue and stunted interactions with those around him fail to reveal his motives and intentions. The casting of Elijah Wood (best known for the *Lord of the Rings* trilogy) adds another element of unsuspecting madness. Wood's boyish good looks do not recall Spinell's downtrodden, craggy face. Wood's Frank looks to be the sort of unthreatening person one would hope to meet in a city. But because the audience can hear his thoughts and see his actions, the terror of *Maniac* lies in its inversion of societal expectations.

Rumors circulated within the industry that both *Martyrs'* Pascal Laugier and *Inside*'s Alexandre Bustillo and Julien Maury were offered chances to helm a remake of Clive Barker's *Hellraiser* (1987) and another sequel to the *Halloween* franchise. These projects never came to fruition, although Bustillo and Maury's prequel to *The Texas Chainsaw Massacre*, entitled *Leatherface*, is set for a 2016 release. Interestingly, *Martyrs* was remade in secret by Kevin and Michael Goetz and released to dismal reviews in 2015. Alexandre Aja returned to the director's chair, adapting Joe Hill's *Horns* in 2013 as a macabre and saccharine fairy tale of lost love that is found again.

These remakes have served as an entrance for French directors to try their hand at a major studio film. Some succeeded, and some did not. As New French Extremity began to decompose, these films were the last of their kind. The ferocity that led these directors to create startling and terrifying visions of the world around them has been all but extinguished.

Conclusion

> We made it known that we were trying to show the reality of
> France. People think of Paris as the city of love or the city of
> light, but where you got love you got hate, where you got light
> you got darkness.—*Mathieu Kassovitz*

In 2015, the *Martyrs* remake was released. Directed by brothers
Kevin and Michael Goetz, from a script by Mark L. Smith, the film is
a decidedly American affair and one that confirms the importance and
singularity of the New French Extremity movement. The *Martyrs*
remake sanitizes the violence of the original and reorients the narrative
thrust of the protagonist. While it is always advisable to transform a
story when remaking it, the American *Martyrs* fails to show any real
knowledge of pain, suffering, love, or transcendence. The marketing
of the film bills it as "the ultimate horror movie" yet, in actuality, it
only serves to reinforce Pascal Laugier's original's place in the horror
canon.

The movement of New French Extremity burned brightly and
quickly. It began in the late 1990s (with murmurs of the movement
occurring decades before) and ended in France with *Martyrs* in 2008—
and a brief, American extension until 2012 with Franck Khalfoun's
Maniac. These French auteurs unknowingly set out as a group to challenge the status quo; they managed to target political and social aspects
of their culture within the art-house movement, yielding debates and
public demonstrations. When the movement progressed into the horror
sphere, the target became France's film industry, which saw the directors
turning outside their borders to gain acceptance while still telling French
stories. Like other movements within film and art, New French Extremity was never planned, it simply grew out of the instability that French

citizens felt every day. The gravitation to horror made perfect sense, as France was living in horrific times.

James Quandt has continued to dismissed the evolution of the sub-genre in his follow-up essay, "More Moralism from that 'Wordy Fuck,'" explaining that his original intention for writing the piece was to examine director Bruno Dumont's movement towards violence and gore with his film *Twentynine Palms* and determine whether it was an evolution or an enslavement to fashion. Further deriding the movement through his piece, Quandt draws no conclusions of which to speak and ends his second essay on contemporary French films by labeling them as "desperate artifacts."[1] It is a strange time indeed when a critic cannot see beyond himself to acknowledge the progressive and transgressive nature of a radical wave of films. Quandt goes on to claim that these films lack a "communal consciousness and coherency"[2] and are unlike the brash violence of predecessors Fassbinder and Pasolini, who used their own brands of extremity to "confront their audiences with grim societal facts."[3] The films which make up this subgenre have been discussed here in the context of a history that highlights the nihilistic worries of a contemporary France, which was still viewed as a bourgeoisie haven seen in such American films as *Before Sunset* and *Midnight in Paris*. New French Extremity illustrated the extremes of France: a country with rioting in its streets, corruption and scandals in politics, rising sexual violence, and a long history of xenophobia. The films of New French Extremity have dealt with all of these issues (and more) and, in doing so, have brought the issues to a wider, international awareness.

The Extremity trend has continued throughout Europe, with directors such as Lars Von Trier, Michael Haneke and Lukas Moodysson, whose films share definite commonalities with New French Extremity, yet their films fail to tether them to any one location, offering instead a broader scope of influence. While these filmmakers focus on their condemnation of contemporary society rather than a look inwards at their histories and backgrounds. New French Extremity looks inward at France's deeds that had previously been unuttered.

Through the works of New French Extremity, a relationship with Artaud's Theater of Cruelty can be gleaned. Artaud created an art form that would assault an audience's senses rather than indulge them. While several experimental theater companies have attempted to mount productions utilizing Artaud's ideas, few have ever managed to make an impact. New French Extremity may be the most fully realized, widest-reaching articulation of Artaud's theory. From the changing lenses of Olivier Assayas's *Demonlover* to the terrifying darkness of Philippe Grandrieux's *Sombre*, the all-encompassing nature of the term New French Extremity has lent itself to a country tied to its past and attempting to maintain a semblance of power as it moves uncertainly towards the future.

The films discussed in this book have taken us down many paths, assumed different forms, and challenged ideals, all in the name of giving voice to concerns that dominate French culture. While these concerns are not unlike those faced by most First World countries, the veracity with which these filmmakers have begun a dialogue with their audiences is something uniquely French, an emblem of the auteur theory. The extremity and terror found in these films is rooted in the soil of France, a country that sought to forget the unpleasantness which grew within its borders. In Grandrieux's *Sombre*, the killer and his would-be victim become intertwined and then separated, leaving them both damaged and angry. In *Irréversible*, Vincent Cassel's Marcus marches down to the depths of hell to seek vengeance for a random crime, which leads his moral compass, Pierre (Albert Dupontel), to break and react. *High Tension* illustrates the terrifying nature of an unreliable narrator and the audience's anger over being duped by a fractured mind. *Froniter(s)* deals with a past that France has made every effort to erase yet is continually confronted by. *Inside* offers a grim look at the uncertain future for France's next generation. *Martyrs* proves that the most vibrant glimmers of light come from darkness. The torment, pain, and fear that the characters in these films experience stems from their inescapable selves, something rooted within them which they cannot shed.

New French Extremity's time as a movement was brief within the larger scale of film history, approximately ten years (give or take), but the impact and discussion it has ignited will continue. Its purpose within the larger context of French films is to offer a radically and violent opposition to the sedate cleanliness of films like *Amélie*, *The Umbrellas of Cherbourg*, and *The Artist*, among others. They reject France's genre film history of the *fantastique* in favor of a reality which exists within France, from its countryside to the darkest streets of Paris. While New French Extremity's absentee father, James Quandt, rejects the notion that these films could mean anything more than the blood and guts which they showcase, he fails to see the impact, actions, and reactions these films have generated. While unpleasant to watch, it is hard to look away from these films.

If there was any further doubt as to the importance of this subgenre, one only needs to watch the remake of Pascal Laugier's masterpiece *Martyrs*; it eschews the aesthetics, technique, and morality of the original and replaces it with a meaningless exercise in artificial appropriation. The films of New French Extremity have pushed boundaries, combining art-house aesthetics with the elements of horror and exploitation films, in an effort to make beautiful the ugliest parts of being French. They have transgressed and transcended. They showed that what France has to fear is itself.

Appendix:
The Business of Violence
An Interview with Colin Geddes

Colin Geddes began programming the genre-centric "Midnight Madness" program at the Toronto International Film Festival (TIFF) in 1998. The importance of TIFF to the New French Extremity movement cannot be understated, and Geddes's role in the emergence of the movement—particularly within genre circles in North America—helped usher in a new era for the horror genre. After programming Alexandre Aja's *High Tension* at TIFF 2003, Lionsgate Films quickly bought the film for distribution in North America. While *High Tension* underperformed on its initial release, buzz steadily grew about the intensely violent film. Part of the appeal of having a film play in TIFF's Midnight Madness program is the palpable energy of the screenings. The excitement at these screenings is immense, allowing distributors, agents, and other industry members to see the films with an audience which understands the subgenre.

After programming *High Tension* in 2003, "Midnight Madness" became an unintentional bastion for New French Extremity, which was still struggling to find an audience. Following *High Tension*'s success, other French filmmakers and distributors began to look to TIFF as a way to garner buzz, recognition, and, hopefully, sales. In 2004, *Calvaire* played the festival; in 2006, *Sheitan* was unleashed; 2007 saw both *Frontier(s)* and *Inside* screened; and, in 2008, an audience member vomited during the screening of *Martyrs*.[1]

While the Midnight Madness program is billed as TIFF's "wild side,"[2] the Vanguard program, which Geddes also programs, is "provocative, sexy ... possibly dangerous. This is what's next,"[3] and has screened films by Gaspar Noé and Catherine Breillat, among many other French auteurs. I had the opportunity to interview Geddes in Toronto in August 2015, to examine the New French Extremity movement from an industry perspective.

Alexandra West: What was your first encounter with New French Extremity?

Colin Geddes: Gaspar Noé was the first director I ever interviewed [in a journalistic capacity prior to working at TIFF]. Back when he had his first film *Carne* at TIFF and I had a press pass. I met him and we talked about Dario Argento films and horror films and I did an interview with him—I don't even know where it went. We struck up a conversation because the film was paired up with a film called *The Lives and the Times*, which was about the pseudo-maybe homosexual relationship that John Lennon had with his manager Brian Epstein. So, two short films paired together, very different films. *Carne* played first and I remember sitting down and watching it and the film has that warning shot where it says, The scenes you are about to see are incredibly graphic. And the next thing you see is a horse, a beautiful horse, which is then just gutted and butchered. So I'm watching the film and the seat beside me is vacant and this woman comes in and she's missed the beginning of the film and she's one of those flustered people going for the guidebook, looking around, trying to figure out what her next screening is and then she looks up and it's the shot of the knife going into the mouth of the immigrant and she just started freaking out, gets up and leaves. Gaspar comes in for the second short film and sits down in her seat, totally unaware of what's just happened. So I remember when I saw *Irréversible* at a press screening at TIFF and the same thing happened, the film had just started, a woman came in late and I thought—oh, not again! But it didn't happen. I interviewed Gaspar and it was a really fascinating interview because it was him just on the cusp of what he would become and it sparked a friendship, and I [still] see him at festivals. And he would contact me when I worked at Suspect Video [an independent video store in Toronto] because he'd be looking for weird, obscure films that were rumored to have real corpses in them, this junkie biography underground film and he'd ask, "Do you know where I could get this?"

AW: What do you feel like your relationship or job is with the filmmakers in terms of getting sales or distribution? It seems to me like it's a lot like matchmaking; you're trying to make sure the right people see it at the right time in the right mood.

CG: The first [New French Extremity film] I picked was *High Tension*. It all probably comes from *Mad Movies* magazine, essentially the French *Fangoria*. It was a magazine that I would always pick up when I could when I was at a French-language bookstore. I picked up a copy and I saw a still from *High Tension* and I just knew I had to get that film; I had to find that film, didn't know anything about it, started doing the research and got a VHS tape of it with the title they were slapping on it for export was *Switchblade Romance*. The first version I got was dubbed in English, but not the dub that they eventually went with. I saw it and it blew me away. The really visceral nature of the violence is what really struck me, but also the woman [Marie] thinking she's the heroine. When we screened it we got a lot of flak for it, but there were also a lot of people who dug it and bought into it. Then there's that camp who says, It doesn't make sense, how'd that car get there, how'd that? how'd that? how'd that? And everyone seems to forget the beginning of the movie, [Marie] is telling you her perspective. If you were reading a book, you'd be doubting your protagonist all the time. And everyone seems to forget that. Also if you look at that same year [2003], *Tale of Two Sisters*, same device. So I got to meet Alex [Aja], and he came to Toronto with his writing partner Greg [Levasseur], and they were great. They were so excited to engage with the audience, to have it screened at the Uptown Theater with a massive stage. So [that experience] really helped firm that relationship with them and also with that scene. The other important thing which happened around that period, that same year we also had *Ong-Bak* which was also picked up by Luc Besson's company Europa which also distributed *High Tension*, so that was a big year for Luc Besson at TIFF and Midnight Madness. But at the same time when I met the agents, by that I mean the American talent agents, so there were a couple guys who introduced themselves to me that year who were agents who represented important U.S. genre directors. That was also the same time I got that validation from the Hollywood industry of what I was doing. They were like, We're paying attention to your programming and your tastes and the filmmakers. As a result, from that [*High Tension*] screening and one of the agents being

181

able to see *High Tension* work big with a crowd, Alex Aja got signed with the William Morris Agency and that's helped Alex go from being a French director to working in America. In the genre scene in France, I believe Alex's film getting the debut in Toronto meant a validation for them. So other directors started paying attention to that and striving for that.

AW: As far as I can tell, these films don't get the kind of recognition they do internationally in their home country. So it must be overwhelming for these directors to come to TIFF and Midnight Madness and experience their films with a receptive audience.

CG: Honestly, the "cool kids" of it all were the guys who did *Inside*. I think they played on the final night of the festival and they had a blast. The audience were their people, and Alex Bustillo, one of the directors, he got his start writing for *Mad Movies*—so the magazine I would go to find these films. When I programmed the French science-fiction film *Eden Log* (2007), director Franck Vestiel said to me, "You have to understand for French genre directors like us, Midnight Madness is our Cannes." That made me understand more of what this meant for them. That said, I still have high standards and there are French horror films that I have not selected because I'm always looking for something that's different. These films are appreciated here [in North America] but the reason why it hasn't continued or we haven't seen a more prolific outbreak of these films is they're beaten down back home [in France]. Back home, the press hates the films because they think the directors made "American" films. The press seems to ignore any of the genre or *fantastique* roots that French cinema has, and accuses them of making dumb American films. To make matters worse, the theatrical chains don't let the films play there, the major theaters where they would need to go to get any kind of success because it's still very much an old white man's world and they think horror films attract "hoodlums." Apparently there was one theater in Paris during the early 1980s where they would do horror film marathons and it was basically like a French Grindhouse scenario, people would get stabbed in the alley, seats would be ripped up. It was a notorious place and I've talked to people who have fond memories of it. As a result of that, theater owners today think these films will only attract people who will rip up their seats and damage their cinemas. So why waste your time booking these films? So the

Otto's Book Store

a booklover's paradise
107 West Fourth Street
Williamsport, PA 17701
(570) 326-5764

Transaction #:00559022
tion:CR2, 18   Clerk:OTTO CR-2
ursday, December 8 2016   12:37 PM

LES:
@   53.27 9781476663487   53.27
ilms of the New French Extremity: Visce
@   8.00 0446352764   8.00
Double Whammy
BTOTAL   61.27

X:
Sales Tax   @6.0000%   3.68
TAL TAX   3.68

AND TOTAL   64.95

NDER:
Currency   64.95
TAL TENDER   64.95

ANGE $0.00

Thank You for Shopping at Otto's

00559022
00559022

films come out, the press were unkind to them, the theater will barely give them a week to play and then they disappear. Then there was the whole scandal with *Martyrs* where it was basically given an "X" rating, the same rating they would have given a sex film even though there was no sex in the film. When I saw *Martyrs* I saw it at Cannes and it was the third "extreme" horror film I had seen that day, in a row. So when I saw *Martyrs*, I hated it but it was because by that point, I felt pummeled. I had already seen two extreme horror films which I didn't think were that good and then there was *Martyrs* which everyone was touting as being *really* good. I was with it for the first act and then as soon as it goes off the rails you don't know what movie you're in. That night was a really intense, boozy debate with Tim League from Drafthouse Films and Mitch Davis from Fantasia and we were all talking about why this film just had to be programmed. And in the course of that thinking I reassessed what I thought. Sure enough, when I left Cannes the film that was *the* film that kept on coming to me. Then the debacle happened with the ratings and then Wild Bunch came to me and said, "You have to help us because if you program the film that will help validate and turn back this decision [on the rating]." Ultimately, I don't think it helped that much. But then reading Pascal Laugier's statement about the film, his statement on victims, and it was fascinating. It's interesting to look, too, at him because his previous film, *St. Ange* (a.k.a. *House of Voices*, 2004), which is a very Euro-horror, gothic-y story. It doesn't quite work, but it's strong, and there is a definite vision.

AW: Cannes is seen as this really glamorous, important film festival. What is it like to go see a New French Extremity film or an "extreme" film at a festival like that?

CG: That's the duality of Cannes. What you see and read in the newspaper is totally different than what is actually going on. You're usually just reading about the films that are in competition which are on the red carpet, which have been selected. However, underneath it all is the Marché du Film [Film Market], which is the sales portion. When someone says they've been to Cannes or they've had their film screened at Cannes—clarify that. Sales agents, producers unveil their project hoping to get as many world sales as they can, hoping to get festival invitations, but the priority really is world sales. Oftentimes, programmers are shunted around and ignored because it's first about getting that sale to the U.S., to England, to wherever. Festival play only matters to some sales agents. You'd be surprised how many don't realize that going to a film festival can really help their film break new ground. So, basically, it's kind of a crapshoot where you have all these different titles and you just don't know about them unless you identify something about the actor, or the director, or the producer, or the writer, or have been tipped off by someone who, say, works for UniFrance, which is the body that helps promote French films abroad, you don't know. You sit down, you watch a film and if it's not working for you in fifteen or twenty minutes, you walk out and go to the cinema right beside it. It's like a hive of these little rooms and cinemas. *Martyrs* might have played in the Star cinema, which is fairly nice; it's pretty big and it was just an intense experience.

AW: In the research I've done, most of these New French Extremity films which played at Cannes were booed by their audiences and it seems like the kind of reaction you would want to get for one of these films because they are anti-establishment and you want to get the audience riled up about them.

CG: So you have the Cannes Film Festival, you have Un Certain Regard, Critic's Week, and Director's Fortnight. *Calvaire*, that was Director's Fortnight, *Alléluia* (Fabrice Du Welz, 2014) was Director's Fortnight, *Blue Ruin* (Jeremy Saulnier, 2013) was Director's Fortnight—that's where you go to find neat, interesting, challenging films. Critic's Week is kind of a mixed bag, but it's had various things, like *Man Bites Dog* [Rémy Belvaux, André Bonzel, Benoît Poelvoorde, 1992] and *Inside* [Julian Maury, 2007]. The theater that Critic's Week is in is The Espace Miramar and is a small cinema. The audiences are predominantly film students, kind of a younger audience and an older international critic audience. *Inside* was not what they wanted to see. They didn't want to see a pregnant woman tormented for ninety minutes. The other thing I'll say about screenings at Cannes which aren't market screenings is the press screenings, that's the one time critics can be vocal. When you hear about the booing at Cannes, usually it's incredibly exaggerated by the press. The press screening will be for the critics and some of the "critics" that are doing the booing are not even proper, valid critics. The people who scream and shout are a minority. But the other thing you need to know about Cannes is the big screenings at the Palais, most of the people who are there aren't cinephiles. Most of the people there have gotten tickets; rich, socialite people dressed up in tuxedos, the [number] of cellphones that are used during those screenings is infuriating. It's a fascinating thing to go and experience Cannes, but it is important to understand that there are two levels—there's the glitz and glamour of the jury, of the films on the red carpet, of a schedule that has to be like clockwork for everything to happen, but the other level is films being bought, sold, put together, packaged, and then so much other sleaze. The films that are screened in the market, that's where the first wave of selling and bidding happens. When a film gets selected at TIFF, that's where we validate it to the buyers and distributors, who then start to heavily negotiate. *High Tension* went to Lionsgate, good investment but when it got released, it bombed, but it's a tough genre film. It's a smart film, it's not a dumb slasher film. Also, audiences aren't going to go see a French slasher film in North America, it's hard enough to get them to go see something which isn't *The Artist*. Dimension bought *Inside* and *Martyrs* because they knew they were perfect titles for their Dimension Extreme label.

AW: To touch again on Martyrs, *a big part of Midnight Madness at TIFF is you coming out before the screening and hyping the audience up for what they are about to see. How do you do that with a film like* Martyrs?

CG: As a programmer, I was struggling to find my voice when I started. I always wanted to get films which were crowd pleasers and I'd get my back up if someone didn't like the film. I took it way too personally. And now, I love programming a film like *Martyrs* because I know half the audience isn't going to get it: half the audience is going to hate it, and half the audience is going to love it, and, afterwards, they're going to engage. The worst thing is having a film where everyone likes it, then walks away. The best is when everyone comes out and you've really split them and they're debating it; some people get won over, some people change their minds. I like having, within the selection, a curveball. The great thing about programming is having that flashpoint afterwards when I deliberately bring the director out to meet the audience on their way out and so they have a chance to engage and talk and it's a moment that directors never really have. *Martyrs* split the audience: someone had thrown up.

AW: That person throwing up at the TIFF screening will go down in Martyrs' *folklore. It will be interesting to see how it holds up against the remake,*

185

which could grow the audience for the original a bit, like how The Strangers *did for* Them.

CG: I've seen the *Martyrs* remake and, watching it, it makes you appreciate the shorthand that Pascal [Laugier] has. He conveys all this stuff that in the American version they have to explain. They have a whole protracted thing about the girls becoming friends in school and maybe becoming lovers and she's still haunted by the ghost of something because she was abducted in the beginning. Then it's a white-bread family, except in the original the image of the ghost creature is terrifying in the remake it looks like a lame version of the woman from *Insidious* [James Wan, 2010]. There's none of the barb wire, nothing threatening.

AW: I think the thing that's so impactful about those images in Martyrs *is that it's an animalistic side of humanity that's been changed by this this metal, industrial, clinical side of humanity. It's a depiction of alteration of desire and changing human desire. It's quite shocking, and it's shocking in its simplicity. Thinking about it in the years since I first saw it, I can't believe no one ever truly got there before to that same extent.*

CG: I was interviewing George Romero for a screening we did at TIFF and he threw back to a quote from Stephen King where people said to him, "They ruined your book," and Stephen King says, "What do you mean? My book's right here." Romero did the same thing. When people said, "They ruined *Dawn of the Dead* [1978]," he was like, "What do you mean? *Dawn of the Dead* is right here." Pascal knows what he made.

AW: I wanted to go back to a film you touched on earlier, which is Calvaire. *I was actually a little surprised when I saw that it had been programmed at Midnight Madness, because it seems like such a quiet film by comparison. It's very twisted and very sinister, but it only reveals that part of itself at the very end.*

CG: Yeah. It just gets weirder and weirder. That's another perfect example where half the audience was like, What the hell was *that*? I'm not going to program something that's easy. I try to give people context. *Calvaire* I might now have put into the Vanguard program, it would seem like a better fit there. It's such a dirty, weird, creepy *Texas Chainsaw Massacre* [clone].

AW: Your allegiance to the characters in Calvaire *is constantly shifting; it's hard to not engage with it.*

CG: The whole beginning of that film, seeing the nursing home and then the woman who plays the head nurse was played by Brigitte Lahaie who was in Jean Rollin films, so she's another part of the history.

AW: The other film we have to talk about is Sheitan *[2006].*

CG: I'm trying to think of how I saw that film.... *Sheitan* is just so crazy.

AW: It's another of those films that just seems to come out of nowhere. But it was developed with Vincent Cassel, who seemed to have a big part in getting it to the screen.

CG: That was because [*Sheitan* director] Kim Chapiron did a bunch of hip-hop videos. Vincent had starred in one of the videos and he really liked the energy that was on set. Everyone was from the projects, mixed race, and Kim is Vietnamese-French. Kim's dad was a journalist who, I think, wrote a book on psychedelic mushrooms, a total counter-culture crazy arts family. And through shooting those videos, Kim was able to put the money together and shoot *Sheitan*. And Cassel is so good in it—the character is racist, horrible, almost unrecognizable, but great! I saw *Sheitan* and I think it played at Tribeca [Film Festival], so I had to shunt it to the final night due to TIFF's policies. And it was such a great, fun screening.

AW: Moving ahead to the 2007 Festival, that seems like a really interesting year because you had Inside *and* Frontier(s), *two films that are hard to watch at the best of times. I can't imagine having them in the same program within ten days of each other at Midnight Madness because there are ticket buyers who go to all ten films. That's a lot of bloodshed for even the most hardened horror fans.*

CG: *Frontier(s)* is just so much fun because there's so much going on. That was Xavier Gens's first film, and he's a neat guy. He had a liver or kidney operation when he was a kid, so he basically couldn't play with other kids, so he learned how to edit off of two VCRs. He would make his own movies and remix off of two VCRs. I really wish he'd make more stuff.

AW: It sounds, from the interviews I've read with Gens, that the process he had on his follow-up film, Hitman *[2007], really hurt him.*

CG: It's weird now seeing they're making a new *Hitman* film—I don't think anyone asked for *that.*

AW: Probably not. There is a weird charge you get watching Frontier(s). You're subjected to all this violence through the film but the way the character Yasmine fights back at the end doesn't feel oppressive, it feels liberating.

CG: I got to meet Karina Testa [who played Yasmine] at Sitges Film Festival in Spain and she was great. I talked to her about how she prepared for that role and she said she got sad Persian love songs on her iPod and she'd sit and listen to those songs and rock back and forth and become that character.

AW: At the end when she's finally driving away and she screams intermittently, it's so powerful.

CG: I remember when *Frontier(s)* played at Stitches and some of my genre friends were like, oh it's just a *Texas Chainsaw Massacre* knockoff. And *Frontier(s)* has influences, you can't make a horror film these days without influences, it's very hard to do something pure.

AW: On the other hand, in 2007 you had Inside, *which is just as nihilistic as* Frontier(s), *but an entirely different beast.*

CG: Watching *Inside*, those guys are really great. The screening was great and it was on the final night of the festival and we were having a gathering at my house for any of the filmmakers who were still in town. They were staring at the residential street I lived on and, I realized, for most of these filmmakers, they never get to come to these areas. They were walking up the street and they were like, You live in Haddonfield [the setting of John Carpenter's *Halloween*]. I guess, to French eyes, this part of Toronto looks like tree-lined small-town America, because it feels somewhat foreign to them.

Chapter Notes

Introduction

1. James Quandt, "Flesh and Blood: Sex and Violence in Recent French Cinema," *The New Extremism in Cinema from France to Europe*, eds. Tanya Horeck and Tina Kendall (Edinburgh: Edinburgh University Press, 2013), 18.

2. Patricia Allmer, Emily Brick, and David Huxley, "Introduction to French Horror Cinema," *European Nightmares: Horror Cinema in Europe Since 1945* (New York: Wallflower Press, 2012), 91.

3. Alan Jones, *The Rough Guide to Horror Movies* (London: Penguin, 2005), 226.

4. Jason Zinoman, *Shock Value: How a Few Eccentric Outsiders Gave Us Nightmares, Conquered Hollywood, and Invented Modern Horror* (New York: Penguin, 2011), 6.

5. Peter Biskind, *Easy Riders, Raging Bulls: How the Sex-Drugs-and-Rock 'n' Roll Generation Saved Hollywood* (New York: Simon & Schuster, 1999), 14.

6. Andrea Subissati, *When There's No More Room in Hell: The Sociology of the Living Dead* (USA: Lambert Academic Publishing, 2010), 3.

Chapter 1

1. Jonathan Romney, "Le Sex and Violence," *The Independent* (September 12, 2004), http://www.independent.co.uk/arts-entertainment/films/features/le-sex-and-violence-6161908.html.

2. Brian Moynahan, *The French Century: An Illustrated History of Modern France* (London: Flammarion, 2007), 29.

3. Tanja Jurković, "Grand Guignol (1897–1962): Introduction to Grand-Guignol, French Theatre of Horror," *University of Sterling—The Gothic Imagination* (January 29, 2013), http://www.gothic.stir.ac.uk/guestblog/grand-guignol-1897–1962-introduction-to-grand-guignol-french-theatre-of-horror/.

4. Colin Jones, *Cambridge Illustrated History—France* (Cambridge: Cambridge University Press, 2011), 276.

5. Kristin Ross, *Fast Cars, Clean Bodies: Decolonization and the Reordering of French Culture* (Cambridge, MA: MIT Press, 1996), 4.

6. *Ibid.*, 9.

7. Danielle Costa, "Decolonization in French Society," *IndyFlicks* (May 1999), http://www.indyflicks.com/danielle/papers/paper06.htm.

8. Ross, *Fast Cars, Clean Bodies*, 11–12.

9. *Ibid.*, 9.

10. Mathieu Kassovitz and Nicolas Sarkozy, "La haine: Kassovitz vs. Sarkozy," Cri-

terion Collection, April 16, 2007, https://www.criterion.com/current/posts/476-la-haine-kassovitz-vs-sarkozy.

11. Slavoj Žižek, *Violence* (New York: Picador, 2008), 199–200.

12. Jon Elster, ed. *Tocqueville: The Ancien Régime and the French Revolution* (Cambridge: Cambridge University Press, 2011), 185.

Chapter 2

1. Rémi Fournier Lanzoni, *French Cinema: From Its Beginnings to the Present* (New York: Continuum, 2002), 142.

2. *Ibid.*, 117.

3. Richard Brody, "The Future of French Cinema," *The New Yorker* (January 2, 2013), http://www.newyorker.com/culture/richard-brody/the-future-of-french-cinema.

4. "Eyes Without a Face," Wikipedia, the Free Encyclopedia (March 2015), https://en.wikipedia.org/wiki/Eyes_Without_a_Face.

5. Roy Armes, *French Cinema: The Personal Style* (Cranbury, NJ: A.S. Barnes, 1966), 18.

6. Guy Austin, *Contemporary French Cinema—An Introduction* (Manchester: Manchester University Press, 1996), 119–20.

7. *Ibid.*, 34.

Chapter 3

1. VICE, "Gaspar Noé," http://www.vice.com/en_ca/video/gaspar-noe-part-1-of-3—2.

2. James Quandt, "More Moralism from that 'Wordy Fuck.'" *The New Extremism in Cinema: From France to Europe*, eds. Tanya Horeck and Tina Kendall (Edinburgh: Edinburgh University Press, 2011), 211.

3. Matt Bailey, "Gaspar Noé," *Senses of Cinema* (October 2003), http://sensesofcinema.com/2003/great-directors/noe/.

4. Liese Spencer, "Cinema to Dishonour France," *The Independent* (January 14, 1999), http://www.independent.co.uk/arts-entertainment/cinema-to-dishonour-france-1046932.html.

5. J Hoberman, "Formal Attire," *The Village Voice* (March 4, 2003), http://www.villagevoice.com/film/formal-attire-6411337.

6. Mitch Davis, "Living is a selfish act: an interview with Gaspar Noé," *Post Script* 21:3 (Summer 2002).

7. Nigel M. Smith, "Gaspar Noé Talks *Irréversible*," *Indiewire* (July 12, 2011), http://www.indiewire.com/article/from_the_iw_vaults_gaspar_noe_talks_irréversible.

8. JW Dunne, *An Experiment with Time* (New York: Faber & Faber, 1934), 133.

9. Tim Palmer, *Brutal Intimacy: Analyzing Contemporary French Cinema* (Middletown CT: Wesleyan University Press, 2011), 11.

10. David Edelstein, "*Irréversible* Errors," *Slate* (March 7, 2003), http://www.slate.com/articles/arts/movies/2003/03/irreversible_errors.html.

11. Jean Tang, "There are no bad deed, just deeds," *Salon* (March 12, 2003), www.salon.com/2003/03/12/noe/.

12. Nicolas Schmerkin, "Interview: Gaspar Noé." *Enter the Void* press kit, Wild Bunch, 2009.

13. David Edelstein, "For a Good Time, *Don't Enter the Void*," *New York Magazine* (September 24, 2010), http://www.vulture.com/2010/09/movie_review_for_a_good_time_d.html.

14. Eric Kohn, "Hardcore Sex Isn't the Craziest Thing About Gaspar Noé's 3D *Love*," *Indiewire* (May 20, 2015), http://www.indiewire.com/article/cannes-review-hardcore-sex-isnt-the-craziest-thing-about-gaspar-noes-3d-love-20150520.

Chapter 4

1. "Catherine Breillat Opens Up About *Romance*, Sex and Censorship." *Indiewire* (September 23, 1999), http://www.indiewire.com/article/interview_catherine_breillat_opens_up_about_romance_sex_and_censorship.
2. *Ibid.*
3. Roger Ebert, "Review: *Romance*" (November 12, 1999), http://www.rogerebert.com/reviews/romance-1999.
4. "Catherine Breillat Opens Up About *Romance*, Sex and Censorship."
5. Martine Beugnet, *Cinema and Sensation: French Film and the Art of Transgression* (United Kingdom: University of Edinburgh Press, 2007), 48.
6. Jean-Pol Fargeau, "Interview with Leos Carax," *Artificial Eye* (n.d.), http://zakka.dk/euroscreenwriters/interviews/leos_carax.htm.
7. *Ibid.*
8. Trevor Link, "Rediscover: *Pola X*," *Spectrum Culture* (n.d.), http://spectrumculture.com/2011/10/31/rediscover-pola-x/.
9. Fargeau, "Interview with Leos Carax."
10. Alix Sharkey, "Scandale!: The Story Behind *Baise-moi*" *The Guardian* (April 14, 2002), http://www.theguardian.com/film/2002/apr/14/filmcensorship.features.
11. *Ibid.*
12. Emily Brick, "*Baise-Moi* and the French Rape-Revenge Films," in *European Nightmares: Horror Cinema in Europe Since 1945*, eds. Patricia Allmer, Emily Brick, and David Huxley (New York: Columbia University Press, 2012), 98.
13. Beugnet, *Cinema and Sensation*, 54.
14. Leila Wimmer, "Sex and Violence from a Pair of Furies: The Scandal of *Baise-Moi*," in *The New Extremism in Cinema: From France to Europe*, eds. Tanya Horeck and Tina Kendall (Edinburgh: Edinburgh University Press, 2011), 140.

Chapter 5

1. James Quandt, "Flesh and Blood: Sex and Violence in Recent French Cinema," in *The New Extremism in Cinema: From France to Europe*, eds. Tanya Horeck and Tina Kendall (Edinburgh: Edinburgh University Press, 2011), 22.
2. Martine Beugnet, *Cinema and Sensation: French Film and the Art of Transgression* (Carbondale: Southern Illinois University Press, 2007), 1.
3. Nicole Brenez, "The Body's Night: An Interview with Philippe Grandrieux," *Rouge* (June 2003), http://www.rouge.com.au/1/grandrieux.html.
4. Jenny Chamarette, "Shadows of Being in *Sombre*: Archetypes, Wolf-Men and Bare Life," in *The New Extremism in Cinema: From France to Europe*, eds. Tanya Horeck and Tina Kendall (Edinburgh: Edinburgh University Press, 2011), 74.
5. *Ibid.*, 76.
6. John Bradburn, "Nothing is True. Everything is Permissible." *Vertigo* (June 2008), https://www.closeupfilmcentre.com/vertigo_magazine/issue-18-june-2008/nothing-is-true-everything-is-permissible/.
7. Jenny Chamarette, "Shadows of Being in *Sombre*: Archetypes, Wolf-Men and Bare Life," in *The New Extremism in Cinema: From France to Europe*, eds. Tanya Horeck and Tina Kendall (Edinburgh: Edinburgh University Press, 2011), 77–78.

8. Darren Hughes, "Bruno Dumont's Bodies," *Senses of Cinema* (March 2002), http://sensesofcinema.com/2002/feature-articles/dumont_bodies/.

9. Beugnet, *Cinema and Sensation*, 104.

Chapter 6

1. Tim Palmer, *Brutal Intimacy: Analyzing Contemporary French Cinema* (Middletown, CT: Wesleyan University Press, 2011), 11.

2. *Ibid.*

3. Laura McMahon, "The Contagious Body of the Film: Claire Denis' *Trouble Every Day* (2001)," in *Transmissions: Essays in French Thought, Literature and Cinema*, eds. Isabelle McNeill and Bradley Stephens (New York: Peter Lang, 2007), 78.

4. Phillippe Piazzo, "Le Film vient de mes émotions, pas d'un principe," *Le Monde* (December 4, 2002), 35.

5. Tim Palmer, "Don't Look Back: An Interview with Marina de Van," *The French Review* 83:5 (April 2010): 1059.

6. Palmer, *Brutal Intimacy*, 84.

7. *Ibid.*, 86.

8. Martine Beugnet, *Cinema and Sensation: French Film and the Art of Transgression* (Carbondale: Southern Illinois University Press, 2007), 161.

9. Kristin Ross, *Fast Cars, Clean Bodies: Decolonization and the Reordering of French Culture* (Cambridge, MA: MIT Press, 1996), 148.

10. Palmer, "Don't Look Back: An Interview with Marina de Van," 1062.

Chapter 7

1. "Interview with François Ozon," François Ozon Official Site, http://www.francois-ozon.com/en/interviews-criminal-lovers.

2. *Ibid.*

3. *Ibid.*

4. James Quandt, "Flesh and Blood: Sex and Violence in Recent French Cinema," in *The New Extremism in Cinema: From France to Europe*, eds. Tanya Horeck and Tina Kendall (Edinburgh: Edinburgh University Press, 2011), 19.

5. *Ibid.*, 24.

6. Martine Beugnet, *Cinema and Sensation: French Film and the Art of Transgression* (Carbondale: Southern Illinois University Press, 2007), 104.

7. Liza Bear, "Bruno Dumont's Lust in the Dust; Talking about *Twentynine Palms*," *Indiewire* (April 9, 2004), http://www.indiewire.com/article/bruno_dumonts_lust_in_the_dust_talking_about_twentynine_palms.

8. *Ibid.*

Chapter 8

1. Kristen Hohenadal, "Peeling Back the Layers of a Man, Clothes and All," *New York Times* (October 14, 2001), http://www.nytimes.com/2001/10/14/movies/film-peeling-back-the-layers-of-a-man-clothes-and-all.html.

2. Kristin Ross, *Fast Cars, Clean Bodies: Decolonization and the Reordering of French Culture* (Cambridge, MA: MIT Press, 1995), 12.

3. "Movies of the Moment: *Demonlover*," *Film Comment* (September/October 2003), http://www.filmcomment.com/article/movies-of-the-moment-demonlover/.

4. David Thompson, "Olivier Assayas Power Games," *BFI Sight & Sound* (May 2004), http://old.bfi.org.uk/sightandsound/feature/260.

5. "Movies of the Moment: *Demonlover*."

6. Thompson, "Olivier Assayas Power Games."

7. Martine Beugnet, *Cinema and Sensation: French Film and the Art of Transgression* (Carbondale: Southern Illinois University Press, 2007), 169.

8. "Movies of the Moment: *Demonlover*."

9. Thompson, "Olivier Assayas Power Games."

10. *Ma mère* Press Release. Mongrel Media, http://www.mongrelmedia.com/Mongrel Media/files/d3/d383801a-63b4-4455-8b26-53f0bd0f58fe.pdf.

11. *Ibid.*

12. *Ibid.*

13. *Ibid.*

Chapter 9

1. Tony Perrello, "A Parisian in Hollywood: Ocular Horror in the Films of Alexandre Aja," *American Horror Film: The Genre at the Turn of the Millennium*, ed. Steffen Hantke (Jackson: University of Mississippi Press, 2010), 17.

2. Matthias Hurst, "Subjectivity Unleashed: *Haute Tension*," in *European Nightmares: Horror Cinema in Europe Since 1945*, eds. Patricia Allmer, David Huxley, and Emily Brick (London: Wallflower Press 2012), 109.

3. Roger Ebert, *High Tension* (June 9, 2005), http://www.rogerebert.com/reviews/high-tension-2005.

4. Devin Faraci, "*High Tension* Director Didn't Like the Twist Ending Either," *Chud* (March 3, 2006), http://www.chud.com/6072/high-tension-director-didnt-like-the-twist-ending-either/.

5. Robin Wood, *Hollywood from Vietnam to Reagan ... and Beyond* (New York: Columbia University Press, 2003), 31.

6. Stacie Ponder, "Take Back the Knife: Revisiting *High Tension*," After Ellen (November 8, 2010), http://www.afterellen.com/movies/81011-take-back-the-knife-revisiting-high-tension.

7. Carol J. Clover, *Men, Women, and Chainsaws: Gender in the Modern Horror Film* (Princeton, NJ: Princeton University Press, 1993), 40.

Chapter 10

1. Milos Jovanovic, "Fabrice Du Welz Interview," Horror Talk (July 22, 2009), http://www.horrortalk.com/features/563-fabrice-du-welz-interview.html.

2. Kristin Ross, *Fast Cars, Clean Bodies: Decolonization and the Reordering of French Culture* (Cambridge, MA: MIT Press, 1996), 145.

3. "Exclusive Interview: Fabrice Du Welz, Director of *Calvaire*," Eat My Brains (December 7, 2005), http://www.eatmybrains.com/showfeature.php?id=39#sthash.bTgYgs20.dpuf.

4. Jovanovic, "Fabrice Du Welz Interview."

5. "Interview: Kim Chapiron," Enterline Media, http://enterline2.tripod.com/kimchapiron.html.

6. *Ibid.*

7. Neil Young, "Exclusive: Interview with *Sheitan* Auteur Kim Chapiron," Neil Young's Film Lounge (May 13, 2006), http://www.jigsawlounge.co.uk/film/reviews/exclusive-interview-with-sheitan-auteur-kim-chapiron/.

8. *Ibid.*

9. "Interview: Kim Chapiron."

10. Jason Lapeyre, "The Patron Saint of Pain," *Rue Morgue Magazine* (March 2009): 20–21.

Chapter 11

1. Pascal-Emmanuel Gobry, "The Truth About French Parenting (and I Would Know)," *The Atlantic* (March 14, 2012), http://www.theatlantic.com/health/archive/2012/03/the-truth-about-french-parenting-and-i-would-know/254521/.

2. Liz Garrigan, "French Children Don't Throw Food (When People Are Watching)," *I Am Carla Bruni's Neighbor* (February 16, 2012), http://lizgarrigan.tumblr.com/post/17712385923/french-children-dont-throw-food-when-people-are.

3. Chris Hewitt, "Interview: David Moreau," *Empire* (n.d.), http://www.empireonline.com/interviews/interview.asp?IID=621.

4. Karen Breslau, "Overplanned Parenthood: Ceausescu's cruel law," *Newsweek* (January 22, 1990), 35.

5. *Ibid.*

6. Hewitt, "Interview: David Moreau."

7. David Marsh, "France goes back to mining as source of national wealth," Market Watch (February 24, 2014), http://www.marketwatch.com/story/france-goes-back-to-mining-as-source-of-national-wealth-2014–02-24.

8. Nigel Finch, "Contemporary Issues in Mining," Palgrave MacMillan (November 2012), http://www.palgrave.com/page/detail/contemporary-issues-in-mining-nigel-finch/?K=9781137025791.

9. James Dennis, "*The Pack* DVD Review," Twitch (June 19, 2011), http://twitchfilm.com/2011/06/the-pack-dvd-review.html#ixzz3j11ac45T.

10. "*The Pack* by Franck Richard, a displaced horror thriller," Cannes Film Festival (May 10, 2010), http://www.festival-cannes.fr/en/theDailyArticle/57589.html.

11. John Kenneth Muir, *Horror Films FAQ: All That's Left to Know About Slashers, Vampires, Zombies, Aliens, and More* (New York: Applause Books, 2013), 218.

12. Carol J. Clover, *Men, Women, and Chainsaws: Gender in the Modern Horror Film* (Princeton, NJ: Princeton University Press, 1993), 35.

Chapter 12

1. Paul Teusner, "Resident Evil: Horror Film and the Construction of Religious Identity in Contemporary Media Culture," *Colloquium Journal*, http://colloquiumjournal.org/back-issues/Coll37.2/169.180.pdf.

2. Carol J. Clover, *Men, Women, and Chainsaws: Gender in the Modern Horror Film* (New York: Princeton University Press, 1993), 37.

3. *Merriam-Webster*, http://www.merriam-webster.com/dictionary/martyr.

4. Virginie Sélavy, "*Martyrs*: Interview with Pascal Laugier," *Electric Sheep Magazine* (May 2, 2009), http://www.electricsheepmagazine.co.uk/features/2009/05/02/martyrs-interview-with-pascal-laugier/.

5. Emma Westwood, "Pascal Laugier (Uncut)," *The Westwood Digest* (August 19, 2010) https://emmawestwood.wordpress.com/2010/08/18/pascal-laugier-uncut/.

6. Thomas Mann, "Interview Pascal Laugier," What's Up, Mann?, http://www.whatsupmann.com/2009/10/pascal-laugiers-martyrs/.

7. Sélavy, "*Martyrs*: Interview with Pascal Laugier."

8. *Ibid.*

Chapter 13

1. Stuart F. Andrews, "Enfants Terribles," *Rue Morgue* (May 2008), 16–21.
2. Ashley Nunes, "Running with Scissors: Abjection and the Archaic Mother in *À l'intérieur (Inside)*," Inter-disciplinary (May 2012), http://www.inter-disciplinary.net/at-the-interface/wp-content/uploads/2012/04/nunesewpaper.pdf.
3. Donato Totaro, "*À l'intérieur*: A Rebirth of French Horror," Offscreen (August 2008), http://offscreen.com/view/french_horror.
4. Stuart F. Andrews, "Enfants Terribles," *Rue Morgue* 78 (May 2008), 16–21.
5. *Ibid.*
6. Totaro, "*À l'intérieur*: A Rebirth of French Horror."
7. *Ibid.*

Chapter 14

1. Aristotle. *Poetics*, *The Complete Works of Aristotle: Volume II* (Princeton: Princeton University Press, 1995), 2316–40.
2. Scott A. Lukas and John Marmysz, eds., *Fear, Cultural Anxiety, and Transformation: Horror, Science Fiction, and Fantasy Films Remade* (Lanham, MD: Lexington, 2010), 15–16.
3. David Konow, *Reel Terror* (New York: St. Martin's Griffin) 127–28.
4. Kathleen A. Tobin, "The Reduction of Urban Vulnerability: Revisiting 1950s American Suburbanization as Civil Defense," *Cold War History* 2.2 (2002), 1.
5. John W. Bowen, "The Evil That Men Redo," *Rue Morgue* 54 (March 2006), 16–20.
6. Tad Friend, "Remake Man," *The New Yorker* (June 2, 2003), http://www.newyorker.com/magazine/2003/06/02/remake-man.
7. "*The Ring*," Box Office Mojo, http://www.boxofficemojo.com/movies/?id=ring.htm.
8. "*One Missed Call*," Rotten Tomatoes, http://www.rottentomatoes.com/m/one_missed_call/.
9. Brad Miska, "*Mirrors* (2008): Red Band Jaw-Rip Featurette" (July 25, 2008), https://www.youtube.com/watch?v=TnKK3Mswkyk.
10. Bloody Disgusting, "*Mirrors* (2008) Exclusive Interview with Kiefer Sutherland!" (August 14, 2008), https://www.youtube.com/watch?v=voU2UKUeRbU.
11. Jeannette Catsoulis, "It's Enough to Make Anyone Blink—*The Eye* (2008)," *New York Times* (February 2, 2008), http://www.nytimes.com/2008/02/02/movies/02eye.html?_r=0.
12. SBS2 Australia, "David Moreau on his Worst Film Experience (*The Feed*)" (March 18, 2014), https://www.youtube.com/watch?v=PCzfGSrvjsQ.
13. John Kenneth Muir, *Horror Films FAQ: All That's Left to Know About Slashers, Vampires, Zombies, Aliens, and More* (New York: Applause, 2013), 326.
14. Joseph McBride, *Steven Spielberg: A Biography* (Jackson: University of Mississippi Press, 2011), 257.
15. John W. Bowen, "Death from Below," *Rue Morgue* 103 (August 2010), 20–22.
16. *Ibid.*
17. *Ibid.*
18. The Gore-Met, "Mother Made Me," *Rue Morgue* 134 (June 2013), 18.
19. Carol J. Clover, *Women and Chainsaws: Gender in the Modern Horror Film* (Princeton, NJ: Princeton University Press, 1992), 177.
20. Susan Sontag, *On Photography* (New York: Picador, 1977), 24.

Conclusion

1. James Quandt, "More Moralism from that 'Wordy Fuck.'" *The New Extremism in Cinema: From France to Europe* (Edinburgh: Edinburgh University Press, 2013), 213.

2. *Ibid.*, 210.

3. *Ibid.*, 211.

Appendix

1. "History of the Toronto International Film Festival's MIDNIGHT MADNESS Programme," *Ultra8* http://www.ultra8.ca/content2/mmhistory.html.

2. "Midnight Madness," *TIFF*, http://tiff.net/festivals/festival15/films#midnight-madness.

3. "Vanguard," *TIFF*, http://www.tiff.net/festivals/thefestivalarchive/programmes/vanguard.

Bibliography

Alexander, Dave. "Only Women Bleed." *Rue Morgue Magazine*, May 2008.

Allmer, Patricia, Emily Brick, and David Huxley, eds. *European Nightmares: Horror Cinema in Europe Since 1945*. New York: Wallflower Press, 2012.

Andrews, Stuart F. "Enfant Terribles." *Rue Morgue Magazine*, May 2008.

Anton, Saul. "Interview: Catherine Breillat Opens Up About *Romance*, Sex and Censorship." Indiewire, September 23, 1999, http://www.indiewire.com/article/interview_catherine_breillat_opens_up_about_romance_sex_and_censorship.

Armes, Roy. *French Cinema*. 2 vols. Cranbury, NJ: A. S. Barnes, 1970.

Artaud, Antonin. *The Theatre and Its Double*. Trans. Mary Caroline Richards. New York: Grove Press, 1958.

Austin, Guy. *Contemporary French Cinema: An Introduction*. Manchester: Manchester University Press, 1996.

Bear, Liza. "Bruno Dumont's Lust in the Dust; Talking About *Twentynine Palms*." Indiewire, April 9, 2004, http://www.indiewire.com/article/bruno_dumonts_lust_in_the_dust_talking_about_twentynine_palms.

Beugnet, Martine. *Cinema and Sensation: French Film and the Art of Transgression*. Carbondale: Southern Illinois University Press, 2007.

Biskind, Peter. *Easy Riders, Raging Bulls: How the Sex-Drugs-and-Rock 'n' Roll Generation Saved Hollywood*. New York: Simon & Schuster, 1999.

Bogdan, Cristina. "New French Extremity: An Exigency for Reality." Notes on Metamodernism, August 14, 2012, http://www.metamodernism.com/2012/08/14/new-french-extremity-an-exigency-for-reality/.

Bowen, John W. "Death from Below." *Rue Morgue Magazine*, August 2010.

_____. "The Evil That Men Redo." *Rue Morgue Magazine*, March 2006.

Bradburn, John. "Nothing Is True. Everything Is Permissible." *Vertigo*, June 18, 2008, https://www.closeupfilmcentre.com/vertigo_magazine/issue-18-june-2008/nothing-is-true-everything-is-permissible/.

Brenez, Nicole. "The Body's Night—An Interview with Phillippe Grandrieux." *Rouge* (2003), http://www.rouge.com.au/1/grandrieux.html.

Brody, Richard. "The Future of French Cinema." *The New Yorker*, January 2, 2013, http://www.newyorker.com/culture/richard-brody/the-future-of-french-cinema.

Clavane, Anthony. "The Radicalism of Fools: The Rise of the New Anti–Semitism." *New Statesman*, January 30, 2014, http://www.newstatesman.com/politics/2014/01/radicalism-fools-rise-new-anti-semitism.

Clover, Carol J. *Men, Women and Chainsaws: Gender in the Modern Horror Film.* Princeton, NJ: Princeton University Press, 1993.

Dixon, Winston, and Gwendolyn Audrey Foster, eds. *A Short History of Film.* New Brunswick, NJ: Rutgers University Press, 2013.

The Gore-Met. "Mother Made Me…" *Rue Morgue Magazine,* June 2013.

Hohenadel, Kristin. "Peeling Back the Layers of a Man, Clothes and All." *New York Times,* October 14, 2001, http://www.nytimes.com/2001/10/14/movies/film-peeling-back-the-layers-of-a-man-clothes-and-all.html?pagewanted=all.

Horeck, Tanya, and Tina Kendall. *The New Extremism in Cinema: From France to Europe.* Edinburgh: Edinburgh University Press, 2013.

Hughes, Darren. "Bruno Dumont's Bodies." *Senses of Cinema* (March 2002), http://sensesofcinema.com/2002/feature-articles/dumont_bodies/.

_____. "The New American Old West: Bruno Dumont's *Twentynine Palms." Senses of Cinema* (July 2004), http://sensesofcinema.com/2004/53rd-melbourne-international-film-festival/twentynine_palms/.

Janisse, Kier-La. "The Cult of Suffering." *Rue Morgue Magazine,* March 2009.

Jones, Alan. *The Rough Guide to Horror Movies.* London: Penguin, 2005.

Jones, Colin. *Cambridge Illustrated History: France.* New York: Cambridge University Press, 1994.

Kaganski, Serge. "Movies of the Moment: *demonlover." Film Comment* (September/October 2003), http://www.filmcomment.com/article/movies-of-the-moment-demonlover/.

Kaufman, Anthony. "Interview: Night Lights; Patrice Chereau Probes *Intimacy.*" Indiewire, October 16, 2001, http://www.indiewire.com/article/interview_night_lights_patrice_chereau_probes_intimacy.

Konow, David. *Reel Terror: The Scary, Bloody, Gory, Hundred Year History of Classic Horror Films.* New York: St. Martin's Griffin, 2012.

Kracauer, Siegfried. *Theory of Film: The Redemption of Physical Reality.* Princeton, NJ: Princeton University Press, 1960.

Lapeyre, Jason. "The Politics of Bloodletting." *Rue Morgue Magazine,* May 2008.

Lazoni, Rémi Fournier. *French Cinema from Its Beginnings to the Present.* London: Continuum, 2002.

Lukas, Scott A., and John Marmysz. *Fear, Cultural Anxiety, and Transformation: Horror, Science Fiction, and Fantasy Films Remade.* Lanham, MD: Lexington Books, 2010.

Mongrel Media. "*Ma Mère.*" Toronto: Mongrel Media, 2004.

Moynahan, Brian. *The French Century: An Illustrated History of Modern France.* London: Flammarion, 2007.

Nunes, Ashley. "Running with Scissors: Abjection and the Archaic Mother in *À l'intérieur (Inside)" Inter-disciplinary* (May 2012), http://www.inter-disciplinary.net/at-the-interface/wp-content/uploads/2012/04/nunesewpaper.pdf.

Palmer, Tim. *Brutal Intimacy: Analyzing Contemporary French Cinema.* Middletown, CT: Wesleyan University Press, 2011.

Paszylk, Bartlomiej. *The Pleasure and Pain of Cult Horror Films: An Historical Survey.* Jefferson, NC: McFarland, 2009.

Price, Brian. "Catherine Breillat." *Senses of Cinema* (December 2002), http://sensesofcinema.com/2002/great-directors/breillat/.

Robb, Graham. *Parisians: An Adventure History of Paris.* New York: W.W. Norton, 2010.

Ross, Kristin. *Fast Cars, Clean Bodies: Decolonization and the Reordering of French Culture.* Cambridge, MA: MIT Press, 1996.

Sehill, Thibaut. "François Ozon." *Senses of Cinema* (April 2004), http://sensesof cinema.com/2004/great-directors/ozon/.

Sharkey, Alix. "Scandale! The Story Behind *Baise-Moi.*" *The Guardian*, April 14, 2012, http://www.theguardian.com/film/2002/apr/14/filmcensorship.features.

Totaro, Donato. "*À l'intérieur*: A Rebirth of French Horror." Offscreen, August 2008, http://offscreen.com/view/french_horror.

Young, Neil. "Exclusive: Interview with *Sheitan* auteur Kim Chapiron." Jigsaw Lounge (May 13, 2006), http://www.jigsawlounge.co.uk/film/reviews/exclusive-interview-with-sheitan-auteur-kim-chapiron/.

Zinoman, Jason. *Shock Value: How a Few Eccentric Outsiders Gave Us Nightmares, Conquered Hollywood, and Invented Modern Horror.* New York: Penguin, 2011.

Žižek, Slavoj. "Robespierre or the 'Divine Violence' of Terror." *Lacan*, n.d., http://www.lacan.com/zizrobes.htm.

_____. "Some Politically Incorrect Reflections on Violence in France & Related Matters." *Lacan*, n.d., http://www.lacan.com/zizekchro1.htm.

Index